Teaching Physical Activities
to Impaired Youth
An Approach to Mainstreaming

Teaching Physical Activities
To Impaired Youth
An Approach To Mainstreaming

Arthur G. Miller, Ed.D.

Educational Consultant, Cotting School for Handicapped Children
Professor Emeritus, Boston University
Boston, Massachusetts

James V. Sullivan, Ed.D.

Professor of Physical Education and Recreation
Chairman, Department of Recreation and Leisure Studies
University of Southern Maine
Portland, Maine

1807 1982

John Wiley & Sons

New York   Chichester   Brisbane   Toronto   Singapore

The book is dedicated to "Dixie" and Ruth

Library of Congress Cataloging in Publication Data

Miller, Arthur George.
 Teaching physical activities to impaired youth.

 Bibliography: p.
 Includes index.
 1. Physical education for handicapped children.
2. Mainstreaming in education.   I. Sullivan, James V.
(James Vincent) II. Title.
GV445.M55   371.9′044   81-11568
ISBN 0-471-08534-0   AACR2

Printed in the United States of America

10 9 8 7 6 5 4 3 2 1

Foreword

The physical education and recreation professions are challenged to provide educational, recreational and rehabilitational programs that involve individuals with handicapping conditions. For some time, participants with handicapping conditions were put in special classes and segregated settings. Some forward thinking professional personnel recognized potential rather than deficiencies, and abilities rather than disabilities of these individuals. They provided this population with meaningful and challenging opportunities in physical, recreational and sport activities within integrated school and community settings.

Legislation during the 1970's established the *rights* of individuals with handicapping conditions and the *responsibilities* of professional personnel in meeting the specific needs of persons with handicapping conditions. More and more, physical education and recreation personnel at all levels are accepting the challenge of meeting the needs of, and providing the services for, individuals with handicapping conditions. As physical education and recreation personnel strive to reach and teach individuals with handicapping conditions, appropriate and instructive ideas, as well as practical assistance, are sought. This type of sharing has allowed many individuals with handicapping conditions to successfully and safely participate with peers, families, and friends in physical, recreational and sport activities. In addition, a great deal of personal satisfaction is derived from these involvements. Active participation in these kinds of activities is a major reason many individuals with handicapping conditions are becoming integral parts of the mainstream of society.

Willingness to share experiences, exchange helpful hints and provide each other with exciting and productive ideas has been instrumental in the progress of meeting these needs. . . . Teaching Physical Activities to Impaired Youth: An Approach to Mainstreaming . . . has resulted from this type of cooperation. Art Miller and Jim Sullivan have demonstrated teamwork at its best in developing and presenting this outstanding text. The authors have blended their background youths. The needed treatment of individuals, program planning and assessment, and the realities of working with individuals with handicapping conditions are all included.

Chapters that deal with the impaired youth focus on ways in which handicapping conditions affect an individual's ability to take part in different physical activities. Recognition of differences is necessary to insure optimum growth and development for each person. The importance of a healthy self-concept and positive body image in building a productive and enjoyable life is given a great deal of attention. The value of active participation in physical activities to foster a positive self-concept and body image comes through loud and clear.

v

Assessment is presented as the basis for, and foundation of, individualizing programs. Such programs in general, and as related to physical education in particular, are addressed in practical ways; an effort is made to reduce apprehension and confusion among individuals responsible for meeting the physical and motor development needs of individuals with handicapping conditions.

While the need for and the role of segregated programs and classes are recognized as part of a sound continuum of placement alternatives, the major thrust of this publication is the integration of students with handicapping conditions into regular programs and activities. Accommodations for individuals and adaptations of activities themselves are expertly addressed. Ways to modify activities, adjust class organization, and provide administrative flexibility are presented so that individuals with handicapping conditions can be a part of the mainstream of society. Individualization is discussed in its truest sense and is conceived as broader than, not synonymous with, one-to-one relationships.

Adapted physical education programs and activities are expertly presently. Unique contributions of professionals from related disciplines emphasize true transdisciplinary cooperation. This book is made complete with appendices that cover a variety of resources, forms and evaluation instruments, films and filmstrips, and other publications.

Many current publications deal with adapted physical education. However, this is one of the few publications that emphasizes integrating students with handicapping conditions into regular physical education programs, when possible, and into adapted or individualized programs when applicable. It focuses on the individual child, not the handicapping condition, and on ways in which handicapping conditions can affect ability to participate in physical, recreational and sport activities.

Miller and Sullivan are to be congratulated and highly commended for a job well done. This is a highly professional text and a valuable contribution to the field and body of knowledge in adapted physical education. The result of this publication will be a greater number of high quality physical and recreational opportunities that involve participants with handicapping conditions. Their lives will be greatly enhanced as they move hand in hand, forward and onward as partners, with ablebodied peers.

Julian U. Stein

Executive Director and Consultant,
Programs for the Handicapped
American Alliance for Health, Physical
Education, Recreation and Dance

Preface

The question that needed to be answered when Public Law 94-142, Education for all Handicapped Children, Section 504 of the Rehabilitation Act, and individual state laws pertaining to the education of the handicapped were enacted was: What are the implications of these mandates? There were many who were concerned about the impact of these laws and the effect they would have at the state and local levels. The concepts of mainstreaming and placement of children in the least restrictive programs were new to many. A need existed to provide administrators and teachers with knowledge about handicapping conditions of children, and planning methods of carrying out physical activity programs for impaired youth.

The belief that *all* people have a right to education prompted us to write this book. Children and adults who have various types of impairments can learn *if* given the opportunity. The extent and degree to which impaired individuals can learn depends on several factors, including the teachers, the facilities, and the content and methods of presentation.

Because we are living in a rapidly changing society, it is necessary to reflect a change in terminology with respect to the handicapped. To some, the word "handicapped" has had a negative connotation and in certain situations has stigmatized people who had "handicapping" conditions. Therefore, we have used the word "impaired" in the title of the book, but throughout have used the two words interchangeably.

The book is designed for students, teachers, and supervisors in the fields of elementary, secondary, special, and adapted physical education. It may also serve personnel in therapeutic recreation and others working in hospitals, clinics, and nursing homes.

The book is organized into three parts. Part I, "Learning About Impaired Youth," has an introduction, description of various types of impairments, and information on self-concept and body image. Part II, "Evaluating and Planning Activity Programs," familiarizes the reader with pupil evaluation, individualized educational planning, the mainstreamed program, the adapted program, and adapted activities. Part III, "Instructing Impaired Youth," provides information on the team approach, tactics for instruction, teaching approaches, and suggestions.

Impaired youths, like their nonimpaired peers, spend many leisure hours at home. These hours could easily be converted into constructive play through participation in some types of physical activities. Parents and other family members will find that the book provides information on what physical activities are appropriate and how to teach them to impaired children.

We would like to recognize the contribution of the late John W. Nichols,

Professor of Psychology, University of Maine at Orono, for the materials on tactics for instruction and self-concept. We are indebted to Drs. Irving L. Kron, Edward A. McCarthy, Jr., Robert W. Scarlata, and Robert B. Waterhouse for their valuable assistance in preparing the section on impairments and impairing conditions. We would also thank John G. Hanna, Ph.D., for his valuable assistance, and we especially thank Rita Douglass for typing the manuscript.

Arthur G. Miller

James V. Sullivan

Contents

One

LEARNING ABOUT IMPAIRED YOUTH

CHAPTER 1

Introduction

Until recent times the fate of the handicapped was one of social indifference and neglect. Today it is possible to see substantial, if not dramatic, changes in social attitudes toward the handicapped. These may be credited to advances in medicine and psychology, to broader humanitarianism, and to changes in both federal and state laws. When "education for all" became a political rallying point, education for the disabled and impaired followed. Add to this the aftermath of two world wars: the Korean and Vietnam conflicts, America faced an enormous rehabilitation problem. Sympathy—that luxury of the sentimental—gave way to empathy; today's generation of the handicapped does not want an emotional response; it wants clear-headed understanding, action, and change for the better.

Society has begun to meet its moral obligations through federal legislation (Public Law 94-142 and selected state laws) that mandates that young people with handicaps be provided with educational programs and related services. Recent census figures reveal that of the 45.8 million school children (aged 6 to 17) in the United States, 12 percent, (or about 1 in 8) are rated as impaired. Some idea of their impact on conventional schooling may be gained from these figures from the U.S. Department of Health, Education and Welfare; and the Department of Commerce:

Blind, Visually impaired	42,800
Deaf, hard of hearing	246,000
Crippled	213,900

3

Speech-impaired	1,497,100
Emotionally disturbed	855,500
Mentally retarded	983,800
Learning-disabled	1,283,200
Multihandicapped	25,700
	5,148,000

"THE RIGHT TO EDUCATION"

In the early 1970's, parent groups launched a humanitarian drive that began with advocating the right of *any* individual to a free education. It became known as "The Right to Education." Subsequently this cause was joined with the work of several advocacy organizations whose efforts led to extensive litigation culminating in a decision long to be remembered among educators and parents of the mentally retarded.

"The Pennsylvania Case" (1971) was a major breakthrough in the right of the handicapped to a free public education. The consent agreement reached by the parties in this case and ratified by a three-judge federal district court had broad implications. Three rulings were handed down, each one of extreme importance to the handicapped. Briefly, the components of the agreement were (1) a policy of "zero-reject" education was to be mandated, which required access to free public education for *all* retarded children, whatever their degree of retardation or associated impairments; (2) each child had to be provided with an educational program or training appropriate to his or her needs and capacities; and (3) the concept of "appropriateness" has to meet the following requirements: (a) on determining appropriateness, schools were forced to consider the issue of "normalization," which became practice under the concept of education in the "least restrictive alternative," and (b) another objective was to be the enhancement of social competence.

The Pennsylvania Case affected not only schools but many agencies and organizations. Challenging the "establishment," activists investigated the possibility of denial of rights in other ways. However, the field of education was most strongly affected: the original court ruling referred to the right to education for all *retarded* children. "In later decisions, the benefits gained by retarded children in Pennsylvania were to be extended to children with *all types of impairments nationally*." One immediate result was that a mechanism had to be created to insure that the educational program actually fitted the child. This task involved a reorganization and revamping of the educational system not only in the state of Pennsylvania but also in other states. In state after state, children who had not been receiving appropriate services were now subjected to the process of identification, evaluation, and placement. A giant step had been taken in fitting education to the impaired. Thus, court rulings have uniformly upheld the concept of alternative education, which asserts that not all students must adapt to conventional modes of instruction. Certainly the blind, deaf, neurologically impaired, educable and trainable mentally retarded, and even many normal students can learn more effectively under alternate systems of education.

Political controversy arose almost immediately over the tremendous cost of funding. A number of other political issues dealing with the mentally retarded were raised by the Pennsylvania Case. Socially, the decision created new parental awareness, pressures were on parents of the handicapped to lead more active roles on the education scene. As a result of the Pennsylvania Case and the "right to education" principle, the handicapped now find a more productive life in harmony with the conscience of a humanistic society.

Chapter 766 of the Massachusetts Acts of 1972—the prerunner to Public Law 94-142—established statutory right to a free, appropriate public education for every child with a special need. *Public Law 94-142 Education for all Handicapped Children Act of 1975**

Six major points are mandated by the law:

1. Equal educational opportunity.
2. Education in the least restrictive environment.
3. Recommended extension of school age from 3 to 21.
4. Development of an individualized educational plan written by a multidisciplinary team for each child served.
5. Parental involvement in diagnosis and program planning as a right.
6. Responsibility for compliance on the states and local education agencies.

Some impaired youngsters may be "mainstreamed" with regular pupils; others may be placed in adapted programs. The term "special education" refers to instruction designed to meet the unique needs, including physical education needs, of handicapped children. The phrase "individualized education program" (I.E.P.) starts with a written prescription for each handicapped child. The problems surrounding special education for the mentally and physically handicapped indicate a need for a clarification of these terms and concepts.

The following definitions are intended as an orientation for teachers, recreation leaders, and parents.

"Impairment" or "Handicap" (used interchangeably in this book) is the effect of any condition that restricts or limits an individual's ability to act in a manner accepted as normal in one's social enviornment, or which limits one's ability to survive independently. As a matter of convenience in a therapeutic sense, impairments may be placed in one or more of four functional classes: sensory, motor, integrative, and mixed.

Education For All Handicapped Children Act of 1975, Public Law 94-142, 94th Congress, November 29, 1975, Washington, D.C.

Sensory impairments are those in which there is a dysfunction in the mechanisms for sensing the environment—such as vision or hearing—but where there is no interference with the ability to act or to combine the results of experience during learning.

Motor impairments are those in which there is a dysfunction in one's ability to act following sensory stimulation—such as walking, using the arms, or moving various body parts as desired. Here the sensory mechanisms and integrative activities are normal.

Integrative impairments are those in which there is difficulty in combining the effects of experience and perception. Integrative impairments are assumed to stem from some sort of neurological damage, although often there are no clinical signs of such. They may also stem from emotional disturbances of various sorts (e.g., pyschosis), from limitations imposed by one's personal history such as fear of walking freely because of previous experiences in bumping into things, or from severe restriction of normal activities at some time in the individual's life.

Mixed or multiple impairments are those in which two or more classes of dysfunctions occur.

Mainstreaming

The concept of "mainstreaming" in education has been evolving over a decade or more. This process involves new methods and attitudes. It calls for the reeducation of guidance and evaluation departments and of all socially related school functions. The success of this educational process depends on the degree of moral and financial support that state and local school administrators give teachers and parents.

An important guideline in "mainstreaming" is that of the "least restrictive alternative." Simply stated, this recommends that students be placed in the environment that best develops their learning capabilities in the most normal setting possible.

Using the individualized educational program (IEP) of students, the standard age-graded classroom is replaced by the multiunit organization, which uses instructional methods based on each student's needs and abilities. The IEP calls for separate and individualized evaluations based on both old and new measurement methods. The upgrading of curriculum materials is recommended in order to insure individual attention.

Opinion varies widely on the relative advantages of mainstreaming unless both integration and segregation are included within the principle. Where the handicapped are concerned, it seems wise to offer both segregated and integrated classes at the present time. The way the student goes will depend on his or her needs and physical, mental, and emotional potential. Usually a pupil-evaluation team, including members of the student's family, make the final decision.

Integrating the handicapped into our nation's schools and communities will not be swift or easy. What will be the immediate effects of federal legislation and what are its long-term implications? To some observers this development, for all its vision and scope, is haunted by the specter of high costs. The American public faces a mandate of its own making that calls for a responsible allocation of funds, creative leadership and, above all, adjusted attitudes in both the public and professional sectors. The benefits of mainstreaming will positively affect both handicapped students and their more fortunate classmates, the nonhandicapped.

Placement

The impaired or handicapped include all who, because of defects or deviations in their physical, mental, or emotional states, are not classified as "normal," "regular" or "typical." While some impairments may be visible, others are not. Some are exhibited only through outward behavior. Moreover, students with *minor* handicaps often perform creditably in *regular* classes with their nonimpaired peers. Still others, from the *moderately* impaired to the *borderline* cases, are enrolled in special classes while attending regular classes on a part-time basis. The *severely* handicapped, however, are usually placed in full-time special classes or in special day or residential schools.

School and class placement of the handicapped demand clear sets of criteria. Should the primary determinant be the student's mental age (MA), chronological age (CA), or the results of perceptual-motor and physical fitness testing? Experience shows that problems of placement in the classroom and in the physical activities program are similar. Both the physical educator and the classroom teacher should have input into the evaluation of the impaired pupil and the selection of appropriate class placement.

Some exceptional children can participate in all aspects of a regular class program; some can safely and successfully take part in certain activities in the regular program for other activities, while others need the adaptive programs only.

A brief description of the different types of classes may help to clarify the placement of impaired students in the broad concept of "mainstreaming."

Regular Classroom

Within the regular class structure some impaired students are able to function successfully. Services offered by consultants provide assistance to the regular teacher by preparing specialized instruction and helping the teacher with supplies, equipment, and materials. On occasion, they may tutor individual impaired students, perform diagnostic evaluations, and counsel both impaired students and their parents.

Regular Classroom Plus Resource Center

For some impaired children, mainstreaming into the regular class is a viable possibility providing they may also receive special assistance in certain areas. Many subjects, including those in which students have academic competency, lend themselves favorably to the mainstreaming process. The subjects that are particularly effective to mainstreaming are art, music, physical education, and vocational training. A supplementary benefit is the use of resource centers. Under this plan, impaired students go to the resource center to be given special services such as physical therapy, psychiatric counseling, and corrective exercises in accordance with their needs.

Full-Time Special Class

Full-time special classes are self-contained or segregated and are located in the regular public schools. While impaired students are separated from nonhandicapped students for the regular class instruction periods, they may have the capability for extra-curricular activities with their nonimpaired peers in school clubs, assemblies, and sports.

Special Day School

Students who have problems of a nature that cannot be "handled" or "treated" in regular public schools may need to be placed in special day schools. In contrast to many of the regular public schools, special attention has been given to the design of physical facilities—to the elimination of architectural barriers and to the installation of equipment that will facilitate movement and learning. Faculty members of special day schools are professionally trained to help impaired children with their physical, emotional, or mental problems. Special medical and psychological needs of students can be met by staff nurses, therapists, and psychologists.

Residential School

Residential schools, administered by state or private agencies, provide educational programs, training, and treatment to students with extreme or severe impairments. In most cases, because of their child's special needs, parents cannot cope with the handicapped child at home nor can they place him or her in special day schools.

The quality of service in residential schools varies from "excellent" to "poor." Ideally, medical care, schooling, recreation, and the needs of daily living are in the hands of professionally trained staff members. Under such conditions, the residential school or facility is the best and probably *only* solution.

Hospitals and Home Care

In some cases, impaired children and youth are confined to hospitals or to their homes for long periods of time. In order to help keep these students up-to-date with their peers, school systems assign itinerant teachers to provide instruction on a tutorial basis. Instruction may last one or more hours per day depending upon the student's condition. In some larger children's hospitals, regular academic classes are conducted by full-time teachers.

Impairments and the Role of Physical Activities

Authorities have long recognized that some form of physical activity is essential to the development of the whole person. The pioneer work of Itard (1962), Sequin (1907), Montessori (1912), and Descoeudres (1928) has consistently stressed body movements of all kinds—games, calisthenics, dance, and gymnastics. Recent research has confirmed that youth with special needs should be given developmental perceptual-motor activities as an integral part of the cognitive process, substituting movement for abstract learning whenever the need arises. The implication is strong that fine and gross motor movements are fundamental to mental, emotional, and physical well-being. It cannot be overemphasized, however, that physical activites should begin with the simplest skills and progress cautiously toward greater complexity of movement. To this end, regular classes may enroll both impaired and nonimpaired pupils as long as activities are kept within reasonable limits. It should be unnecessary to remind teachers that the handicapped youngsters should be treated first as human beings with normal needs and desires. Only after this clear recognition should the pupil be thought of as impaired. Lack of regular physical activity results in motor regression, which leads in turn to weakened muscles, poor posture, and general awkwardness. Regardless of their impairments, children must develop motor skills if they are to improve, not only in physical fitness but also in psychosocial and emotional maturity.

GOALS

Physical activity programs with a developmental approach are aimed at four major goals: general motor ability, physical fitness, psychosocial adjustment, and emotional adjustment. The teacher should strive to offer each student ample opportunity to develop each of these goals to his or her maximum ability.

General motor ability refers to one's ability, either potential or actual, to perform motor movements with some degree of proficiency. Examples of gross motor abilities include crawling, walking, running, jumping, skipping, throwing, and balancing. Examples of fine motor abilities are printing, cutting, coloring, folding, threading, bead stringing, and drawing.

Because of the nature and needs of impaired youth, much of the instruction should be in the area of motor-skill development. The potential and capacity to learn motor skills need to be carefully examined by the teacher, since skill acquisition is of the greatest importance.

Locomotor and nonlocomotor movements should be taught first. Handicapped pupils need to be given the opportunity to explore, investigate, and move in their own particular way through movement exploration; ball skills such as tossing, throwing, catching, kicking, and batting can be added.

Physical fitness refers to one's ability, either potential or actual, to develop and maintain strength and stamina sufficient for daily living and the enjoyment of leisure. Physical educators and recreation specialists universally regard it as one of the cardinal teaching objectives. Not surprisingly, handicapped youngsters capable of running, performing calisthenics, and practicing weight-training noticeably improve their physical fitness, but all such activities must be carefully adapted. It has been observed that a narrow concern for physical fitness has sometimes resulted in neglecting the pupil's fundamental and perceptual-motor activities, and possibly psychosocial and emotional development as well. Fitness should therefore be looked upon as a by-product of the physical activity program, not as its primary objective.

Psychosocial adjustment refers to the ability, either potential or actual, to behave and interact in a socially acceptable manner. For all of us, self-confidence comes with the recognition we gain through accomplishment. For the handicapped, physical activities are often the key to an improved self-image. It follows that teachers must create a positive climate for learning and eliminate barriers to socially acceptable behavior. The problems are, of course, multiple: family patterns, peer relationships, and classroom social hierarchies all influence physical performance. The effective teacher of the impaired understands and confronts these psychosocial forces.

Self-respect, honesty, sportsmanship, freedom from racial and religious prejudices: these signs of adjustment should emerge from a physical activities setting. Other benefits are obvious: a congenial atmosphere in a play area, gymnasium, or pool enables the handicapped to release their tensions, express themselves freely, and forget past failures. Clearly, learning to meet daily challenges is vital to the sound adjustment of normal and handicapped youngsters alike.

Emotional adjustment refers to one's ability, either potential or actual, to express feelings in a manner acceptable to oneself and society. Impaired youngsters are not exempt from the burden of coping with success and failure. The teacher's task becomes one of identifying gaps in children's ability to respond appropriately in the affective area and providing remedial intervention to fill those gaps.

Instructors interested in teaching physical activities should be familiar with the regulations of P.L. 94-142, especially Section 121a. 307 from the *Federal Register,* Vol. 42, No. 163; 8/23/77:

(a) Physical education must be made available to every handicapped child receiving a free appropriate education.

(b) Each handicapped child must be afforded the opportunity of participating in the regular physical education program available to nonhandicapped children, unless:

(1) The child is enrolled full-time in a separate facility.

(2) The child needs specially designed physical education as prescribed in the child's individualized education program.

(c) If specially designed physical education is prescribed in a child's individualized education program, the public agency responsible for the education of that child shall provide the services directly, or make arrangements for it to be provided through other public or private programs.

(d) The public agency responsible for the education of any handicapped child enrolled who is full-time in a separate facility, or who is not able to participate in a regular physical education program, shall take steps to insure that physical education provided to that child is comparable to services provided to nonhandicapped children.

Stein, Consultant for the Physical Education and Recreation Programs for the Handicapped (American Alliance of Health, Physical Education, Recreation, and Dance), has submitted the following recommendations to supplement the preceding sections:

1. Aquatics shall be included in physical education.

2. Intramurals, extramurals, and interscholastics shall be added "modifiers" and "describers" of athletics.

3. Leisure education shall be expanded to include therapeutic recreation and recreation programs, both of which should be conducted in a community setting.

Following are arguments for and against the proposition that handicapped children should be mainstreamed into regular physical education classes:

PRO	CON
Impaired children are more normal than they are different.	Adverse behavioral effects (withdrawal, defensive antagonism) are multiplied.
Advantages from play with normal children outweight the disadvantages.	Excessive time is spent on planning, conducting, and evaluating an integrated program to meet all individual needs.
Integration allows the more capable handicapped person to grasp motor skills and body concepts.	Many of the handicapped lack basic skills.
The nonimpaired develop compassion rather than pity for the impaired.	Strategies, competition, and team spirit are little known concepts to the hand-

Note: For futher assistance with reference to P. L. 94-142 and its application to Physical Education, see pages 52–56 and 68–70.

PRO	CON
Integration helps with the social-emotional adjustment to school activity and society—an equalizer and a vehicle for social interaction.	icapped child, which therefore preclude their successful participation.
Attention and retention are reinforced by teacher and students.	Few physical educators are sufficiently trained in teaching the impaired.

PRO	CON
Money, time, and personnel are saved.	Many mental age groupings fail to perform at expected levels for their chronological age.
Integration embodies the highest democratic values.	"Normals" should be relieved of having to wait for slow learners.
Pupils are exposed to human "feats" and "defeats."	Teaching and behavior problems should be minimized for teacher's sake.
Pupils develop self-direction and confidence.	Impaired children require special facilities, methods, techniques.
	The impaired pupil, sheltered from failure and frustration, encounters overwhelming difficulties.
	Auxiliary services of psychology, guidance, and speech will be disregarded.

A course of action must be articulated for teachers and recreators to understand students who are handicapped or impaired physically, mentally, or emotionally. Both experienced teachers as well as teachers in training need to take courses in the nature, needs, and characteristics of handicapped persons of all ages. They must acquire a working knowledge of the psychology of the physically and mentally impaired. They should also attend in-service conferences and symposia on children with handicaps to become knowledgeable about the latest methods and teaching techniques.

CHAPTER 2

Understanding Youth with Impairments

How can a teacher or recreator help impaired students cope with the many adjustments to "normal" living that make up a typical day? Perhaps one of the best answers to this question is by having a thorough understanding of the pupil's impairment (s). First, a comparison should be made between non-handicapped and handicapped youth. What are their similarities and their differences? What effect does the impairment have on their level of functioning? How can a teacher help these youngsters gain self-esteem and self-confidence?

Teachers and recreation personnel who are concerned with impaired youth should have an understanding of the stages of normal "growth and development." "Growth," in the context of this book, means the process of experiencing changes in body size and proportion. "Development," on the other hand, refers to the process of attaining improvement in skill or functional capacity. Although children generally follow the same sequence of growth and development, each child tends to grow at his or her individual rate and pattern. The handicapped, however, may deviate from these norms. A working knowledge of growth and development will assist the teacher and recreator in choosing appropriate physical activities for youth with impairments.

Health and Medical History

Teachers should have ready access to health and medical histories and, whenever possible, to input from the family or school physician. A knowledge of medical

13

backgrounds can help the teacher better understand the pupil's health status. The two main reasons for obtaining a health and medical assessment are to determine health status and to discover any impairments, disorders, or disabilities. A medical examination should be compulsory before pupils enter school for the first time and either yearly or every two years thereafter. Students who have physical disorders and have had serious sickness may require more frequent medical examinations. Some school systems have their own physicians perform the medical examinations while other systems depend upon the family doctor. A family physician who knows a pupil's family and background has a distinct advantage in completing the health and medical history.

Numerous health and medical examination forms are in use by examining physicians. A sample of a school health and medical examination form used by a department of health in a city school system may be found in Appendix A. After reviewing health and medical data and the physician's recommendations, the teacher is in a position to select those activities most beneficial to the pupil, whatever the type of impairment.

The school nurse or classroom teacher should conduct yearly visual and auditory acuity screening tests. Selected visual screening tests appear on page 57 and in Appendix B. On page 58 is an auditory screening test.

Classification of Impairments*

Impairments may be classified under one of the following categories: *visual, auditory, neuromuscular, orthopedic, cardiovascular, respiratory, mental,* and *emotional*. In the pages that follow, each of these impairments is described medically. The chapter concludes with a discussion of *multiple* impairments.

VISUAL IMPAIRMENTS

Youngsters with diseases or conditions affecting their vision are classified according to the degree of their impairment. Blindness or visual impairment may be caused by abnormalities in the eye itself, in the muscles of the eye, or in the central nervous system. Blindness may also result from trauma to the occipital lobe of the brain, the center for visual identification. Injury to the optic nerves themselves may also cause blindness, but this is rather infrequent. In children, accidents rank as the primary cause of blindness. Genetic factors may also be responsible for blindness in children. The primary cause of blindness in adults is the result of diseases such as diabetes, typhoid fever, measles, and smallpox.

*Most of the descriptive information was provided by Irving L. Kron, M.D., Edward A. McCarthy, Jr., M.D., and Robert B. Waterhouse, M.D., of Maine Medical Center, Portland, Maine, and Robert W. Scarlata, M.D., Clinical Director, Pineland Hospital and Training Center, Pownal, Maine.

The Snellen Chart* is utilized to reveal quantitative measurement of visual acuity. Many school systems use the following classification to group and describe visual impairments.

Terminology	Description	Snellen Measurements
Legal Blindness	Inability to see at 20 ft what a non-impaired eye can see at 200 ft	20/200
Travel Sight	Inability to see at more than 10 ft what a non-impaired eye can see at 200 ft	5/200 to 10/200
Motion Perception (sees shapes or movement of shapes)	Inability to see at more than 5 ft what a non-impaired eye can see at 200 ft (pertains almost entirely to motion)	3/200 to 5/200
Light Perception	Ability to distinguish a strong light 3 ft from the eye despite inability to detect motion of the hand at the same distance	Less than 3/200
Total Blindness	Inability to recognize a strong light shown directly into the eye	

AUDITORY IMPAIRMENTS†

Children with auditory impairments include the *hard of hearing,* those who can hear most sounds in the speech frequencies and enough speech to learn how to speak, either with or without a hearing aid. Those who are considered *deaf* cannot hear well enough in these frequencies to comprehend the spoken word.

Deafness may be *congenital,* that is, the individual is born deaf or has an inherited tendency toward deafness. Most congenital auditory impairments are caused by such contagious diseases in the pregnant mother as *rubella* (German

*This chart and how to administer the test to measure visual acuity are found in Appendix B.
†A screening hearing test may be found on page 58.

measles) or mumps. The impairment is a result of malformation of the bones of the middle ear, or structural defects of the tympanic membrane (the eardrum).

Deafness may also be *acquired,* caused by damage to the organs of the ear or auditory nerves by either disease or trauma. Acquired loss may be attributed to infections such as meningitis, measles, and chronic ear infections in childhood. It may be produced by a trauma, such as puncture of the tympanic membrane or continual exposure to sounds over 130 decibels. *Total* hearing loss or auditory impairment (either unilateral or bilateral) may be caused by structural abnormalities of the auditory system itself or the central nervous system.

There are three common types of hearing loss. They include *conductive,* which is damage to the outer or middle ear, causing sound waves to be blocked and all sounds to be faint; *sensory-neural,* which is damage to the inner ear or brain, causing some sounds to be perceived incorrectly; and *mixed,* which is a combination of conductive and sensory types.

The motor movements of the deaf are often vague and distorted because of the loss of background noises by which they might perceive space and motion. Individuals with hearing loss often have problems that affect balance. The eighth cranial nerve is the ''nerve of hearing,'' as well as the nerve that transmits input from the vestibular apparatus (balance). This points up the relationship between a sensory-neural impairment and balance problems. Deafness or hearing loss is usually accompanied by psychological problems, such as withdrawal because of the difficulty of communication. The psychological effects of deafness depend upon when it occurs in life; but, regardless of when it occurs, deafness creates an emotional strain in adjusting to a hearing society.

NEUROMUSCULAR IMPAIRMENTS

Those who have neuromuscular impairments are affected by diseases or trauma involving the neurological and muscular systems. These impairments are primarily caused by defects in the central nervous system, the spinal cord, the peripheral nerves, or the muscles. They may range from mild impairment, such as momentary loss of muscle coordination, to complete paralysis.

Cerebral Palsy

Cerebral palsy is a general term for a group of neuromuscular abnormalities that adversely affect motor performance. Cerebral palsy is *not* a disease. The exact cause of cerebral palsy may often be unknown; disease, injury, malformation of brain cells or congenital absence of the upper motor neurons may all produce symptoms similar to cerebral palsy. Damage usually occurs before or during the birth process or during the first two years of life. Approximately 90 percent of the cases have prenatal or natal origins. Some of the principal causes are listed below, classified according to the time of their apparent onset.

Prenatal causes. There are two basic categories—functional and metabolic. Included in the functional category are infections that may be contacted during pregnancy such as German measles (*rubella*), syphilis, and toxoplasmosis (microorganisms that may damage the nervous system). The metabolic disturbances are diabetes, anoxia (lack of oxygen, which may be associated with severe prematurity), toxemia (abnormal condition associated with the presence of toxic substances in the blood), excessive radiation, and severe jaundice due to rh incompatibility. Prematurity is one of the major causes of cerebral palsy.

Natal causes. The most common causes are excessive pressure on the head, trauma, and insufficient oxygen exchange for the baby. Among the conditions that can cause these problems is a prolonged or difficult delivery.

Postnatal causes. Several infections may be sources, including whooping cough, mumps, toxic poisons, meningitis, and encephalitis. Traumas may also cause cerebral palsy during this period.

Any of these causes may lead to lesions in various parts of the brain, and the seriousness of their effect may vary from very slight lack of muscular coordination to total inability to control muscular movement. Movement is generally impaired and awkward postural problems are common. Speech is often affected. Visual defects also occur, including such perceptual impairments as strabismus, or inability to focus both eyes simultaneously on the same object. Some individuals also experience hearing loss. The condition is frequently complicated by multiple handicaps, such as epilepsy, behavior disturbances, hyperexcitability, and mental retardation. Seizures and mental retardation occur in approximately 50 percent of cases. Cerebral palsy is a nonprogressive and nonhereditary condition. Primitive reflexes play a part in the muscular problems associated with cerebral palsy. These are reflexes that are present in all newborn infants but that normally persist only a number of weeks and gradually lessen in strength, eventually disappearing. In a person who has cerebral palsy, these reflexes may not disappear, explaining many involuntary movements seen in these individuals.

People who have cerebral palsy may be classified according to the extremities involved: *monoplegia* refers to involvement of one limb; *paraplegia* involves only the legs; *diplegia* involves primarily both legs and, to a lesser degree, the arms; *hemiplegia* is involvement of the limbs on one side of the body; *triplegia* is involvement of three limbs, usually two legs and one arm; and *quadriplegia* involves all four limbs.

Cerebral palsy may also be classified according to the syndrome or type.

Spastics constitute about three quarters of the cases of cerebral palsy. Spasticity is thought to be the result of damage to the extra-pyramedial tract and is manifested by a lack of inhibitory control. It is evidenced by hyperactive reflexes and by contracted flexor muscles, which produce stiff, jerky movements. The spastic cerebralpalsied child has suffered destruction of the nerve centers that control or minimize the stretch reflex, so that the slightest movements or tensions produce exaggerated antagonistic muscle movements. With the spastic, whose reciprocal inhibition is lost, an attempted movement in one direction produces a poorly timed, jerky movement in the opposite direction, severely limiting such movements as reaching or maintaining posture. In extreme cases, the joints of the body are held in partially flexed positions, making the spastic less normal in appearance than those with other types of cerebral palsy. When spastics are inactive and not tense, however, they do not appear different from normal children. Contracture (shortening or distortion of muscles caused by prolonged hypertonicity) may occur if motion exercises are not performed daily. Mental impairment is often associated with this type of cerebral palsy.

Athetoids display exaggerated overflow from slight exertion or tension. Some overflow is even present during their inactivity, so that an athetoid is almost constantly squirming or wriggling the affected parts of the body. The extraneous movement is involuntary and hard to control and always confuses purposeful movements. Uncontrollable tremors, usually pendular or patternlike in nature, may be present. There are two types of athetoid cerebral palsy; the rotary type involves those muscles that take part in rotary movement, making slow circular movements as overflow; the tremorlike type causes irregular contraction and relaxation of those muscles that produce flexion, extension, abduction and adduction.

Ataxic cerebral palsy, a less common type, is thought to be the result of damage in the cerebellum or cerebellar pathways, which involve the integrating center for balance and direction. Ataxia produces poor motor coordination and a disturbed sense of balance and direction. The impressions are not integrated properly in the coordinating center of the cerebellum. As a result, a person is unable to make balance adjustments easily or control the direction and force of movements. "Timing" is off with some parts of bodily movement in disaccord with other parts. Ataxics have to concentrate to keep from falling and they walk with hesitant, faltering steps. In most ataxics, muscle tone is poor and muscle strength is weak.

Rigidity is a form of cerebral palsy characterized by resistance to slow, passive movements resembling the movements of a cogwheel. It is generally believed that the destruction of motor cells is diffused throughout the brain as opposed to a localized lesion. Such destruction may be caused by diseases like encephalitis or by cerebral hemorrhages in later life. Children with this type of cerebral palsy have impaired stretch-reflexes, which show in the hyperextension of body parts. With severe muscle rigidity, the child lies helplessly in a "windswept" or arching position.

Tremor is a type of cerebral palsy that produces involuntary movements of the flexor and extensor muscles. A tremor that is increased by voluntary motion is called an "intention" tremor, which stems from damage to the cerebellum. "Rest" tremors, on the other hand, are caused by damage to the basal ganglia; these *decrease* during voluntary movement. Individuals with either "intentional" or "rest" tremors may develop increased muscle tone, or "dystonia," a condition sometimes leading to bony deformities of a disabling nature.

Mixed patients are those who display cerebral palsy symptoms of more than one type, and they are classified as having "mixed" cerebral palsy. They are usually more impaired than people who exhibit symptoms of a single type.

Spina Bifida

Spina bifida is a birth defect in which the formation of the vertebral bodies is incomplete. One or more vertebral arches fail to close properly, allowing exposure of the spinal canal. Neurological manifestations may range in severity from none (little or no evidence of paralysis) to severe (total paraplegia, bowel and bladder incontinence). There are three types of spina bifida:

> *Spina bifida occulta.* This benign condition, which may go unnoticed, is a defect in the fusion of the posterior vertebral arch and does not require treatment. It is a condition in which the skin and the spinal cord are normal.

> *Meningocele.* In this condition, the meninges (coverings of the spinal cord) protrude through the defective opening in the vertebrae in the form of a sac which contains the pia mater, dura mater, and arachnoid and which is filled with cerebrospinal fluid. The spinal cord and nerve roots remain in normal position. Surgical closure may be necessary to prevent rupture of the sac; and if successful, no neurological disability results. However, there may be some paralysis, and even urinary and bowel dysfunction. Sensation may also be lessened or completely lost.

> *Meningomyelocele.* This, the most serious form of spina bifida, exists when the sac protruding throught the defective vertebrae includes portions of the spinal cord itself, as well as the meninges fluid. This condtition requires surgical closure. Some paralysis below the waist usually exists as well as bowel and urinary dysfunction. The nature of the involvement depends on the location of the spinal cord lesion that accompanies the condition.

Epilepsy

Epilepsy is a brain disorder consisting of disturbances in the normal biochemical/electrical activity of the brain. Epileptics represent from two to three percent of the general population. The frequency, however, is much higher with certain neuromuscular disabilities. The disorder may be divided into two categories: (1) *primary* or idiopathic, in which the exact etiology is unknown, and (2) *secondary* or acquired, which is in addition to some other brain abnormality. The latter may be a head injury or a brain irritation (resulting from a complication of encephalitis, meningitis, or localized lesions such as brain tumors or cerebral abscesses). Epilepsy must be distinguished from simple febrile convulsions, frequently found in children between the ages of six months and three years. Some metabolic disorders accompanied by seizures or convulsions are not classified as epilepsy. These include low blood sugar (associated with insulin reaction in the diabetic), low blood calcium, and barbiturates withdrawal. Although epilepsy is described according to an international classification, most types fit the following descriptions.

The first is called major motor, or generalized *tonic-clonic* ("grand mal"). This form of epilepsy usually has its onset before the age of twenty years. It has four phases. The first known as the aura, or "premonition" phase, consists of a warning of an oncoming attack. Usually an epileptic has the same warning—a vague sensation or strange feeling. In the second, or *tonic* phase, a generalized stiffening of the entire body occurs. During this seizure, which lasts 15 to 30 seconds, the individual falls, loses consciousness, and becomes blue (cyanotic) from lack of oxygen. The third, or *clonic* phase, is marked by repetitive and severe muscular contractions of all four extremities and the head. It is approximately two to five minutes in duration, and may be accompanied by frothing of the mouth and loss of bladder or bowel control. In the last phase, the individual enters the so-called postictal, or postseizure, state of deep sleep, which extends from minutes to hours. Upon awaking from a seizure, epileptics are usually disoriented, complain of headache, severe muscle soreness, or amnesia.

The next three types of epilepsy belong to the "petit mal" triad characterized by extreme frequency, short duration, onset in childhood, and limited postictal or postseizure duration. The "absence" type, a blank spell, is a sudden arrest of motor activity in which the person stares into space, his or her eyes blinking and hands twitching slightly. This seizure lasts from 2 to 5 seconds, after which the individual, though somewhat confused, generally resumes usual activity. A second type of minor motor triad is the akinetic/atonic type, or a "drop attack," in which the epileptic suddenly loses muscle tone but rarely consciousness. Also of short duration, this seizure may cause injury as a result of falling. The third in the triad is the myoclonic type, a sudden strong contraction of the muscles of the extremities, that is brief and without loss of consciousness.

The last type of seizure described is one of the most common types of seizures and it is at times very difficult to diagnose and treat. This is a complex, partial seizure alternately termed a psychomotor or "temporal-lobe" seizure, in which the focus of irritation is in the temporal lobe of the brain. Such seizures are distinguished by sudden arrest of normal activity, sensations of fear, and visual, auditory or olfactory hallucinations. Motor activity during this seizure is often semipurposeful: scratching one's head, rubbing an arm or a leg, buttoning or unbuttoning a coat. Other activities associated with the mouth area are also observed: chewing motions, swallowing, and lip smacking. Persons may turn pale, become sweaty (diaphoretic), have dilated pupils and a tachycardia (fast heart rate). Occurring at any time in one's lifespan, these seizures may last from minutes to hours, though usually a few minutes only. Loss of awareness, confusion, and disorientation often join with an impulse to sleep for a short period of time. Such epileptics may respond to the spoken voice but may experience difficulty in expressing themselves. Common in adults, the psychomotor or temporal lobe type can occur at any age.

Other types of seizures that may be encountered are of the "focal" type. These can be either motor or sensory and originate in specific areas of the brain that correspond to clinical manifestations involving certain areas of the body.

The major motor seizure brings about a condition called *status epilepticus,* a generalized "grand mal" seizure followed by repeated tonic-clonic activity without any regaining of consciousness. A medical emergency, it must be brought to the physician's attention immediately. With respect to epilepsies, many people may have several different types of seizures, a so-called mixed seizure disorder.

Seizures may be aggravated by many factors such as anxiety, stress, alcoholic beverages, menstrual periods, hyperventilation, bright lights, loud noises, or general illness. These triggering factors should be eliminated as much as possible consistent with normal daily living. Only in this century have anticonvulsant medications exerted control. In 1908 Phenobarbital was introduced; in 1937, Dilantin; since then, research in the development and use of psychotropic drugs on motor performance has expanded. The goal of therapy is to obtain maximum control of seizures with minimal side effects. The method used by most physicians is a careful history-taking and a thorough examination—neurological, EEG, general, physical, and diagnostic. All are intended to identify the nonepileptic. Such tests also classify the type of seizure or seizures so that appropriate medications may be prescribed. Frequently, trial and error is the sole means of finding the right medication or combination of medications that will help keep the seizure under control with minimal side effects. Education is the greatest tool to dispel the many misconceptions about epilepsy.

Muscular Dystrophy

This condition is described as being a progressive degeneration of the muscles of the body. The disease is of a genetic origin and is characterized by progressive muscular weakness. The exact etiology is unknown; however, it is recognized that the condition is brought about by changes that take place in the muscle fibers. Differentiation of types of muscular dystrophy is frequently made according to the area of the body primarily affected and the age of onset of the disability. These types are

Facioscapulohumeral. Usually affects the facial muscles first, then slowly progresses to involve the shoulder girdle, then the muscles of the upper arm. The onset of this type of muscular dystrophy is usually around puberty.

Juvenile or Limb-Girdle. Slow progress and limited involvement of the pelvic girdle or shoulder girdle muscles. The onset is usually in early childhood, and the youngster becomes severely disabled, generally dying in his or her 30's or 40's from respiratory or cardiac problems.

Duchenne or Pseudohypertropic. The most prevalent, most severe, and most progressive form of muscular dystrophy. The etiology is a sex-linked trait that is passed on through women to men and occurs almost exclusively in young males. This type of muscular dystrophy usually leaves the youngster completely helpless six to twelve years after the first signs of its onset. Death usually results from involvement of the respiratory muscles or cardiac failure. The first weakness begins in the hip, pelvis, and abdomen, progressing upward and outward throughout the body. Most often seen in the calf, pseudohypertrophy occurs when the fat and connective tissue replace degenerating muscle fibers; thus, the body appears to have well-developed musculature when, in actuality, the muscles have little strength and endurance.

Muscular Atrophy

The shrinking of muscles because of nutritional deficiencies, caused either by lack of exercise, disease, spinal cord injury, or interference with the nerve or blood supply. Muscular atrophy commonly results from a neurological dysfunction whereby the lower motor neuron cell-bodies degenerate and become incapable of transmitting impulses to the motor nerve-fibers, which normally supply the muscular system. Characteristics are paralysis, shrinking of muscles, fasciculations (erratic twitching fibers), loss of reflexes, and lack of sensation.

Poliomyelitis

The Salk and Sabin vaccines have eliminated this dread disease. In cases where the vaccine has *not* been used, polio may still be encountered. It is brought about by an acute viral infection that causes motor-neuron cell injury and destruction to those cells mainly located in the anterior horn of the spinal cord. The injury and destruction to these cells affect any number of muscle groups in the body. For example, the individual's deficit may be a mild weakness of an arm, or may range to a more extensive impairment such as total paralysis that in itself may result in death. Polio may occur in any one of three stages: acute (lasts for several days), convalescent (may last from one, two or three weeks to several months), and chronic (may persist for years).

Multiple Sclerosis

A chronic, progressive disease of unknown cause, usually affecting persons between the ages of 20 to 45. It is characterized by the degeneration of the myelin nerve axon sheaths. The resulting scar tissue replaces the disintegrating myelin tissue. Individuals with this disease exhibit a wide variety of symptoms; some of the most common are spastic paraplegia with slight speech problems, poor motor coordination, muscular weakness, and bladder and bowel difficulties.

Parkinson's Disease

A progressive degenerative disease of the central nervous system that usually begins in the fifth or sixth decade of life. The symptoms are rigidity, tremors, and a slow gait consisting of short, shuffling steps. As the disease progresses, the patient experiences extreme difficulty in all voluntary movements, walks with an abnormal gait, has poor balance, and displays emotional stress and pain. Those with "Parkinsonism" are in urgent need of physical activity if they are to lessen its effects.

Spinal Cord Injuries

Damage to the spinal column in the form of dislocated or fractured vertebrae may result in a severed or compressed spinal cord. Since it does not regenerate, injuries to it may result in a permanent disturbance of the motor and sensory functions below the level of the trauma. Such effects will be of varying degrees of severity. The location of paralysis is directly related to the site of the injury. For instance, a severed spinal cord caused by a neck injury will result in upper and lower bilateral paralysis, whereas a similar injury to the lower spine would result in paralysis of the lower body only. The term *paraplegia** is used to refer to paralysis of both legs and of the lower part of the trunk; such paralysis usually results from damage to the spinal cord at the thoracic or lumbar level. *Quadriplegia* refers to paralysis affecting all four limbs and the upper trunk as well as the lower, although it may vary in extent. Usually the result of lesions at the sixth or seventh vertebrae, it may allow use of the biceps but not the triceps.

ORTHOPEDIC IMPAIRMENTS

This class of impairments involving the musculo-skeletal system affects either the bones, joints, or tendons and prevents proper motor functions of the body and body parts. Orthopedic impairments are congenital or acquired and have varied causes.

Congenital

Congenital orthopedic impairments of structure or function are apparent at birth or are genetically caused, although they usually do not appear until later in life. They may be the result of chromosomal abnormalities and inherited enzyme or hormonal defects.

Paraparesis is the term for disablement of the lower trunk and legs, which is not complete, i.e., there is still some use of the affected area.

Clubfoot is the most prevalent of all congenital orthopedic impairments. The foot is twisted out of shape or position in such a way that the individual is forced to walk on the outside edge of the foot, causing further bone deformities and posture problems. There are several types of clubfoot, and the functional impairment varies with the degree of the anatomical deformity. Treatment involves therapy and special footgear.

Congenital amputation refers either to the absence of limbs or parts of limbs at birth. This condition is often associated with thalidomide cases, in which women using the tranquilizer thalidomide in the early stages of pregnancy gave birth in many cases to babies with such birth deformities.

Dysplasia, or *congenital hip dislocation,* is the result of partial development or complete displacement of the femoral head in relation to the acetabulum. There are two types of dysplasia. In *subluxation,* there is only partial development of the femoral head. In *luxation,* the femoral head is completely displaced and moves above the acetabulum edge.

Dwarfism refers to retarded growth resulting from damage of the anterior lobe of the pituitary gland in childhood. Tumors, disease, or an anomaly of the gland are among the causes.

Achondroplasia is a congenital skeletal anomaly in which the trunk and head of the individual is approximately normal size with asymmetrically shorter arms and legs. Because of this anomaly, the individual has limited extension of the elbows, the abdominal and gluteal areas protrude with substantial lumbar lordosis, and one exhibits a waddling type of gait.

Osteogenesis Imperfecta is an hereditary disease characterized by the increased fragility of the bones, which are easily fractured by slight trauma. Some children who have this disease are unable to walk. However, by the late teens, bones strengthen and there is a more normal condition in the bone structure.

Acquired

An injury to the musculo-skeletal system or any surgery that removes or limits the function of a limb is called a "trauma" and comes under the classification of "acquired."

Amputation is the removal of a limb or part of a limb, either as the result of an accident or as a surgical procedure necessary to arrest a disease. Surgical operations may be required by the presence of a malignant tumor or by diseases that cause circulatory problems wherein a lack of blood circulation in a limb makes it impossible for dead cells to be replaced (such as diabetes and arteriosclerosis). Another purpose of elective amputation may be to arrest the spread of infection. Amputations are classified according to the level of the limb at which they are performed. Disarticulation is the term for amputation through a joint. Amputations are also classified according to the nature of the closing. An open amputation leaves a surface wound that is not covered with skin. A closed amputation is one that creates a stump suitable for the use of an artificial limb. Most prosthetic devices for amputees require an extensive period of training.

Slipped femoral epiphysis, or adolescent coxa vara, may be the result of trauma to the hip area. In this condition, the epiphysis, either gradually or all at once, slips downward and backward in relation to the neck of the femur. The exact cause of this dislocation is unknown, and hormonal disturbance may also be a factor. This displacement usually occurs during a period of abnormally rapid growth in adolescence. Pins are sometimes placed across the epipyseal plate to keep the femur in correct position until union between the bones takes place.

Burn injuries are, by definition, those injuries that damage the skin, whether as a result of fire, chemicals, or electricity. Contact with very hot or very cold liquids over an extended period of time are also causes. Disabilities resulting from thermal injuries include possible amputation and hypertrophic scarring, in which thick scar tissue forms across joints. Fusion of finger-web spaces results in a condition known as *burn syndactyl.* Range of motion is limited, and skeletal anomalies such as scoliosis are evident, as well as varying degrees of shortening of affected muscles. Severe burns may require several years of rehabilitation before full use of the limbs is regained.

Fractures, dislocations, sprains, bruises and contusions, and wounds are categories of trauma that may lead to impairment, especially if not properly treated. Many different types of fractures may require surgical reconstruction and extended periods of therapy before useful mobility is restored. Original strength and range of motion may never be recovered. Hip fractures, severe crushing injuries and damage to tendons and ligaments may be as severely debilitating as amputations.

Osteochondrosis

This is a disorder in one or more of the ossification centers during children's growth period, which may result in orthopedic impairment.

Coxa plana or Legg-Calve-Perthes Disease is a disease of the hip(s) that causes the flattening of the head of the femur bone because of circulatory disturbance from strain or trauma to the hip area. It is more prevalent in males than females and occurs between the ages of 4 and 10 years. The disease runs a definite course lasting from one to three years and eventually heals. It may leave a deformity of the hip area, such as a shortening of the diseased leg or extensive destruction of the femoral head, and severe impairment of hip function. Weight-bearing activities that focus on the hip area should be avoided.

Osgood-Schlatter Disease is a condition in which osteochondrosis occurs in the tuberosity of the tibia, causing separation of the tibia tubercle (to which the kneecap is attached) from the tibia, in much the same manner as *coxa plana.* This condition is almost certainly caused by chronic trauma to the tibial tuberosity.

Scheuermann's Disease is a condition of the spine, probably a developmental abnormality that causes kyphosis (hunch back). The vertebral epiphyses are affected. This disease frequently requires bracing to lessen the pain and to prevent deformity.

Infection and Disease

Infection and disease account for many cases of orthopedic impairment.

Rheumatoid arthritis is a condition of inflammation of the joints along with pain, heat, redness, and swelling resulting from rheumatism. It attacks both joints and connective tissue structures with painful inflammation that may cause erosion of the cartilage over a period of time. Several joints at once are usually affected, particularly those of the hands and feet. This condition is accompanied by general muscular weakness and fatigue. The resulting arthritis becomes progressively worse.

There are other forms of arthritis that may afflict the individual, such as *osteoarthritis,* or degenerative joint disease, a natural effect of aging; *arthritis resulting from rheumatic fever; arthritis resulting from known infectious agents;* and *arthritis resulting from trauma.*

Osteomyelitis, a bone infection that most often occurs between the ages of 5 and 14, is caused by the body's reaction to the presence of staphylococcus, salmonella, and other pathogenic bacteria. The effects of the disease are pain, hardening of the overlying tissues of the body, distension of neighboring joints that fill with fluid, and movement hindered by pain. The disease is described as acute in its early stages; if the infection persists or becomes recurring, it is in the chronic phase, a condition that may linger for years. An outward symptom of osteomyelitis is the forming of a subperiosteal abscess on the surface of an affected bone, which leads to the formation of a pus-discharging sinus in the skin over the bone.

Tuberculous infection is a disease caused by the presence of *bacillus tuberculous.* The disease can affect tissues and organs as well as bones and joints. The bones most often affected are the femur and tibia.

Rickets is a childhood metabolic disorder of the bones usually caused by Vitamin D deficiency. Some of the skeletal changes are soft and pliable bones, exaggerated curvatures of the long bones, and bone deformities (knock-knees, bowlegs, and malformation of the chest).

Posture Deviations

Poor posture and poor body mechanics occur when the body and body parts are not in correct alignment during standing, walking, running, sitting, or lying. Poor posture tends to produce more strain and stress on the supporting body structures, thus resulting in improper balance both while in static (stationary) or dynamic

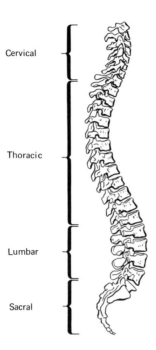

(moving) positions. The years of childhood are best for correcting postural deviations, for then deviations can often be identified by screening tests.*

There are several causes of poor posture and poor body mechanics. Among these are weak postural muscles that fail to maintain proper posture and congenital orthopedic impairments such as shortness of one leg, forward head, or rounded shoulders. The etiology, or complex of causes, is long: visual and auditory impairments, general fatigue resulting from lack of sleep or rest, malnourishment, injuries that cause the individual to shift weight to avoid pain, mental and emotional factors such as stress, worry, fear, and insecurity, rapid structural growth caused by some body parts developing faster than others, environmental factors such as poorly fitted shoes and clothing, poor lighting and poor bed mattresses, and finally, lack of posture knowledge.

Postural deviations are classified as "structural," referring to permanent changes, and "functional," referring to temporary involvement of muscles and ligaments—deviations that can be corrected by prescribed corrective exercises.

The normal spine is divided into four curves: cervical, thoracic, lumbar, and sacral, as shown in the diagram.

The spinal column is the focal point for the three most common postural deviations: *kyphosis* (round upper back or shoulders), *lordosis* (exaggeration of the

*A posture screening test may be found in Appendix C.

lumbar curve), and *scoliosis* (lateral curvature of the spine). Other common and observable deviations include forward head, flat back, protruding shoulder blades, round shoulders, flat feet, and either ankle pronation (ankles roll inward) or supination (ankles roll outward).

Obesity*

As a clinical term, "obesity" refers to the presence of excess body weight. Persons approximately 20 percent above ideal weight qualify as "obese." Standardized reference tables indicate ideal body weight, or norms, for a given age, sex, and height, but their accuracy is questionable.

A person becomes obese when there is an imbalance between calorie intake (food) and the total energy needed to sustain physical activity and growth. As a result, fat is accumulated and stored as adipose tissue. Obesity, in most cases, is due to simple overindulgence of food associated with familiar and emotional factors and is rarely due to endocrine or metabolic disease.

Overeating, poor eating habits, and lack of physical activity comprise the first and most common cause of nonendocrine obesity. It is during early childhood that the child formulates eating habits. To control a child's weight, parents should, if possible, plan the largest meal at mid-day since the period of greatest physical activity is usually in the afternoon. "Snacks" during the afternoon and evening can upset a whole day of dieting.

Psychological dependency is a second cause of obesity. Some people overeat out of nervousness or as a substitute while withdrawing from smoking and alcohol, while others overeat to avoid doing an unpleasant task. It is well established that psychological problems can cause obesity.

Hypothyroidism is a common endocrine disorder due to a low level of the hormone thyroxine and may on occasion be a cause of obesity. The basal metabolic rate in this instance is slow, thereby decreasing the individual's response to usual environmental stimuli. Food, for example, will be slowly broken down and taken up as fat. Hypothyroidism can be controlled by drug-replacement therapy.

Diabetes Mellitus may actually be brought on in certain individuals by obesity. By itself, it may contribute to obesity.

Cushing Syndrome results from the overproduction of cortisone by the adrenal gland. Most cases are due to the bilateral adrenal hyperplasia. A rare type of obesity, it is exemplified by unusual fat distribution such as hump in back of the neck ("buffalo hump"), rounded face ("moon face"), and trunkal obesity with thin extremities.

Gonadal deficiency is due to the effect of the sex hormones on basal metabolism. Children may be obese before they reach puberty, but once this state is reached, their weight tends to decrease.

*Screening tests used to determine obesity may be found on page 60.

CARDIOVASCULAR IMPAIRMENTS

Cardiovascular impairments are those that affect the heart or blood vessels. Such abnormalities are extremely varied, causing mild to severe symptoms depending upon the type of defect and the degree of involvement. Some can be alleviated while others are life-threatening.

Congenital Cardiovascular Malformations

Heart defects in younger people are most commonly congenital and often involve a malformation of the valves or the chambers of the heart or of the large blood vessels near the heart. The cause of congenital heart malformations, though usually indeterminate, has been linked to a maternal history of virus infections, vitamin deficiencies, or excessive exposure to radiation during pregnancy. Heart surgery can correct most of these heart defects. Special post-operative exercises are necessary to rehabilitate the muscles involved in the large incision made for heart surgery. After correction of the defect and rehabilitation, no limitations in exercises should be necessary.

Many of the congenital heart defects can be thought of in terms of their method of causing physiologic impairment. The great majority cause *left-to-right shunt*. In the left-to-right shunt, most of the blood flow, seeking an alternative path, preferentially circulates through the lungs. This eventually results in permanent damage to the pulmonary arteries and lungs and may result in right-sided heart failure. Three types of lesions may cause left-to-right shunts: ventricular septal defect, caused by a hole in the wall between the two ventricles; patent ductus arteriosis, an abnormally persistent connection between the aorta and pulmonary artery; atrial septal defect, a hole in the wall between the two atria.

The other basic physiologic abnormality is the *right-to-left* shunt. Here, the circulation preferentially by-passes the lungs, causing *cyanosis* (blue baby). This defect is usually caused by *Tetralogy of Fallot,* consisting of pulmonary stenosis, ventricular septal, enlarged right ventricle, and overriding aorta.

Coronary Heart Disease

Coronary heart disease occurs when there is a blockage of the coronary arteries because of atherosclerosis. Blockage of the coronary arteries will decrease blood flow to the heart and damage the heart muscle. *Atherosclerosis,* hardening or degeneration of the arteries, can affect not only the heart but other vital areas such as the kidneys, brain, and peripheral circulation. Possible causes of this condition, in which the inner linings of the arteries thicken and become rough and resistant to blood flow, are an upset in cholesterol metabolism, hereditary defects, poor physical habits, and the normal aging process.

Angina *pectoris* is a manifestation of coronary artery disease caused by deficient oxygenation of the heart muscle. It is marked by brief paroxysmal attacks of chest pain usually following exertion.

Hypertensive Cardiovascular Disease

Hypertensive heart disease results from the strain put upon the heart when there is high blood pressue and constriction of the smallest arteries of the body. Resistance to blood flow makes the heart work harder to circulate the blood. Although hypertension can be relatively well controlled today through early detection and drug therapy, the disease may lead to any of several manifestations that warrant serious attention. Among them are stroke, heart failure, renal failure, and myocardial infarction.

Heart Infections

Heart disease may be brought about by infection. *Endocarditis* involves the valves; *pericarditis* is an inflammation of the outer lining of the heart; and *myocarditis* is an inflammation of the heart wall. All of these conditions may be the result of childhood diseases such as rheumatic fever.

Valvular stenosis consists of narrowing or stiffness of the heart valves. If this affects the pulmonary valve, it may lead to "right" heart failure. If aortic stenosis is present, there is a diminution of blood flow to the rest of the body and the possibility of "left" heart failure.

Coarctation is a narrowing of the aorta, which results in decreased blood flow to the lower extremities and hypertension to the upper extremities.

Rheumatic Heart Disease

Occurring most often during childhood, one or more rheumatic fever attacks may inflict lasting damage on the heart, usually by scarring the heart valves. Such attacks are caused by the sequalae of untreated beta hemolytic streptococcal infections of the upper respiratory tract (pharyngitis, tonsillitis, and scarlet fever). Once a child has rheumatic fever, he or she becomes increasingly susceptible to another attack. Recurrence may result in chronic heart disease. Inflammation of the joints usually accompanies this disease.

Some of the signs associated with rheumatic fever attacks are poor appetite, recent sore throat, fatigue, fever, and pain in the joints. During the fever, the child is confined to bed and, on recovering, is instructed to follow doctor's orders for all physical activities.

Heart Conditions

Poor oxygenation of the blood and insufficient cardiac output often affect a person's total performance. One may suffer from a number of symptoms: dizziness, shortness of breath, chest pain, rapid pulse, general sensation of exhaustion, profuse perspiration, blurred vision, and a numbness or tingling sensation in the extremities. Heart conditions are classified in four groups according to the degree of functional capacity and of limitations on activity. Those in *Group I* have not been limited in their physical activity at all. *Group II* individuals have slight limitation; ordinary activity results in fatigue, palpitation, and either dyspnea (difficulty in breathing) or anginal pain. Those in *Group III* have suffered marked limitations on their physical activity. Even mild activity causes them to feel the above danger symptoms. *Group IV* heart cases are unable to carry on any physical activity whatsoever without discomfort; the symptoms of fatigue, anginal pain, etc. are present for them even when they are at rest.

RESPIRATORY IMPAIRMENTS

Several common lung diseases may lead to respiratory impairments that affect both the ability to breathe and the function of breathing.

Bronchial Asthma

The clinical manifestations are usually wheezing and marked shortness of breath. Physiologically, an asthmatic has three basic abnormalities in the bronchial tubes: edema, or swelling of the tubes; mucous plugs, which are thick and tenacious; and constriction of the muscular layers of the tubes, which causes the tubes to clamp down. Medically, the most severe case of clinical bronchial asthma is so-called *status asthmaticus*. In this condition, the asthmatic develops a severe, prolonged, and intractable attack that does not respond to the usual medical therapy without hospitalization. Attacks may be triggered by a viral infection, even the common cold, and an asthmatic may be more predisposed to bacterial pneumonia than a normal individual. Emotional strain, fatigue, and overexertion are contributing factors.

The two basic types of asthma are allergic, or extrinsic asthma, and intrinsic asthma. The first, which occurs in children and young adults, is often related to an allergic history. The individual, having become sensitized to such agents as animal hair, pollen, or dust, develops wheezing attacks on contact with them. By contrast, intrinsic asthma occurs in adults who often have no previous history of allergy. Asthma is reversible.

Children with asthma tend to be in poorer physical condition than their contemporaries because concerned teachers and parents fear that overexertion may trigger an attack. Restricted in their physical activities, such children develop poor muscle tone. Any form of even mild physical activity may bring on another attack that further reduces their activity as well as their incentive. Weight problems and undermined confidence are the inevitable result. It should be emphasized, therefore, that asthma in itself is not a contraindication to physical activity.

Emphysema and Chronic Bronchitis

Chronic lung disease has three manifestations: *emphysema, chronic bronchitis,* and *restrictive lung disease.* In the case of *emphysema,* which occurs in the fourth or fifth decade of life, the lungs and body are constantly working to maintain a normal oxygenization of blood despite the abnormality of the lungs. Hence, the descriptive term for the affected—"pink puffers." Any hindrance to this effort will cause a severe breakdown of one's ability to maintain blood oxygenization. Physiologically, emphysema is characterized by lungs that cannot expire the normal amount of air during respiration. They become stiff and enlarged, losing their normal patterns through failure to expire carbon dioxide. Clinically, persons with emphysema are distinguished by their larger anterior-posterior rib-cage diameter and their inability to breathe adequately with the respiratory muscles alone. Instead, they often resort to the use of neck and abdominal muscles as well.

The chronic bronchitic persons cannot attain normal physiologic parameters. Living as they must with less oxygen in their blood, they are unable to exert themselves as those with pure emphysema. Often dusky in complexion (from cyanosis), they experience attacks accompanied by the production of purulent sputum from their lungs. Obstructions from chronic bronchitis have similar clinical findings as those from emphysema. However, most individuals with the so-called chronic obstructive lung diseases usually are a mixed type; they have some of the characteristics of both emphysema and bronchitis. It is probably more reasonable to deal with this group under the single heading of chronic obstructive lung disease. The final stage of this disease is often heart failure or respiratory failure, the latter a result of both infection and continuous deterioration. Smoking is related to these conditions.

Restrictive lung disease refers to severe chest deformities that can also lead to respiratory difficulties. This condition, in contrast to obstructive lung disease, refers to either a neuromuscular or a structural abnormality that impairs the ability of the lungs to expand adequately, such as after extensive removal of lung tissue or severe kyphoscoliosis.

Cystic Fibrosis

Cystic fibrosis is inherited as a recessive trait. Clinically, sticky mucous obstructs the bronchioles of the lungs. The child is prone to a recurrent infection that can further damage the lungs. The long-term prognosis is poor; patients sometimes die at an early age from either deteriorating lung functions or continuous infections. Numerous screening devices are now available to pediatricians, including the so-called sweat test, which often shows an elevated amount of sodium chloride excreted from these children's sweat glands. They are usually quite limited in physical activity because of poor lung function.

MENTAL IMPAIRMENTS

Mental retardation refers to significantly subaverage general intellectual functioning, with the I.Q. usually below 70. Existing concurrently with mental retardation are deficits in adaptive behavior or activity of daily living skills. It is manifested during the developmental period before 18 years of age. The level of retardation is determined both by measured intelligence, the number of standard deviations below the mean I.Q., and the degree of impairment in adaptive behavior. This condition is caused by anything that interferes with development before or during birth, or in early childhood. The principal causes, conditions, and diseases associated with mental retardation are listed below.

Genetic. Chromosomal abnormalities, including Down's Syndrome; these include such biochemical disorders as those caused by inborn errors of metabolism, or nutritional, endocrine or growth dysfunctions that can damage the nervous system. These include hypothyroidism, galactosemia, or phenylketonuria (PKU).

Prenatal. Prenatal infection or disease, such as rubella (German measles), toxoplasmosis, and syphilis; prenatal trauma—an accident in pregnancy that affects the fetus—resulting in retarded fetal growth; X-ray irradiation, particularly during the first trimester of pregnancy; severe jaundice due to RH factor incompatibility; toxic agents such as drugs, lead, and carbon monoxide that poison the fetus and result in brain damage; unknown prenatal influences that cause such cerebral malformation as absence of part of the brain (*anencephaly*); craniofacial anomalies of unknown origin such as microcephaly anomalies (small cranial cavities); faulty closure of the neural tube, such as *spina bifida* and *hydrocephalus* (excessive cerebrospinal fluid, causing enlargement of the head).

Perinatal. Gestational disorder, including low birth-weight, premature birth, and postmature birth; asphyxia (lack of oxygen to the brain); brain injuries (as in breech or difficult forceps deliveries); labor difficulties; umbilical cord strangulation.

Postnatal. Head and spinal injuries that cause damage to the brain; cerebral infections (encephalitis and meningitis); cerebral damage caused by such toxic agents as lead poisoning, or gross brain disease in which there may be combined lesions of the skin and nervous system such as *neurofibromatosis* and *tuberous sclerosis*. Retardations of this type show easily identifiable skin lesions.

Familial-Cultural and Environmental Retardation. This may result from nutritional, chemical, psychological, and mechanical factors. This type is accompanied by sensory deprivation or severe defects of the senses.

Down's Syndrome or Mongolism. This is a form of retardation made up of three types—standard trisomy, translocation, and mosaic. The type could account for much of the variance seen in motor skills in the Down's Syndrome population. The individual exhibits abnormal physical growth and development. Such physical deformities as posture defects, dislocated hips, pigeon-breasted chest, club feet, and lax ligaments are common, the latter of which leads to such problems as flat feet and hyperextensible joints. Congenital heart problems and general immaturity of the circulatory system are also closely associated with Down's Syndrome.

The individual usually has a round shaped face with mongoloid features, short stubby fingers, and muscular flabbiness (hypotonia) the last of which decreases with age. Persons with Down's Syndrome are generally thought of as well-mannered and responsible. Teachers invariably describe them as cooperative and friendly.

The cause of Down's Syndrome is relted to the defective separation of chromosomes during the development of the egg or sperm, or in the initial cell division of the fertilized egg. Rather than the normal 46 chromosomes in each cell, these individuals have 47. A connection between Down's Syndrome and older maternal age exists.

Educational Categories of Retardation

Mental retardation falls into several educational categories based on the severity of the condition.

Mild retardation. Individuals in this category have I.Q. scores ranging from about 50 to 70. They are close to normal in motor performance, height, and weight. Some deficiency in their verbal communication is likely, and they are slow in mental development, but they are usually capable of learning some academic skills, and their communication skills can be developed adequately for most situations.

Moderate retardation. The group includes all those with I.Q.'s ranging from about 35 to 50. Such youngsters need special education; those most severely affected may have to live in residential facilities. Most of this group show some possibility of learning to care for their personal needs, of adjusting socially, and of performing in a work situation. But some care, supervision, and economic support will be required throughout their lives. The social age of these individuals is more important than their chronological age; a "moderately retarded" adolescent, for example, may have reached a social age of seven years. Down's Syndrome children are variable but usually function at this level of retardation.

Severe retardation. This embraces all those with I.Q.'s ranging from 20 to 35. Possessing few, if any, communication skills, these children evidence a developmental motor lag. Nevertheless, they may respond to training in self-help (in feeding and toilet duties). As a group, however, they need constant direction and supervision.

Profound retardation. These youngsters have an I.Q. below the 20's, are grossly retarded, and have minimal functional capacities in psychomotor movements. As a group they have developmental lags in all areas and are usually nonverbal. Yet, if taught and supervised carefully, they can be trained to use their hands and legs. They need continued nursing help, as they are usually incapable of most self-care skills.

Until quite recently both the "severely" and the "profoundly" retarded were placed in institutions, state hospitals, or treatment centers. A movement is afoot, however, to bring some of these young people into the public school system. As the idea of integrating them begins to spread, outmoded definitions of "education" will give way to new concepts. The time may soon arrive when education may mean a process whereby individuals are helped to develop new behaviors to cope more effectively with the environment.

The labeling and classifying of mentally retarded children may soon be terminated. The I.Q. measurements, along with knowledge of the child's adaptive skills, will be used in developing the individualized education program.

EMOTIONAL IMPAIRMENTS

"Emotionally impaired" people are unable to function normally as individuals in society or to relate either to themselves or others in expressing feelings and reactions because of severe personality disturbances or misperceptions of reality.

Problem Behavior

"Emotional disturbance" in a child refers to behavior that clearly deviates from societal norms to such a degree that adults concerned with the child's development feel the need to request outside assistance. Quay and Werry (1972), in a recent multivariate statistical approach to the classification of childhood psychopathology, report at least three dimensions of problem behavior: aggression (conduct disorder), withdrawal (personality disorder), and immaturity.

Aggression. Children who manifest a conduct disorder are typically seen as disruptive, destructive, disobedient, and openly aggressive, either physically or verbally or both. As a result, they often find themselves in conflict with authority figures both in and out of school. They are impulsive and they have difficulty in delaying gratification. Much of their misbehavior stems from poor impulse-control and low frustration tolerance. They also experience difficulty in profiting from past experience; attempts to change their behavior by appealing to their consciences or by pointing out the negative consequences of future similar behavior are usually of little value. They habitually have a lowered self-concept; but unlike the child with a personality disorder who withdraws in order to hide this deficiency, children with conduct disorders utilize their misbehavior as an attention-getting device to gain status with their peers. Much of their behavior in the classroom has an overactive, restless, disturbing quality to it that generally results in their being described as ''problem children.'' Although underachievement in academic subjects is likely, these children, unlike children with personality disorders, rarely display withdrawal, inhibition, or fearfulness.

Teachers of children with conduct disorders will have to work very hard to avoid being manipulated. Strict adherence to rules and immediate penalties for misdeeds are a must. Moreover, teachers should realize the importance of clear-cut instructions for this type of child; they should be willing to directly confront those who fail to meet expectation.

Withdrawal. The behaviors, attitudes, and feelings of children with withdrawal or personality disorders clearly involve a different pattern of social interaction than do those of children with conduct disorders. They generally imply withdrawal rather than attack. This disorder is characterized by seclusiveness, detachment, sensitivity, shyness, timidity, and general inability to form close interpersonal relationships. In marked contrast to the characteristics of children with conduct disorders are such traits as feelings of distress, fear, anxiety, physical complaints, and open and expressed unhappiness. Fears, both general and specific, are central features of children with personality disorders. The impact that these types of children make upon their environment is less repugnant to both adults and their peers than that made by children with conduct disorders. They are less likely to stimulate others into action. If anything, they display too little rather than too much behavior, and their excessive avoidance-behavior may be so widespread as to make them appear to be behaviorally paralyzed. Although they may sometimes exhibit antisocial behavior, these children are generally minimally aggressive; they accept authority and are receptive to attempts to help them to change. Repeated delinquences are very uncommon. It is their lack of self-confidence, their inhibited, dutiful, and conforming behavior, that not only render delinquency unlikely but make them particularly apprehensive in unfamiliar situations. At times their generalized anxiety levels lead to attempted avoidance of participation in class, or even in school. Unfortunately, children with a personality disorder, because of their lack of overt misbehavior, are often seen by school personnel as the "good child." This often delays recognition of the child's problem.

Teachers of children who show personality disorders will need to encourage verbal interaction. In general, they must become emotionally involved with these children, making sure that they themselves are "open" so that feelings can be dealt with openly and honestly. Above all, teachers must understand that outward behavior is only a front for what lies behind.

Immaturity. Children who obtain high ratings on the immaturity dimension are typically seen as preoccupied, clumsy, passive, and daydreamy. They are frequently picked on by others and often prefer younger playmates. Their behavior is inappropriate to their chronological age. Unable to cope with a complex world, they frequently impress teachers as incompetent.

Teachers of children who score high in the dimension of immaturity should be aware of a constant need for attention and reassurance. Since these children habitually "wander off" mentally, their teachers must cultivate a patient, flexible, and, above all, informal teaching style.

Psychoses

In addition to Quay's three dimensions of problem behavior, attention should be given the most severe type of emotional impairment manifested by children: psychoses—the psychiatric term for serious and prolonged behavioral disorder. The most severe among the emotional impairments in childhood disorders of this type include schizophrenia, early infantile autism, and symbiotic psychoses.

Schizophrenia in children typically involves a gradual onset of such symptoms as marked social withdrawal, looseness of associations in thinking, preoccupation with fantasy life, and a break in reality testing. Development of this disorder typically occurs between the ages of six and twelve. Stereotyped motor patterns such as rocking and whirling may also be present. In the past, speculations regarding etiology have focused on the mother-child relationship. Mothers of childhood schizophrenics were seen as overintellectualized, and the idea of a schizophrenogenic mother gained wide clinical acceptance. Empirical support for such a hypothesis, however, is clearly lacking; and there is no clear evidence that the parents of schizophrenic children are in any way unique in terms of personality functioning.

Early infantile *autism,* a syndrome identified by Leo Kanner (1943) has four key symptoms: (1) inability to relate to people since birth, (2) absorption in fantasy as escape from reality and aloneness with little need for human contact, (3) obsessive insistence on the preservation of saneness, and (4) language disturbance, including a failure to develop speech. Hypotheses concerning the etiology of autism range from parental personality to neurobiological factors to genetic factors, but clear support for any particular hypothesis is lacking.

Symbiotic psychoses is a syndrome proposed by Margaret Mahler (1952). Symptoms include an unusual dependence on the mother, manifested by intense separation anxiety. Regressive behavior, frequently seen during times of stress, includes giving up of previously acquired speech. Symbiotic psychoses are conceived to represent a failure on the part of the child to move past the natural symbiotic relationship of infancy and to separate so as to develop an identity apart from that of the mother. The frequency of this condition is much less than either childhood schizophrenia or early infantile autism.

Treatment of psychotic children is primarily either educational, psychodynamic, behavioral, or organic. None of these approaches, however, has been able to show significant improvement in the actual psychotic behavior of the child, at least not in large groups of psychotic children. Behavioral approaches have had some limited success in improving adaptive behavior; this includes the acquisition of speech. Some evidence indicates that psychotic children who begin to improve before age five have better prognoses than those who do not. In general, the prognoses for childhood psychoses is poor.

MULTIPLE IMPAIRMENTS

Only a few handicaps commonly associated with one another are identified here even though there are many other combinations involving physical, mental, emotional, and social impairments.

Cerebral Palsy and Mental Retardation

Studies of the intelligence of the cerebral palsied tend to agree that the incidence of mental deficiency is high—roughly 50 to 60 percent have I.Q.'s below 70. Five percent have I.Q.'s above 115, while those between 70 and 115 make up about 35 to 45 percent of those with cerebral palsy.

Cerebral Palsy and Epilepsy

Evidence exists to suggest an association between the occurrence of cerebral palsy and epilepsy. Depending on the degree of involvement, the type of cerebral palsy, and the degree of control, epileptics may lead active lives with few modifications.

Epilepsy and Mental Retardation

Persons afflicted with these combined handicaps are generally more limited than those suffering only from epilepsy. However, the epileptic's lack of ability to cope emotionally with recurrent seizures may cause difficulties. Care should be taken to insure that children take their proper medication at prescribed times. In modifying activities of persons with these impairments, teachers should exercise care to avoid excessive fatigue but offer the same activities that are applicable to the peer group.

Mental Retardation and Cardiac Impairments

Congenital deformities of the heart are found to occur frequently with Down's Syndrome. Because of the predisposition to early fatigue and low endurance levels, this multiimpairment may constitute a profound disability in terms of physical activity, depending, of course, on the extent of the heart defect.

Auditory and Visual Impairments

The combination of deafness and blindness is a condition that may be acquired or hereditary. This combined handicap may be acquired throught diseases, such as German measles (*rubella*), scarlet fever, or meningitis.

CHAPTER 3

Self-Concept and Body Image

In order for learning to take place, one must be in the right frame of mind. How much more urgent it is, then, for insecure students to be helped to more positive feelings toward their impairments, their chances for improvement, and the opening up of their futures.

Although it may take weeks, months, or even years to alter negative images of the self existing in a youngster's mind, one fact is clear: no matter how low the self-regard, one can be helped in raising it. Fortunately for thousands of impaired and often depressed young people today, proven techniques to promote positive feelings are within the reach of teachers and counselors.

SELF-CONCEPT

The self-concept may be defined as a system of ideas, attitudes, appraisals, and commitments intimately related to one's own person. Oddly enough, each person experiences these concepts as if they are one's own, no matter how universally they are shared.

Psychology recognizes three components of the "self." The *perceptual component* is based on objective data as to the image of one's appearance, its effect on other people, and the effect of one's actions on the physical world. The *conceptual component,* on the other hand, consists of a knowledge of one's distinctive mental and emotional characteristics, abilities, and faults. Part of the conceptual self is awareness of origin and background, present impulses and temptations, role or roles in life, obligations and responsibilities. The third component, the *attitudinal* or *valuative component,* is made up of views of one's self as meriting either pride or shame and of views of one's present and future status.

How Johnny responds to a physical activity program or whether he responds at all is largely dependent on his self-concept. How will he react to the prosthetic device he may have to wear? Visible structural peculiarities may bear a social stigma. How does he see himself in relation to his handicap and to others similarly impaired? What adjustment has he made? Will he interpret his friend's attitude toward his condition as a reflection on his value as a person?

By contrast, heart or lung impairments may be less conspicuous or even unseen, but they usually limit motor activities, which are taken for granted by the rest of the world. Unable to be like the others on the playground, Mary may become frustrated, then angry, then—worst of all—self-recriminating.

Bodily stress and pain drastically reduce one's self-concept, and result in a brooding reluctance to undertake anything unfamiliar. Orthopedic impairments, for example, obviously make some movements difficult, often painful. A blind boy must avoid reckless movement or suffer embarrassment and a jarring collision. A girl with a breathing problem may be so fearful of a respiratory attack that she constructs a sort of fence around her normal desires to be active.

Any handicapped child's response to a prescribed physical activity program will therefore depend on a person's view of his or her body. Tedford and Sawrey (1977) have described four modes of adjustment to an impairment: one may succumb to it, deny it, accept it, or cope with it.

If Jody *succumbs* or takes a more or less hopeless view of the impairment as incurable or irremediable, he fancies himself to be totally lacking in the resources for dealing with the challenge. His response to outside "help" is passive. Although he may tolerate the help from others, he will usually shun active participation. Assuming a hopeless outlook, Jody abandons the very goal he has set for himself. In short, he overinterprets the impairment and underinterprets his own adaptive resources.

The second mode of adjustment is *denial* of the existence of the impairment. Not only has Beth, a paraplegic, rejected the reality of her situation but she attempts, and fails in, activities beyond her potential. She underinterprets the severity of the impairment and overestimates her own potential. Oftentimes this exaggerated self-concept is accompanied by her refusal of therapeutic treatment. In a sense, the mode of denial is beneficial because her activities, even though misguided, are positive efforts to maintain normality. Unfortunately, her chances of frustration have been increased.

Johnny, whose *acceptance* of his handicap exemplifies the third mode of adjustment, knows only too well the hampering effect of cerebral palsy. He goes along with measures that are prescribed. This reaction may be described as "good" in the sense that he is reacting positively to the management of his impairment. Although acceptance should never lead to a sense of a personal failure, nor to a defeatist attitude toward new activities, Johnny's acknowledgment of his impairment is an indication that he will probably find life more pleasant.

The most favorable reaction to therapeutic and corrective measures usually follows from the fourth mode of adjustment, *coping*. Consider an illustration of this mode. Theresa, a blind 13-year-old, deals positively with her impairment. She is not only energetic but she finds ways to progress toward goals she has set. Although young, Theresa continually evaluates herself, taking pride in what she does. She is patient, she adjusts quickly, she overcomes barriers and is willing to take advice from others. From what she has demonstrated to date, Theresa has all the qualities of one destined for a happy life.

Relation of Impairments to Self-Concept

The two basic types of impairments are *congenital* (present at birth) and *adventitious* (acquired after birth). In general, adjustments to living are best among the congenitally impaired. The adventitiously impaired adjust less successfully, especially those whose impairment occurred at a later period of life. This difference is presumably conditioned by the concepts people have of themselves. In the case of congenital impairments, individuals often develop from infancy a more realistic self-concept. With no memory of a normal lifestyle, they picture themselves as "handicapped persons." In the case of adventitious impairments, however, individual expectations, fortified by past experiences, have been rudely shattered; goals are suddenly denied, and the consequences are frustrating. The original picture or plans must be modified and new ones developed. The older the person is at the origin of the handicap, the stronger the impact usually is on the emotions.

Youths with *adventitious* impairments often go through several emotional stages before they can realistically accept their new status. Having withdrawn from social contacts, they may become totally self-absorbed, returning only gradually to reality. Teachers who work with the adventitiously impaired should be aware of these stages, for each requires a different approach. The teacher must establish a rapport with the student before any program can be prescribed. It is a mistake to assume that the congenitally handicapped are always better adjusted than those adventitiously handicapped. Individual cases vary so widely that no rule of thumb can apply.

The *degree of intensity* of an impairment often determines the degree of adjustment necessary. Those with minor visual or auditory problems, for example, may experience only minor adjustments after glasses or a hearing aid are prescribed. On the other hand, serious visual impairments such as 20/200 vision require special techniques and facilities.

One of the problems in indicating the degree of an impairment has to do with its quantitative level. Each kind of impairment has its own intensity scale and each scale has its own degree of clarity. For some persons, the intensity is obvious. For example, in limb paralysis, the degree is specifiable in terms of the *number* of limbs rendered nonfunctional, [*monoplegia* (one, diplegia or paraplegia (two, quadriplegia (four)].

In some cases, a minor or minimal impairment may demoralize a youngster more than a severe condition could possibly do. Reggie, whose left thumb and index finger are missing, is "expected to keep up" on the gymnastic apparatus only because others with worse handicaps have done so. Because he cannot, however, he runs the risk of an inferiority complex and related emotional problems. Reggie's deficiencies merit closer attention.

David, a nine-year-old with cerebral palsy, perceives himself as a failure in physical education. He is not wheelchair-bound and he has fairly good mobility. Obviously, his parents have spent little if any time helping him to develop his body, for he lacks coordination and his muscles are weak. Dave enjoys watching his classmates perform on various pieces of apparatus; but when his turn comes to participate, he flatly refuses. Yet the instructor is convinced that Dave could handle some of the basic gymnastic skills if he would only try. Individual counseling is needed in this case to provide support and motivation to initiate participation.

Extensity is another way in which an impairment may be specified. As used here, "extensity" refers to impairments that go beyond the physical or mental to other aspects of one's behavior and personality. Epileptics, for example, are characterized not only by unusual motor activity, but also by a syndrome known as "the epileptic personality." Similar behavior-personality correlations exist for a number of diseases. Two explanations have been advanced. First, an inherently fixed causal relationship exists between personality and behavior; where one is found, the other is also. A second explanation is that many of the handicapped child's behavioral traits and most of one's personality characteristics are learned modes of adjustment.

The unsocial, morose, suspicious behavior of Glen, a six-year-old deaf boy, may be an expression of his uncertainty in social relations; for he cannot hear what other children are talking or laughing about. In other words, Glen's impairment is far in excess of his primary condition. Deafness has deprived him of activities he hungers for. If deaf children are taught lip reading or some other form of communication, such negative behavior is often reduced or eliminated.

BODY IMAGE

While it is tempting to define "body image" simply as a mental picture of the physical self or, alternately, what we imagine we look like to others, the facts of the case are complex enough to demand closer attention. Most of us fantasize the impression that not only our bodies as a whole make on the world, but also our body parts. An example of heightened self-consciousness is an adolescent's preoccupation with mirrors—a form of narcissism never quite obliterated by adulthood. We are increasingly aware of various positions in space and how the body relates to the multitude of objects about us, whether they are stationary or in motion, animate or inanimate, pleasant or unpleasant.

The complexity of the body image is enriched by time as well as space. Like the body itself, our concept of it is shaped and influenced throughout life. Physical factors, feelings, emotions, moods, attitudes, and personal perceptions of how the world "sizes us up" all come into play. Thus the body image interacts with the larger, deeper, more comprehensive "self-concept." Although in childhood these subjective appraisals of both the body and the self are virtually identical, in adolescence they veer off from one another. Ongoing life experiences thereafter, together with a myriad of personality factors such as the conscious will to change, bring about profound shifts in both the body image and the self-concept—not always, unfortunately, for the better.

In recent decades the evolution of the body image has been traced to the prenatal period, when various parts of the fetus begin their first tentative movements. Walters (1965) reported that an unborn child whose motor behavior is active and extensive usually exhibits above-average motor development during early infancy. It is generally assumed today that the unborn infant acquires a special capability for motor activity several months before birth. The apparent result is a body image superior to that postnatal infant whose activity was less pronounced.

A developmental lag in body image is common among impaired children. Since emergent perceptions of the body during childhood are crucial, many children need guidance in their continuing self-appraisal. The size and shape of the body, the "looks" and functional value of the body's parts, the level of motor performance, personal mannerisms, and psychological traits are the common concerns of all children. Each child makes judgments as to his or her physical and social acceptability. These unformulated judgments of the self also explore the relationship between body build, personality, and social adjustment.

All children, whether handicapped or not, eventually perceive their bodies as the mechanism that performs physical activities with greater or lesser skill and strength. The perception is thus both the cause and the effect of the child's performance level: confidence develops coordination, which in turn produces greater confidence. A low level of physical ability may reflect a poor body image as surely as improved performance enhances that image.

Environmental Factors

Environmental factors, such as accidents and disease, together with psychological traumas, have an adverse effect on the body image. A positive body image is often a sign of adequate adjustment to family, schoolmates, and teachers. Conversely, those youngsters with a negative body image are usually below average in motor ability, feel socially rejected by classmates, possess negative attitudes toward parents and teacher, and often exhibit an excessive dependence on others. The task of changing a student's body image is, at best, a formidable one. But of all the school programs offering some hope of success, physical education promises the most dramatic results. To cite an instance of a measurable change: Ann, a bright nine-year-old, does not mix socially with her peers but she enjoys classes in the gym, with one exception—she avoids anything in physical education involving her left hand, which had received second-degree burns. She is self-conscious about it and even refuses to switch hands when turning a jump rope. Ann must be shown that once she puts her left hand to work, she will acquire new skills that affect everything else she does. Ann's natural zest for games must be channeled if her disability is not to threaten the full development of her personality.

Numerous cases exist in which a prosthesis has helped a schoolchild develop a more positive body image. If the device in question is fitted properly and used continually, it will be integrated with the wearer's body image and lifestyle. Assume for a moment that a boy loses an arm following an automobile accident. An amputation of the arm calls for a replacement with a "facsimile" reasonably normal in appearance and function. With the proper explanations, no prosthesis should be rejected; but the boy in this case will not develop a body image he can tolerate unless the value and benefits of the device are promptly and regularly demonstrated in exercise. The teacher's words must be translated into movements that are vigorous enough to achieve progress.

There is understandable sensitivity in the child who has athetoid movements, wears braces, sits in a wheelchair, or suffers any other bodily changes that attract attention. Even a handicap like epilepsy or a heart problem, though unseen, may be a greater deterrent than an impairment plainly visible to the world. Lack of motivation, low spirits, self-disgust, apathy, or bitter negativism may be the consequences of parental neglect. To illustrate: George's parents spent generous amounts of time and money on their emotionally disturbed 13-year-old son. But they postponed an important phase of his development: feeling secure in the water. As a result, George is terrified at the thought of learning to swim. Whenever asked to join in basic aquatics, he withdraws to the far end of the pool and broods. The instructor's attempts at "remedial intervention" are futile until these guidelines are observed:

- *Indirect methods* should be used that involve the simplest skills at the shallow end of the pool.
- *Reinforcement* by repetition and progress building of skills to sustain interest: material rewards may be used.
- *Evaluation* of progress should be expressed only in positive and reassuring terms.
- *Encouragement* from classmates may work better than the instructor's technical advice.

Close associations between teachers and students are highly recommended as a means of enhancing the body image. Kathy, a 12-year-old student with Down's Syndrome, is a trainable mentally retarded girl. Chubby and uncoordinated, Kathy

Body Identification   Particularly for young children and older ones who are retarded, there is need for identifying body parts and direction: for example, right/left; up/down; in/out.

will not try the balance beam because of a deep-seated fear of falling that is traceable to the constant anxieties of her protective parents. The instructor is faced with trying to change the body image of Kathy, whose physical sensations are intense but whose reasoning is clouded. A number of suggestions are open to the instructor:

- Kathy must be convinced that she is fully capable of walking the beam at floor level; appeal should aim at having her "at least, try it."
- Once she *tries* the beam and *walks* it successfully at a low level, she should be challenged to walk it farther and at successively higher levels.
- Try to convince her that, by performing, she will get "better and better" until she can walk forward and backward.
- Compliment Kathy regularly on how gracefully she walks the beam.

Creating a positive body image requires constant attention and patience. Kathy's attitude toward herself and her abilities are what is meant by an improved "body image" and its effect on the "self-concept."

Most physical educators observe four ways of improving a child's body image:

Identity of body parts—hands, feet, head, ears, and other features, while naming the parts touched.

Directionality—up, down, under, high, and low, in relation to space and to the body.

Laterality—awareness of the body's right and left sides.

Verticality—relationship of objects to a vertical axis above, below, or on the midline of the body.

Cratty's scale entitled "Steps in the Formation of the Body Image and the Body's Position in Space" together with an evaluation procedure step for each stage may be found in Appendix D.

PART TWO

EVALUATING AND PLANNING ACTIVITY PROGRAMS

CHAPTER 4

Pupil Evaluation

The pupil-evaluation team consists of professional and lay persons in the school community whose initial assessment includes procedures to determine levels of function in educational, psychological, medical, sociological, and adaptive-behavior areas. The team also prescribes teaching methods and objectives that meet closely defined criteria; the psychomotor domain should be an integral part of assessment procedures in one or more of the areas listed above. Since instruction in physical education is a defined part of special education, individualized planning committees are expected to review the motor, physical, movement, and fitness needs of each child to determine whether or not specially designed physical education programs are required.

Other concerns beyond these parameters that are essential to a full and accurate evaluation include the handicapped child's psychosocial behavior, emotional traits, self-concept, and body image. The evaluation team should, before prescribing any physical activity at school, consider the *total* child.

Two basic approaches to pupil assessment for physical education are widely recognized. One is informal and subjective. It includes observation of student performance in self-testing activities and in exploration activities; discussions with students, professionals, and volunteers who work with students; and the use of rating scales, checklists, inventories, questionnaires, and screening activities. The other approach to pupil assessment is more formal and objective. Tests of the impaired child's perceptual-motor functions, coordination, gross motor ability, and fine motor skills fall into this category as do tests of physical fitness, cardiorespiratory function, anthropometric characteristics, and specific sport skills.

The evaluation team and the teaching staff determine each pupil's learning potential. Thereafter, tests should be based on behavioral or instructional objectives that reflect the child's actual performance in class.

It is unproductive, however, to test students merely to label them "very good," "good," "fair," or "poor." The data should be applied, for it can show pupil improvement and reveal the most effective activities, methods, and techniques. Slow progress implies the need for more practice in that skill, or a shift of strategy. A rating of "good" or "fair" suggests more emphasis on the skill or activity that resulted in such a rating. "Very good," on the other hand, indicates the pupil's readiness for new challenges. For comparative purposes, pupil records should be maintained from year to year or over a period of several years.

The teacher may also wish to reexamine normal developmental stages using these ratings as a baseline for the impaired. To illustrate: a normal child begins running and kicking a ball at approximately eighteen months. A trainable mentally retarded or emotionally disturbed child may or may not be a match for his normal counterpart; early and regular training could help close the gap. If neglected, however, the impaired youngster is bound to fall behind.

The motivation of many handicapped youngsters is often low or lacking until they have witnessed the performance of classmates with similar disabilities. Instructors should be prompt in capitalizing on any sign of freshly aroused interest. Imagine a teenage boy with mild cerebral palsy (spastic) whose attention is caught by the performance of golfers with the same affliction. Intrigued, he is for the first time eager to swing a golf club. Will he receive instruction while his incentive is strong?

It is important that the pupils' strengths and weaknesses be shared with them so that teaching strategies can be developed. In many cases pupils can be helped if the teacher utilizes the principle of "attention to individual differences." Although some pupils may be no more handicapped than others of even the same age or sex, they may be incapable of performing the same skills or activities.

Clear guidelines for assessing and screening are, therefore, critically important to evaluators and teachers alike. The provisions of PL 94-142 containing these guidelines and their application to physical education are listed as follows:

IMPLICATIONS OF ASSESSMENT AND EVALUATION PROVISIONS FOR PHYSICAL EDUCATION*

PL 94-142 Provision	*Application to Physical Education*
Be provided and administered in the child's native tongue or other mode of	• Give necessary instruction for physical fitness, motor development,

*"Individual Education Programs: Assessment and Evaluation in Physical Education," *Practical Pointers,* American Alliance for Health, Physical Education, and Recreation, Washington, D.C., Vol. 1, No. 9, Feb., 1978.

communication unless it is clearly not feasible to do so.

Be validated by trained personnel in conformance with instructions provided by the producer of the instrument.

Be tailored to assess specific areas of educational need and *not* merely those designed to provide a single general intelligence quotient.

skills, and other tests in child's primary language if other than English.

- Include other modes of communication as necessary; that is, sign language for deaf children, Braille or audio-cassette instructions for blind students, pictures for nonverbal students, coaction for deaf-blind individuals, combinations of various methods for multiply involved persons.

- Use physical education, adapted physical education, motor-development specialists, or other personnel with appropriate background, training, and experience in these specific areas in processes by which test batteries and individual test items are validated.
- Use same types of personnel as listed above whether process to determine if test instruments and assessment devices measure what they say consists of research or statistical approaches or is determined through face validity procedures.

- Use tests designed to assess physical fitness performance for this purpose and not as a means of determining basic motor development or ability in sport skills.
- Use test items designed to assess function and ability in specific components of physical fitness, gross motor ability, fine motor skill, or sports skills only for that particular purpose—balance test items are not appropriate as indicators of muscular strength or endurance.
- Make generalizations cautiously; because an individual does well or

poorly on a specific test item cannot be interpreted as strength or weakness in more than that particular movement, pattern, or skill.

- Avoid a single general physical or motor quotient in the same way and for the same reasons a single general intelligence quotient is prohibited.
- Do not make generalizations or assumptions about physical and motor performances on the basis of categorical information about handicapping conditions. Base decisions about physical and motor needs on appropriate input about physical and motor function.

Be selected and administered so as to best ensure that when a test is administered to a child with impaired sensory, manual, or speaking skills, test results accurately reflect the child's aptitude or achievement level or whatever other factors the test purports to measure rather than reflecting the child's impaired sensory, manual, or speaking skills, except where these skills are factors that the test purports to measure.

- Remove or adapt specific test items that do not reflect an individual's level of physical and motor fitness, fundamental motor skills or patterns or skill in aquatics, dance, individual and group games and sports and lifetime sports but rather how his or her handicapping condition affects achievement and performance in these areas. For example, eliminate carrying and picking up objects on shuttle run for blind students; substitute wheelchair dashes or wheels for sprint, run-walk, and running events as indicators of power or cardiorespiratory endurance; develop balance activities involving crutch use in place of traditional static and dynamic balance activities.

Not be a single procedure as a single criterion for determining an appropriate educational program for a child.

- Use a variety of sources and procedures to determine specific physical and motor needs of each child; formal and informal devices, quantitative and qualitative measures, objective and subjective data, and observational and anecdotal input are *all* necessary to determine each child's needs in terms of actual cause and effect relationships. A single procedure promotes attacking symptoms, not basic causes of a problem.

Use of information obtained solely from a single performance sequence or progression does *not* provide input about the child's social, emotional, and intellectual factors that can affect physical and motor performances. Often these nonphysical and motor factors are more important considerations than physical and motor ability in determining performances in these areas.

Be conducted by a multidisciplinary team or group of persons including at least one teacher or other specialist with knowledge of the area of suspected disability.

• Obtain input from other school personnel and specialists so that the most accurate assessment of *why* the child has particular physical and motor problems can be determined. Input from regular classroom teachers, special education teacher and resource personnel, physicians, nurses, physical therapists, occupational therapists, recreation and therapeutic recreation specialists can be very helpful in this process.

• Keep focus and emphasis on the *child,* not the program activity, therapy, or modality.

• Strive to have input from or active participation by physical education personnel or motor development specialists in *every* individualized planning meeting to foster two-way communication regarding physical and motor needs of the child.

• Recognize that a physical educator,

adapted physical educator, motor development specialist, or other person with background, training, or experience in the physical motor areas/psychomotor domain *must* be considered the specialist to provide input about a child's needs in these areas.

Deal with all areas related to the suspected disability including, where appropriate, health, vision, social and emotional status, general intelligence, academic performance, communicative states, and motor abilities.

- Recognize positive and negative effects of particular disabilities on physical and motor function and performance in individual children as well as the positive and negative effects of physical and motor activities on the disability itself.
- Deal with only those characteristics, traits, and functions that affect the particular activities under consideration.
- Avoid making categorical generalizations based on handicapping conditions.

Suggestions for Conducting Motor and Fitness Tests

Suggestions for conducting motor and physical fitness tests of any kind should begin with the obvious reminder that impaired students must be treated with care. Those with cerebral palsy, spina bifida, muscular dystrophy, and either severe or profound retardation may well be incapable of performing a number of the tests. At the same time, however, teachers should accept the challenge of devising new ways to gauge the performance and progress of any pupil with a physical disability or a mental disorder. No one who finds pleasure in it should be excluded from the satisfaction of a physical movement. However, a few general observations on testing the handicapped may prove useful. All directions, for example, should be given clearly and should be repeated whenever necessary. Some of the test items may need to be demonstrated. Patience and a relaxed, friendly attitude do wonders with the impaired, who appreciate an instructor's willingness to allow more than the usual number of free trials. Only a few test items should be given in one class period. If aides are used, they should be familiar with the test items and testing procedures. Some test batteries require that each student's performance be recorded on an individual score card. Many tests are given in the fall and, for comparative purposes, in the late spring. Others are repeated monthly or even weekly throughout the year. Ideally, the test data should figure prominently when charting student progress or in revising the curriculum.

After instructors have familiarized themselves with the guidelines and suggestions for conducting various kinds of motor and fitness tests, it is important that they know which tests, scales, and checklists are specifically designed for students who have one or more impairing conditions. In some cases, the same test, scale, or checklist may be used with students even if the types of impairments differ.

The remainder of this chapter is organized into categories of impairments under which tests, scales, and checklists are identified and described where applicable.

Vision

The *Snellen Vision Test* (Appendix B), possibly the best single measurement of visual acuity, is easily administered, economical, and practical. It comes in two versions. The first utilizes a chart restricted to the stylized letter "E" in four symbolic positions. It is designed to test young children as well as illiterates. The second, a mix-letter version, is used with pupils above the third grade and with adults. Each chart consists of nine separate lines decreasing in size from top to bottom. The largest letters are designed "200 feet;" succeeding lines test reading acuity at 100, 70, 50, 40, 30, 20, 15, and 10 feet.

Several other more sophisticated tests for vision are available: the *Denver Eye Screening Test,* the *Massachusetts Vision Test,* the *Titmus Vision Tester,* the *Keystone Ophthalmic Telebinocular,* the *School Vision Tester,* the *Sight Screener,* and the *Atlantic City Vision Test.**

Although the Snellen Vision Test is beneficial in determining visual acuity, the *Visual Tracking Scale* (Appendix E) gives an assessment of the pupil's ability to track objects. Since motor skills sufficient for even the modest ability in sports are dependent on competency in visual tracking, most instructors can readily appreciate the value of a rating scale that is convenient and reliable. Used at the start of the school year during regular activity periods, the scale will accurately identify visual problems for prompt referral to the school physician. It determines, with a minimum of delay, whether pupils can follow a moving object—its speed, direction, and relationship in space. In short, it tests and rates the coordination of the eye and brain in selected motor activities. The student's performance, once transferred to an easily read scale, points to below-average responses that are in need of special attention.

---

*If more information is desired on vision tests and testing, contact The National Society to Prevent Blindness, 79 Madison Ave., New York, NY 10016.

Hearing

The *puretone audiometer* is by far the most reliable means of measuring auditory acuity. The student is given a set of earphones and is asked to listen for high- and low-level tones. On a special form, students write down the numbers they hear. Each ear is tested separately; one side of the record is for the right ear, the other side is for the left ear. Nine or more errors constitute a hearing loss. This device measures the pupil's ability to hear a series of pure tones of varying frequencies (pitches) at different sound intensities (loudness). The testing procedure is as follows: an "intensity" knob first is set at 15 decibels (units of sound) and a "tone" knob is turned quickly through 500, 1000, 2000, 4000 and sometimes 6000 frequencies. If the student hears the first tone, he or she responds by raising the hand. Some pupils, though capable of hearing the initial frequencies, cannot detect any of the higher pitches. To speed up the testing, the so-called sweep method is utilized. This allows the teacher to complete all the frequencies quickly. Any student who hears each tone is said to have normal hearing. Group audiometers are impracticable for most children below the third grade or for the handicapped who cannot write the numbers from dictation.

Posture

In public education few teachers pay sufficient attention to children's posture problems. Posture screening, even in mainstreamed and special classes, has been perfunctory at best. An impressionistic appraisal, while better than no appraisal at all, cannot possibly do justice to the numerous postural deviations and anomalies encountered in any cross section of the American schoolroom. Furthermore, quite aside from those minor defects that still fall within the range of the "normal" are those more serious posture conditions that accompany various disabilities. The future classroom, whether regular, mainstreamed, or special, will reflect in ever-increasing numbers such posture problems as those of the blind, the deaf, the amputee, or the child with congenital anomalies of the arm or leg. As mainstreaming of the handicapped into our public school system swells, a head-on confrontation with numerous postural faults is inevitable. The child who is emotionally disturbed, the educable mentally retarded, the trainable mentally retarded—all of these must receive observation, appraisal, and screening essential to effective remediation. But how?

To begin with, teachers must be genuinely concerned with the proper identification of postural problems. Second, they must be familiar with screening methods and devices, from the simplest to the most sophisticated. Some of these have been widely used for several generations, but others are new on the educational scene.

The *Plumb Line Test* is unmatched for convenience of installation, ease of operation, and low cost. It is the irreducible minimum approach to the posture screening process; a description of the test follows:

1. The teacher holds the plumb line or suspends it from the ceiling.
2. The pupil stands sideways to the line, and the teacher takes up a position to observe the pupil's head and body in profile, the line intercepting the teacher's vision.
3. The pupil's posture is recorded as satisfactory if the line seen against the pupil in profile passes through the lobe of the ear, the center of the shoulder, the center of the hip, the back portion of the kneecap, and the outside of the ankle bone.
4. If any deviations from the line are detected, the pupil's opposite side should be viewed; if deviations are still evident, the pupil should be referred to the school's health service.

More complicated but more accurate is the widely adopted *New York State Posture Rating Test.** The procedure utilizes a line suspended from the ceiling almost to the floor. Directly under the plumb bob a straight piece of one inch wide tape is placed on the floor. Three feet from the tape a white screen is placed as a background for observation. Crossing the tape at right angles, just under the plumb bob, a second strip of tape runs ten feet to the teacher's location. The student is 3 feet from the screen and the examiner is 13 feet from the screen.

The student is viewed in two positions. In assuming the first position, he or she straddles the end line with the feet comfortably apart. The screen is faced with the student's back to the teacher. From that 10-foot vantage point, the plumb line should bisect the student's head, spine, legs, and feet. For the second position, the pupil is asked to make a quarter turn to the left, sideward to the teacher, so that the plumb line passes through the middle of the ear, shoulder, hip, knee, and ankle.

The chart for the New York State Posture Rating Test shows a series of thirteen posture profiles. In each profile, three figures are shown with three degrees of deviation: (1) correct posture, awarded a score of five points; (2) slightly incorrect, with a score of three points; and (3) markedly incorrect, scored at one point. Each of the 13 posture areas is rated on a 5-3-1 basis; the total score representing the pupil's overall posture rating is entered under his grade level (4–12) for future reference.

Photographs are a third means of screening students for posture. The following procedures are recommended:

1. Use an instant film development camera.
2. For the first picture, position the pupil in front of the grid with his or her back to the teacher. The second picture is a side exposure.
3. Ask the pupil to remove all clothes from the waist up, including shoes and stockings. Older girls may, of course, be asked to wear bras. Swim suits may be used for the pictures.
4. Long hair must be pinned up so that the complete spine is clearly seen in both pictures.

*See Appendix C.

5. Consistent distance, lighting, and camera are essential.

6. For corrective purposes, pictures should be shown to students, then placed with their permanent records.

After all pupils have been screened, those who are found to have postural deviations should be referred to the school's medical staff. The staff determines the causes of the condition and prescribes the treatment. Posture problems are either structural (cannot be corrected) or functional (can be corrected by exercise). Usually, the physical education adaptive specialist can, under medical supervision, provide corrective exercises for most functional deviations.

Obesity

Five ways to assess obesity are now available to teachers. *Teacher Observation* is the first and most obvious way. Second, *Pupil Observation* allows students to judge themselves with considerable objectivity by means of a mirror and with the instructor's tactful assistance. A third method involves the use of *Weight Tables* with norms and comparisons indicating the desired body weight relative to age, sex, and height. Fourth, a *Pinch Test* can be used whereby the teacher lifts a fold of skin between his or her thumb and index finger. One of the major test points for both sexes is the triceps (back of the upper arms). The size of the lifted fold varies according to age and sex. Minimum allowance for girls aged 6 to 11 is two-thirds of an inch. This measurement increases gradually up to age 18, when it exceeds one inch. For boys in the age range of 6 to 11, the allowed maximum is one-half inch; ages twelve to fourteen, three-quaters of an inch, and ages 15 to 18, back to one-half inch.

The fifth and most reliable method is the *Skin-Fold Measurement*. A fold of skin is selected at three areas: triceps (rear of upper arm), side of abdomen (at the umbilical cord level), and tip of the subscapular region (upper back). A set of skin calipers is applied to the fold, and a measurement in millimeters is taken to determine thickness. These measurements are totaled and compared to established norms.

After screening, students classified as obese should be referred to the school's physician for evaluation and prescription. The adaptive physical educator can help combat obesity by providing an individualized program in conjunction with a prescribed diet.

Activities of Daily Living*

After assessing some of the physically handicapping conditions, probably one of the first checks to be done with some impaired pupils is to determine their abilities in

*See Appendix F.

performing routine activities of daily living. A checklist of the activities of daily living (ADL) may be found in Appendix F.

Physical Fitness

Teachers should familiarize themselves with the 10 components of physical and motor fitness, either potential or actual. A subjective rating scale of physical fitness components may be found in Appendix G.

1. *Agility.* Controlling successive body movements and changing directions quickly and easily.
2. *Balance.* Maintaining a specified body position and equilibrium by distributing and controlling the weight of the body.
    a. Static Balance: holding the body in a stationary position.
    b. Dynamic Balance: holding the body in motion.
3. *Coordination.* Performing a complex activity efficiently by the simultaneous use of several muscles or muscle groups.
4. *Muscular endurance.* Continuing a physical activity that involves strength without undue fatigue.
5. *Circulatory-respiratory endurance.* Sustaining a physical activity that involves the body's efficient utilization of oxygen so as to develop the circulatory and respiratory systems.
6. *Flexibility.* Moving body parts easily through a full range of motion; that is, maximum flexion and extension without strain.
7. *Speed.* Performing rapid successive movements within a short, timed interval.
8. *Strength.* Exerting force by using specific muscles or groups of muscles in a concentrated effort.
9. *Power.* Combining strength with speed to perform an explosive type of movement.
10. *Reaction time.* Perceiving a given stimulus, starting the movement, and completing the movement.

A *Special Fitness Test Manual for Mildly Mentally Retarded Persons,** ages 8 to 18, was published by the A.A.H.P.E.R. together with the Kennedy Foundation. Included is the table of national norms and standards for judging performance in the following events: flexed-arm hang, one-minute situp, shuttle run, standing broad jump, 50-yard dash, softball throw for distance, and 300-yard run-walk. All seven of these activities can be adapted to more moderate types of mental retardation. Only two or three, however, are applicable to severe mental conditions.

*American Alliance for Health, Physical Education, and Recreation, "Special Fitness Test Manual for Mildly Mentally Retarded Persons," Washington, D.C., 1976.

In 1976 Leon Johnson and Ben Londeree coauthored a *Motor Fitness Testing Manual** exclusively for the moderately mentally retarded. Teachers can secure a physical fitness profile by using only six test items, specifically, flexed arm-hang, situp for thirty seconds, standing long jump, softball throw for distance, 50-yard dash, and 300-yard run-walk. This test, which is for both boys and girls, ages 6 to 19, includes percentile-scoring tables.

Motor Ability

Four motor ability rating scales are included in the Appendices *H* through *K: fine motor skills, gross motor skills, ball skills,* and *movement skills.* The teachers make judgments of the student's ability or inability to perform the various movements identified in the scales.

Motor Development Tests for the Retarded

The *Lincoln-Oseretsky Motor Development Scale*† measures the motor abilities of mentally retarded youth, aged 6 to 14, with reference to chronological-age norms. There are six categories in all: static coordination, dynamic manual coordination, general motor coordination, motor speed, simultaneous voluntary movements, and asynkinesia (unwilled associated movements). The Lincoln-Oseretsky Scale consists of 36 distinct motor tasks.

The *Stott Moyes and Henderson Test of Motor Impairment** (SMHTMI) was developed after years of researching the original Oseretsky test and the revised Lincoln-Oseretsky test. From the battery of six categories, only five were retained; the sixth—synkinesis—was excluded. The test was modified chiefly because it required an excessive amount of time. Of the 45 items on the SMHTMI, only 16 were derived from the Oseretsky and, of these, only 2 were used with the same pass/fail criteria and at the same age level. The revised form contains sets of 5 test items each, one set for each year, ages 5 to 14. This streamlined version of the Oseretsky can be given to most pupils in approximately twenty minutes. The objective of the test is to ascertain and assess motor impairment of functional or presumed neurological origin.

Balance

An important part of the evaluation process involves measuring the different types of balance needed to perform most motor skills. All three of these tests measure stationary or static balance.

---

*American Alliance for Health, Physical Education, and Recreation, "Motor Fitness Testing Manual for the Moderately Mentally Retarded, Washington, D.C., 1976.

†See Appendix L.

*See Appendix M.

The *Stork Stand Test* is designed for both boys and girls, ages 10 to 21 years. The only equipment needed is a stopwatch with a second hand. The pupil stands on the ball of the dominant foot, and places the other foot on the inside of the supporting knee. Hands are resting on the hips; this balance position is maintained as long as possible without moving the foot. Three trials are allowed, and scoring is simply in terms of the longest holding period in seconds.

The *Bass Board Test* (crosswise version) is a balance test for boys and girls, ages 10 to 21. The supplies needed are individual pieces of oblong board 1 in. × 1 in. × 1 in. (one for each student) and a stopwatch. Boards are placed on the floor in a line, spaced far enough apart to prevent students standing behind them from touching each other. Upon command, one student at a time places the ball of the foot on the board crosswise, shifting his or her entire weight to that foot, with the other foot lifted off the floor. This position is held as long as possible, up to a maximum of 60 seconds, while the teacher counts the seconds off aloud. Six trials are permitted, three on each foot. The score is the total in minutes and seconds for all six trials.

The *Bass Board Test* (lengthwise version) is identical to the previous test *except* that boards are placed lengthwise.

Measuring balance while the body is in motion is considered an indispensable part of any comprehensive motor-skill appraisal. A subjective rating scale that can be used to assess the pupil's ability or inability to perform dynamic balance skills may be found in Appendix N.

Range of Motion

Range of motion pupils have in each part of their bodies, can be evaluated separately. Movements may be executed from a sitting or standing position. See Appendix O.

Perceptual-Motor Abilities

Tools for assessing perceptual-motor abilities include standard norms based on national data. For all practical purposes, teachers should rely on comparative scores within the class or on scores in the same school system. The following tests for perceptual-motor ability are widely used and are best known for identifying students who may have perceptual-motor problems.

The *Purdue Perceptual-Motor Survey* (PPMS). The PPMS is a qualitative scale used to assess areas of perceptual-motor abilities in children, ages 6 to 10. It is designed to allow the teacher to observe perceptual-motor behavior while the pupil is performing a series of specific movements. The information gathered from this instrument can be used to develop remedial programs. See Appendix P.

Southern California Perceptual-Motor Tests. Included in this battery are six test items designed to assess the perceptual-motor abilities of children from four to eight years of age. It is important that the child understands simple verbal directions. Since five of the six items call for adequate motor responses, extreme caution must be taken in testing pupils with neuromuscular impairments. This battery can be administered by either the teacher or a trained examiner in approximately 20 minutes. The equipment is simple—a watch, a table, and chairs. See Appendix Q.

Aquatic Skills

Evaluating the aquatic skills of impaired students is important. The skills to be taught and measured vary, depending upon the student and the impairment(s). The skills listed in Appendix R should be most helpful to the instructor in evaluating and motivating impaired students.

Psychosocial and Emotional Behavior Traits

Subjective scales can be used to ascertain the social and emotional behavior traits of impaired children (Appendix S). A *Student Social/Emotional Profile* is also included that may assist teachers in their ratings of students and in determining progress or regression over a period of time (Appendix T).

Self-Concept and Body Image

The following section relates to self-concept and body image. The *California Test of Personality* for elementary and secondary students is a test designed to provide teachers with data on how students view themselves.

The students' perception of their bodies and body parts should receive high priority, since body image is more closely allied to performance than was formerly envisioned. The *Goodenough-Harris Drawing Test* for youngsters, ages 3 to 15, is a revision and extension of the popular Goodenough Intelligence Test.

Teacher/Parent Conferences

In order to obtain information from parents about their impaired children, classroom teachers and physical educators should hold frequent conferences, preferably at school.

After the teacher has had a personal conference with a parent, a short summary of the remarks should be written up and placed in the pupil's school records. No particular reporting form is necessary for these teacher/parent conferences, but two or three paragraphs explaining what transpired at the meeting may be included.

Discussion topics could include some or all of the following items:

- Problems that may exist between the pupil and teacher.
- Problems that may exist between the pupil and parent.
- Type of information the pupil gives to the parent about school and the teacher.
- The chief interests of the pupil at school and at home.
- What the pupil does in his or her leisure hours.
- The pupil's relations with playmates at school and at home—impaired or nonimpaired.

CHAPTER 5

Individualized Educational Planning

Any handicapped child identified as having "special needs" must, according to the federal mandate (PL 94-142), be provided with an *individualized educational program* (IEP). The law is very explicit and it includes physical education as an integral part of special education and related services. A prescription identifying those motor activities appropriate to the child's handicapping condition should be included under the comprehensive IEP.

Classroom teachers and physical educators should be involved in the practical implementation of IEP's, which provide three different instructional settings: the large group, the small group, and the "one-to-one." While teaching under the IEP requires considerable focus on one student, its main thrust is the accommodation of each youngster in the *most appropriate* learning setting. The IEP in the context of PL 94-142 refers to a comprehensive process in which the activities of each handicapped child may or may not be integrated with those of other children. That process encompasses four distinct procedures: (1) testing and evaluation, (2) program alternatives designed to accommodate the individual, (3) placement in a program based on the individual's needs, and (4) the selection of methods and techniques that match the student's limitations and potentialities.

Records and Forms

Through a close working relationship with medical personnel, instructors should have access to student records and forms. From these, they can extract pertinent data useful in teaching children with impairments in the mainstreamed and adapted physical education programs. The so-called "cumulative folder" is a repository of information on the general health of the youngster and his or her family, the results of screening tests, a record of physical examinations, and immunizations (Appendix A). Data pertaining to participation in the adapted programs may be obtained through use of forms that are found in Appendices U through W.

Under the provisions of the law,* the IEP requires that the following data be provided by schools or agencies on each handicapped child:

- A statement of the child's present levels of educational performance.
- A statement of annual goals, including short term instructional objectives.
- A statement of specific special education and related services to be provided to the child and the extent to which the child will be able to participate in regular educational programs.
- The projected dates for initiation of services and the anticipated duration of the services.
- Appropriate objective criteria and evaluation procedures and schedules for determining whether the instructional objectives are being achieved.

The physical educator should be an advocate of the following guidelines:

- Perform an active role in the evaluation process.
- Provide information about the pupil's physical, motor, movement, and fitness needs.
- Be responsible for seeing that each student is placed in an appropriate physical education class, either a mainstreamed physical education class, or in an adapted class.
- By testing and observing performance, predict, at least to a certain degree, a student's physical and motor fitness potential.
- Classify a student's motor fitness as either "beginning," "intermediate," or "advanced," carefully considering the method by which he or she can progress, and the reasonable expectations of improvement.
- Choose instructional formations that best suit the child's individual needs, avoiding those that block optimum learning.
- Introduce different activities and challenges even if the students find these formidable at the start.
- Know the instructional material: supplies, equipment, adapted devices, and facilities, both indoor and outdoor.
- Plan special events and special days as part of the program.
- To strengthen motivation, strike a balance between overexertion and a sluggish semblance of activity.

*Federal Register, Vol. 42, No. 163, Tuesday, August 23, 1977, Section 121a 346, p. 42491.

- Include programs with activities of a risk nature as long as safety precautions are strictly enforced.
- Maintain concern for safety in all activities.

Provisions and Applications

Because PL 94-142 provisions, as they refer to the individual education program, are stated in general terms, they must be interpreted before they are applied to specific curricula. The information below, arranged in chart form, correlates the key provisions of the law with the application of each to physical education:*

PL94-142 Provision	*Application to Physical Education*
Statement of the child's *present levels of educational performance*	• Statement of the child's present levels of development in (1) physical and motor fitness, (2) fundamental motor skills and patterns, and (3) skills in aquatics, dance, individual and group games and sports, including lifetime sports. This statement must be based on information obtained through assessment processes designed to provide input about the child's levels of physical and motor development.
Statement of *annual goals* including *short term instructional objectives*.	• Statement of *annual goals* in areas of physical and motor development, determined analysis and interpretation of assessment results in these areas for each child. Annual goals provide direction for the child's program throughout the year and ultimately for daily instruction.
	• Statement of *short term instructional objectives* in terms of specific movement patterns, fitness components, and aquatics, dance, games, and sports skills needed to reach the

*"Individualized Education Programs: Methods for Individualizing Physical Education," *Practical Pointers*, American Alliance for Health, Physical Education, and Recreation, Washington, D.C., Vol. I, No. 7, Dec., 1977, pp. 6-8.

long term more general annual goals. Short term instructional objectives provide the focus of day-to-day instruction.

Statement of *specific special education* and *related services* to be provided to the child and the *extent to which the child will be able to participate in regular educational programs.*

- Statement of specially designed physical education required by the child to attain specific short term instructional objectives based on needs identified through the assessment process—that is, individual tutoring or one-to-one relationship in special adapted aquatics program; adapted aquatics program; small homogeneous group based on swimming ability or handicapping condition for special adapted aquatics program; regular beginning swimming program with supplementary one-to-one/small group assistance; regular beginning swimming program with additional adapted aquatics session weekly.
- Statement of related services necessary to enable the child to benefit from specially designed physical education services—that is, transportation to and from the pool; aide to assist in dressing/undressing, getting to/from locker room/pool.
- Statement indicating those periods and activities the child can take part in in regular physical education program—that is, stay in adapted aquatics program until child enters pool independently; divide time equally between regular and adapted aquatics programs; full time beginning swimming program with supplementary one-to-one small group assistance; 80 percent, 15 minutes of each period in beginning swimming program.

Projected dates for *initiation of services* and the *anticipated duration of the services*.

• Statement specifying when specially designed physical education services are to begin and how long they are to be provided. These dates are to be provided. These dates are to be projected for *both* annual goals and short term instructional objectives. Readers are reminded that final rules and regulations did not require any agency, teacher, or other person be held accountable if a child does not achieve growth projected in annual goals and objectives. Individualized education programs are not contracts; they are simply guides to progress and growth.

Appropriate *objective criteria* and *evaluation procedures* and *schedules* for determining on at least an annual basis whether short term instructional objectives are being achieved.

• Basic approaches that can be considered to insure that objective criteria and evaluation procedures are used including:
  • *Standardized instruments* with normative data to assess individual progress and make comparisons with other children of comparable chronological age, handicapping condition, and related characteristics.
  • Criterion referenced approaches in which progress is readily assessed and defined as students move from one level in a progression to the next.
  • Informal techniques including observations, anecdotal records, case studies, rating scales, self-evaluation, and similar items should not be overlooked in this process, especially when tempered with experience, knowledge of activities, understanding of children in general and the individual child in particular, and good judgment.

Planning Factors

In order to produce measurable results, teachers should work closely with the pupil evaluation team from the very start. This means sharing the initial responsibility for determining, as accurately as possible, each child's physical, mental, social, and emotional status. In this first, or planning stage, the data should be reliable enough to assure proper program placement. The data should also be comprehensive enough, however, to indicate the child's potential. In addition, the data should suggest what may reasonably be expected with reference to any rate of improvement and to eventual goals. Without such an evaluation, planning for an IEP tends to be unproductive.

A brief discussion of the more common terms and concepts associated with growth and development, terms that have gained wide acceptance among educators in recent years, seems justified in light of individualized educational programs as they relate to the physical educator of the handicapped. Although these terms may seem self-evident, they acquire a new perspective when viewed against special problems and challenges encountered in physical activity.

In the broadest sense the term "development" refers to that process of growth in which one's unique genetic constitution is expressed within a continually changing context of environmental influences. *General* characteristics are determined primarily by *heredity,* and *individual* characteristics are determined primarily by *environment.* These two determining forces—heredity and environment—operate together to produce the unique child. That is, one's genetic constitution establishes a range of *potential* structural and functional reactions, but the possible reactions *within* this range are essentially a matter of environmental influences.

Several commonly accepted *principles of development* are important to instructors of the impaired. These principles are useful in establishing a good mental set from which the specialist can teach physical activities, and they also provide a general conceptual framework for a long-term program.

Continuity. Development continues from conception until death. The relative strength of the two shaping forces—heredity and environment—varies with the chronological age of the individual. Prior to birth, when the various structural systems of the body are being established, heredity exerts the strongest influences. The bases from which the adult structures will develop are laid down here. At birth, and for the two years following, heredity begins to lose its importance as a major determinant. During this period the physical forces of the environment, as opposed to the psychological, become more influential. This is the time of the filling out and completion of the structures begun in the prenatal period. It is also a time when the importance of nutrition, exercise, and rest is confirmed.

At approximately the third year of life, the psychological environment begins to assume an importance that grows with increasing age; only through learning will functional efficiency be sharpened. Beginning with puberty, when most of one's physical and physiological processes have matured, the psychological environment, which is intimately associated with learning, becomes the strongest determiner of development. Yet, despite this change in salience, both physical and psychological forces affect changes that continue throughout a person's life.

Interaction. The critical feature in the principle of continuity is that in the interaction of heredity and environment, the influences of these two forces are at no time perfectly equal. Heredity may dominate during one phase or moment, environment during another. An important question arises: To what extent can the process of development be modified through manipulation? For all practical purposes, at the present time at least, heredity is more difficult to manipulate than environment is.

In light of contemporary knowledge, therefore, certain generalizations about manipulation of human development may be made. On the one hand, some human traits are basically dependent on heredity—species characteristics, height, and sex, for example, all of which are related to one's structural growth. For the most part such individual traits are difficult, if not impossible, to control through environmental manipulation; only by providing substitute or alternate structures or functions is modification possible. Similarly, a new auditory system cannot be transplanted, but a deaf person can be taught lip reading. Another example is the child with a thalidomide-stunted limb; this can be replaced with a prosthetic device that is reasonably normal in appearance and function.

Environment can influence the nature, intensity, and precision of many human functions. For one, the autonomic nervous system appears to be profoundly affected by the prenatal environment. It is theorized that some biochemical effects on the fetus may predispose to a highly responsive infant, others to a phlegmatic infant. Such modifications are questionable, however, on the grounds of medical ethics.

Greater success in manipulation is achieved when the instructor works directly with the student and with the function to be corrected. In this case the nature of the impairment is assessed, a program plotted, and methods and techniques applied that lead to the desired outcome.

One might generalize from the foregoing that to the extent that an impairment involves *structure,* manipulation will be difficult; to the extent that it involves *function,* manipulation will be less difficult. In light of the discussion on continuity, it might be said that control of the heredity-environment interaction early in the life of the individual will be difficult, while control later in life will be less difficult. The older person, because of relative physical, mental, and emotional maturity, may be able to manage the environment more readily.

Sequence. In general, development goes on according to known sequences. Growth proceeds from head to toe and from the spinal axis outward to the limb extremities. The head and upper torso develop first; then growth extends to the lower part of the body. Growth also occurs first in the hip and shoulder region preceding development of the foot and hand. Following birth, locomotor activities develop along the same general lines. The infant is able to raise the fore part of the body before managing the legs. One crawls before one creeps and one creeps before walking upright. There is some evidence to suggest that certain cognitive and emotional processes develop in the same general sequential way.

Each step in a sequence seems to prepare the individual for the development of the next step in the sequence. While given steps in a sequence often appear to be "skipped", that is, not observed, the succession is consistent within a given species.

Tempo. As explained above, the sequences within the individual's development are fixed. However, the rate at which human beings grow through those sequences is unique. Some persons can be classified as slow developers, others as rapid. For some, this rate of growth, or tempo, is uniform from birth to maturity. For others, there may be a period of slow initial growth in which the person lags behind normal age-peers. This lag may be followed by a period of rapid growth during which the individual overtakes those in the same age group. Or, there may be an initial period of rapid development, followed by a slower period.

The *tempo* of development, while it appears to depend on genetic factors, does seem to be amenable to environmental manipulation, within limits. For example, a child whose academic performance is slow, or "retarded," may sometimes be stimulated to perform at a significantly higher level (normal tempo). Similarly, a youngster with significant leg damage from burns may, under appropriate medical and physiotherapeutic care, achieve a performance level equal to or superior to his or her age-peers. If the student in either of the foregoing cases is not provided with increased tempo-training, functioning will remain at a low level. In other words, the permanent reduction in the tempo occasioned by such conditions as retardation or severe burns can be compensated by treatment. As a result, the drop in the developmental curve is leveled off.

Accommodations and Adjustments

When an individualized conference is held to develop a child's educational program, the physical educator should be invited to attend if the problem is motoric. An essential topic for discussion deals with the accommodations and adjustments that must be made if a youngster is to be successfully mainstreamed into the regular or adapted physical education program.

No child should be denied the opportunity to participate in such programs and activities solely because of an impairing condition. It is of utmost importance, therefore, that instructors familiarize themselves with model accommodations. They should also realize that, regardless of program placement, other accommodations and adjustments are often necessary. The following accommodations should be useful to teachers who bear in mind that their focus should be on the individual student and not on the program per se. Children with various handicapping conditions will be assisted in the implementation of their IEP through use of:*

- Problem solving, exploratory, movement education and station/circuit approaches at elementary school levels.
- Flexible or optional unit scheduling, especially at middle, intermediate, and junior high school levels.
- Elective or selective program patterns emphasizing lifetime, recreational, or leisure time activities, especially at senior high school and college/university levels.

Various other approaches can be introduced so that students with special needs can be accommodated in regular physical education programs:

- A buddy system that pairs a child with a handicapping condition with an able-bodied partner for specific activities.
- Peer tutoring.
- Students as squad leaders.
- Circuit or station organizational patterns.
- Contract techniques.
- Cross-age teaching.
- Team teaching involving regular physical education teachers and adapted physical education teachers or resource teachers.
- Preteaching certain activities to select students with special needs.
- Additional physical education classes to supplement, not replace, regular physical education classes.

Within adapted classes, types of accommodations that can be considered include:

- Letting blind or partially sighted students hit a beeper ball, bat off a tee, or hit out of their hands in softball.
- Letting physically impaired students serve in volleyball or take foul shots for both teams in basketball.
- Having students in wheelchairs on the sideline, in sideline basketball, receive a certain number of passes prior to the shot at the basket.
- Organizing locomotor activities, fleeing-chasing games, and similar activities involving movement so that the physically impaired may take part on scooter boards, gym scooters, or in wheelchairs.

*"Questions and Answers About P.L. 94-142 and Section 504," *Update*, American Alliance for Health, Physical Education and Recreation, Washington, D.C., June, 1979, pp. 12-13.

- Using individuals on crutches or in wheelchairs as goalies in activities such as soccer or floor hockey.
- Organizing relays in ways to compensate for individuals in wheelchairs, with braces, or on crutches when situations do not permit the same number of these students on each team or squad.
- Giving some individuals more than three strikes in games such as softball or kickball.
- Applying decathlon scoring approaches so individuals are competing for points against records applicable to their conditions, and then devising ways in which points attained are compared to all individuals.
- Developing and using appropriate assistive and adaptive devices.

Creative thought, innovation, and resourcefulness are keys to successful application and implementation in the accommodations and adjustments of physical activity programs.

Establishing Behavioral Objectives

Recent theory, substantiated by wide-scale laboratory experimentation, has dispelled much of the confusion surrounding educational objectives. Human behavior is divided into four basic learning domains: cognitive, psychomotor, affective, and psychosocial. Students who aspire to competency in any of these areas are asked to meet specific individualized goals known as "behavioral" objectives.

To assure the validity of a behavioral objective, instructors first assess the student's specific skills. Thereafter, a forecast is submitted by the teacher that estimates the probability of reaching a certain level of skill within a designated time or space or both. If a youngster fails to meet these requirements, the question should be asked, "What kind of instruction, and how much, is needed to gain a reasonable degree of competency?" It should be understood that behavioral objectives in physical education are usually as measurable as those in any other field. Thus, it is possible for a teacher to observe an impaired youngster's response to tests, and to measure, record, and evaluate them. A teenager with poor eye-foot coordination may, for example, kick a moving ball three times out of three trials, a performance that fulfills a behavioral objective according to five criteria:

The Situation. The name, background, and overall qualifications of the performer.

The Movement. The physical activities concerned with gross motor development such as crawling, creeping, walking, running, balancing, jumping. Various degrees and combinations of motor activity will be specified.

The Condition. The term refers here to everything of an auxiliary or facilitating nature, from prosthetic devices to direct physical aid by the teacher to no assistance at all.

The Challenge. Stipulations relating to the amount of space and time involved in performing an activity. Thus, a handicapped student may be "challenged" to walk eight blocks, or half a mile, in half an hour, or more, or less.

Degree of Achievement. To what extent, the teacher and the student may both ask, has the "challenge" been met in accordance with the prescribed device or aid?

These five criteria, useful though they may be as practical steps toward the fulfillment of behavioral objectives, should not be issued to any teacher or evaluation team without several cautionary remarks. Administrators, teachers, physicians, and parents should *agree,* first of all, on the relevance and appropriateness of the objectives. Second, these objectives must be capable of *duplication;* when other teachers wish to offer similar or identical activities to their students, the model should be available for immediate implementation. Third, not only ends but also *means* must be scrutinized. Everything considered instructional—methods, techniques, equipment, supplies—should be consistent with the end in view. That end is, quite simply, a measurable achievement.

The following minicase histories can serve as examples for preparing and recording behavioral objectives. In each case, however, the first criterion ("situation") should be more detailed regarding home situation, body image, and both physical and emotional readiness:

Situation: Noreen, a 10-year-old with Down's Syndrome (trainable mentally retarded).
Movement: Running ("as fast as you can").
Condition: Unassisted.
Challenge: 50 yards in 11.5 seconds.
Degree of Achievement: Having succeeded in covering the distance within one or two seconds of the designated time, Noreen was allowed to go on to other activities.

Situation: Joe, an eight-year-old with cerebral palsy.
Movement: Walking ("as best you can").
Condition: With braces, but unassisted (unless necessary).
Challenge: Without stopping, along a straight plastic tape twenty feet in length, placed on the floor.
Degree of Achievement: Joe did wobble in his braces and was once assisted by the teacher, but his diligence and delight earned him recognition for a successful performance.

Situation: Joanne, a deaf pupil, 11 years old.
Movement: Balancing on the low balance-beam.
Condition: Unassisted.

Challenge: For 10 seconds on each foot, three times out of three trials.
Degree of Achievement: Joanne's balancing skill enabled her to reach 10 seconds only twice, but otherwise not less than 7 seconds. Passed.

Even a brief glance at these cases will indicate the central importance of behavioral objectives. Teachers should clearly understand how each objective is developed and how it relates to the pupil in question. Each articulates the "What," "Why," and "How" of a youngster's performance level, whether he or she is impaired or nonimpaired. Finally, each objective, once recorded, provides instructors with a measurable account of progress, and youngsters with some degree of achievement.

Developing the IEP for Physical Education

Faced with the data on a youngster's physical and motor fitness, an instructor must translate these, together with the evaluation team's overall recommendations, into one of the three alternative programs that are available. The *first* program placement is the regular or mainstream program in which the handicapped are integrated with the nonhandicapped. This placement enables students who need special assistance to be assigned right along with classmates who need no special provisions. Each student is assigned activities within the combined class on the basis of physical condition, individualized abilities, and personal limitations. Provisions of the individualized educational program may be fulfilled in the regular class.

The *second* alternative is one in which the impaired are enrolled in both regular and adapted classes. Dual placements provide students opportunities to take part in special physical education classes on certain days (to carry out a specially designed program) and to take part in a regular class and participate with their peers on other days.

A *third* alternative is the adapted program. It joins the handicapped student with others whose degree of impairment requires basic skills and modified games, sports, and dance. This special class placement provides students opportunities to be assigned special or different activities with other, more impaired students when regular activities are prohibitive, or when specially designed physical education activities are prescribed.

Setting Goals

Before goals can be set, data on a handicapped boy or girl should be gathered from all sources. The youngster's present performance level, attitudes and general behavior, prospects for improvement, school and medical records, test results, the comments of parents and teachers—all these factors should be reinforced by the instructor's personal observation.

A "goal" usually refers to a higher level of competence in any one of a number of skills or games. In an IEP, neither the number nor the complexity of the movements and activities that comprise a "goal" is fixed; specifications are always relative to individual needs and are never absolute.

Within the long-term "goals" are short-term "objectives," which are steps that can be reached over a period of several days or weeks. They are usually regarded as interim checkpoints indicating a youngster's progress. The immediate advantages of such a "pacer" are that it discourages slowdowns and reduces needless deviations from the year-long plan. It also provides frequent rewards for even the most modest signs of progress. The written form of instructional objective is strongly recommended, since it reminds a teacher where the student under IEP stands in the developmental sequence. The importance of written records in logging progress should be obvious.

Following are two representative examples of Physical Education IEP that detail in chart form descriptive information on each pupil. Other charts may be developed by instructors for each pupil who has one or more special needs.

Special Strategies

Physical educators who hope to improve their teaching should recognize the central importance of *strategy,* especially as it applies to the individualized education program. In this IEP context, a *strategy* is defined as a plan designed or employed by an instructor to enhance learning. Discussed below are the major terms and concepts related to these special strategies. Each has its place in a variety of teaching situations—one-to-one, small groups, or large groups. Though not the exclusive property of the IEP, such terminology has long been associated with physical activity programs. Two in particular should be defined at the outset: *sequence* and *progression.*

A *sequence,* as used in an instructional unit, is any series of continuous and connected movements performed in correct order. If, for example, an adolescent's IEP called for skill development in team sports, the youngster would need direct teaching in each of the sports: flag football, basketball, volleyball, and softball. To illustrate, flag football might be used to teach passing. The correct sequence would include: gripping the ball behind its midpoint, raising it behind the ear, both stepping in the direction in which the ball is thrown and pointing the shoulder in the same direction, swinging the arm forward overhand at shoulder level, releasing the ball off the finger tips, and lastly, following through with arm and fingers extended, both pointing at the receiver.

Another term that refers to a strategy is a *progression.* There are two types of progressions, *vertical* and *horizontal.* The first suggests an increase in the level of difficulty, known as "graduated" levels of performance. A *vertical* progression may also range from simple to complex; for example, from crawling, creeping, walking, and running to relatively sophisticated skills used in trampolining—vertical control, "killing the bounce," heel clicking, quarter turns, and seatdrop. The second, *horizontal* progression, suggests increasing the number and variety of activities to insure a wide selection on the basis of appropriateness and appeal. The difference between vertical and horizontal progression is important: in selecting activities, the teacher must consider the student's mental age rather than chronological age. An illustration will clarify the difference.

In a *vertical* progression, the student first executes a sit-up by using a rocking chair movement with the instructor's help; later he or she performs the sit-up unaided and still later undertakes as many or even more sit-ups on an inclined board. Horizontal progression, by contrast, is keyed to a youngster's chronological age, mental age, physical response, and emotional response. Hence, appropriate and appealing activities are important. *Vertical* progression works best with the blind, the deaf, amputees, the burned, and others who are "normal" or near normal in mental development. *Horizontal* progression, on the other hand, is recommended for the mentally retarded as long as they react favorably to juvenile games. Teachers should be warned, however, that retarded adolescents are inclined to resent any activity that appears childish. They are substantially different from younger children of comparable mental ages, not only physically, anatomically, and psychologically, but socially and emotionally as well. Thus, consideration must be given to their chronological age so that horizontal progressions are as challenging and appealing as vertical progressions. Mentally retarded adolescents are bored or resentful if taught "Drop the Handkerchief," a game appropriate to children of elementary school age. It would be far better to introduce a game like "Squat Tag," which, though no more demanding than "Drop the Handkerchief" avoids the appearance of childishness.

Although *repetition* is usually associated with weight training and calisthenics, it is one effective way of progressing in any skill. For a breathing exercise, an asthmatic boy may start with 4 repetitions 3 times a week until he can perform 20 or more. Students who are constantly urged to go through the full range of an exercise "one more time" invariably make greater progress than those denied such challenges.

Similarly, a young girl with hydrocephalus, having once successfully tossed a ring from her wheelchair to the post five feet away, should be encouraged to "do it again." If she can repeat these movements, with occasional rests, she often discovers after three or four weeks that she can toss 20 rings in succession, thanks to the teacher's persistence.

Repetition has other virtues. Often an instructor finds that repeating the same skill in different ways is well received. Running, for example, is a skill that can be performed alone, and can be varied—running in place, forward, backward, sideward, in circles, in squares, or diagonally. It can be done to music, with or without a partner, or holding hands in groups. Other ways can easily be improvised, and the

Physical Education—IEP

Name ___Mark*___ Age—9 ___Birthdate___ P.E. __X__ Swim __X__

Long-Term Goals: Mainstream in physical education and swimming.

Annual Goals:

School Yr.	Program Level	Goals	Comments
1980–81	Primary–PE 5	Increase tolerance for structured work activity. Improve basic sports skills (i.e.) throwing, catching, kicking, hitting). Establish concept of teamwork.	Contact sports are contraindicated

80

Objectives: (Include Performance Criteria)	Strategies: (Include methods and materials)	Evaluation of Performance	Completion Date	
			Ant.	Actual
Mark will . . .				
1. Practice each newly taught skill for a minimum of five minutes with minimal supervision.	1. Verbal reminders. Removal of play privileges until work is finished. Praise.	1. Observations of performances.	12/80	
2. Learn to perform the following sports skills on a 70% accuracy basis: kick an 8″ ball, throw a softball, throw an 8″ ball, and bat a whiffle ball of a tee.	2. Directive teaching and skill drills.	2. Skill tests.	6/81	
3. Use each of the above skills in an appropriate lead-up sport game (i.e., line soccer, modified basketball, newcomb, modified softball).	3. Game play, filmstrips for soccer, basketball, and softball.	3. Oral rules quizzes. Observations of game play.	6/81	

*Mark is a multiply handicapped boy with a spina bifida and low mildly mentally retarded combination. He is ambulatory with a somewhat restricted gait pattern. Although short for his age, he loves physical activities and is fairly well coordinated. He lacks maturity and would rather continue to play using skills he already has mastered rather than learn and use new ones; a deep-water swimmer.

Date ___ 9/80 ___

Person(s) Responsible _____ Position _____

LEA Representative _____ Position _____

Parent _____

Reprinted by permission of the American Alliance for Health, Physical Education, Recreation and Dance, 1900 Association Drive, Reston VA 22091.

Physical Education—IEP (Front)

Laura*   Age—16   P.E. __X__   Swim __X__

Name   Birthdate

Long-Term Goals: · Participate actively in most games and sports including mainstreaming for swimming.
· Develop active leisure skills.
· Become a knowledgeable spectator in at least three sports.

Annual Goals:

School Yr.	Program Level	Goals	Comments
1980–81	Secondary	Broaden skills and knowledge of leisure sports and games skills. Develop ability to select individualized activities for self-enjoyment	Currently casted for heel cord stretching. She may wish to use a wheel-chair for some activities.

Objectives: (Include Performance Criteria)	Strategies: (Include methods and materials)	Evaluation of Performance	Completion Date	
			Ant.	Actual
Laura: Select and participate in at least three individual leisure activities including disco dance, table games, and one activity yet to be selected.	1. Filmstrips, officiating, library books, lecture-discussions.	1. Observations of performances. Oral and/ or written tests.	6/81	
	2. Verbal instruction. Use of phonograph records.	2. Observations of performances.	6/81	
*Laura is a quadraplegic cerebral palsied female who walks with long crutches. Since her intelligence level is in the high moderately mentally retarded range, she has been in a special school since kindergarten. Laura is not a strong competitor but does enjoy physical activities and has completed swimmer level requirements.				

Date _____ 9/80

Person(s) Responsible _____

LEA Representative _____

Parent _____

Position _____

Position _____

Reprinted by permission of the American Alliance for Health, Physical Education, Recreation and Dance, 1900 Association Drive, Reston VA 22091.

list is long. A few variations include running zigzag, through a turning rope, slow motion, full speed. Relay races and distance running are, of course, obvious choices. Teachers will find that repeating the same skill or skills in different ways results in their focusing upon the individual child. Obviously, such repetition facilitates the mastery of the skill. The diversity of teaching situations requires that instructors familiarize themselves with various *grouping alternatives.*

In some cases, the one-on-one may be the ideal pupil-teacher relationship. Some cases call for small groups, others for large groups. These groupings imply that the instructor divides his or her time among individual students within the group. Homogeneous grouping involves pupils with the same handicapping condition, whereas heterogeneous grouping brings together those differently handicapped. Groups can be homogeneous in one activity and heterogeneous in another. In circle dodgeball, or in three-on-three basketball, teams consisting exclusively of trainable mentally retarded members with approximately the same ability play well together.

By contrast, participation in individualized activities such as swimming, tumbling, or performing on a trampoline does not require such homogeneity. Students with handicaps that are widely different in kind and degree can perform within their individual limitations. Instructors must decide which skill, game, or sport lends itself to one or the other of these two clearly differentiated types of groupings. Although children are able to progress and develop in either homogeneous or heterogeneous classes, the latter have distinct advantages. The performance of more skillful classmates provides positive role models, hastens learning, and deepens emotional and social maturity.

A *learning center,* another name given to a *circuit* or a series of *stations,* is a designated location that provides impaired pupils an opportuniy to perform activities and individualized programs. The activities performed at such centers may be either related or unrelated. In a circuit of related tasks, each station could involve separate activities such as two arm curl, tricep pushdown, front press, supine press, leg curls and sit-ups. In contrast, unrelated activities might include crawling, climbing, skipping rope, tumbling, ring tossing, and basket shooting.

These circuits or stations can be organized in almost any type of setting—gymnasium, playground, athletic field, classroom, and pool. Furthermore, almost any type of activity—physical education, recreation, sports, and swimming—can be performed there.*

Since impaired students are seldom alike in their *interests* and *abilities,* efforts should be made to understand their differences and to individualize their programs as far as time and money will allow. This challenge to the educator often starts from

---

*More information on circuit or station activities may be obtained from *Practical Pointers* booklet, Vol. 1, No. 2, Aug., 1977, American Alliance for Health, Physical Education, and Recreation, 1201 16th St., N.W., Washington, D.C. 20036.

assumptions that may later have to be discarded. If classes begin with activities that motivate only those who can meet general performance levels, some individuals will suffer. When a growing minority of poor performers and stragglers appear, their teachers should take a closer look. Sheer inability, fear or boredom may compel a reassessment of needs. A few reminders may serve that end:

- Early in the year make sure that everybody in class performs fundamental movement well enough to attempt more.
- Identify students without motivation. Encourage them, praise them, help them to take pleasure in movement.
- Freely dispense rewards for extra effort so that those who persevere may learn early that everyone's a winner, no one's a loser.
- Teach skills, games, and sports that are within "reach," that is, at a youngster's ability level no matter what his or her handicap.
- Through trial and error, use only those methods and techniques that are effective; promptly drop those that fail to motivate.
- Recognize personal pride and the desire to achieve regardless of how faint or dormant they may be.
- Teach activities that are within the pupil's present performance level yet present a challenge.
- Reconcile group instincts with individualism: a student's desire to belong is often accompanied by self-assertiveness.

Without getting, and holding, a handicapped child's interest, an instructor cannot be expected to teach either skills or fitness activities. To make this possible, teachers should make a diagnostic evaluation of physical and motor fitness levels. Close on-the-scene observation is also imperative. Too often, wide discrepancies exist between test results and in-class performance, although the cause of these discrepancies is uncertain. Has the pupil's nervousness made test scores fall short of actual functioning levels? Have the tests themselves failed to measure areas where the child's skills and strength actually lie? When instructors feel overwhelmed by a student's repeated failures, have they lost sight of the potential indicated by test results? Finally, do they become so deeply involved in the IEP itself that they tend to minimize the ability of the student for whom the program was designed?

It is important that teachers accept pupils at their present ability level and proceed from there. Teaching skills have top priority in any IEP; but physical fitness, social adjustment, and emotional maturity must also be given consideration.

Once pupil interests and abilities are taken into account, instructors can turn to problems of utilizing personnel. The apparent luxury of individualized instruction and the challenge it presents in methodology prompts the frequent question, "Where do I get help?" This is no easy task but, with some effort, assistance can be found in *peer-tutoring,* a strategy for enlisting the aid of classmates with special talents. Or the instructor can assign *student leaders,* a means by which everyone gets a turn at teaching. Next on the scale of potential merit is the *career education aide*. These are high school students enrolled in career education programs, who receive credit for their volunteer work. A fourth alternative is the *practicum student,* who can be a major in physical education, special education, or elementary education; a physical or occupational therapist; or a major in social welfare or therapeutic recreation. All of these assistants are assigned by a college or university. However, one of the top prospects is the *teacher's aide,* who is employed by the school system to render a variety of services. Sometimes the role of the aide is assumed by the parent of an impaired child as a *volunteer*. Numerous other opportunities present themselves: interested high school students, members of service clubs or fraternal organizations, or church organizations. Such possibilities for utilizing personnel are reminders that problems need not be faced single-handed. Help is available to those who will only look. In this way handicapped youngsters get the attention they deserve, in spite of shortages in trained personnel.

Learning a skill in parts requires a breakdown of a movement into its interrelated and sequential components. Although more time-consuming for both teacher and student, this process is easier in the long run. For example, the "forward roll," a challenge for many youngsters, can be learned faster when its parts are clearly identified. The following sequence, with its division into subunits, clarifies this strategy: spread feet, gradually bend knees to a squatting position, place weight on hands and balls of feet; while squatting, place hands on mat in front of feet a shoulder-width apart; place chin on chest, head between knees; push with hands and feet to roll over. The body must be kept tightly curled while executing the skill.

Impaired children are often capable of *learning a skill as a whole* rather than in parts. In fact, some seem to respond to this strategy better than to learning a skill in parts; their very impatience to learning a skill all at once is an incentive. It can be a time-saver as long as the pupil can reproduce the model without omitting steps in the sequence. Again, the forward roll is used as an example. While teaching this activity, instructors would complete the entire skill without interrupting its continuity.

Short instructional sessions extended over a long period have their place in the IEP. The pupil's age, grade, physical and motor fitness, and present functioning level are factors. Specialists in the field recommend two ways to determine the length of a period. Short instructional periods range between 20 and 30 minutes, 5 to 10 of which are allowed for toilet and wash-up. Unlike long sessions, these may meet as often as three to five times a week, extending from a month to a whole school year.

Longer instructional sessions concentrated over a short period of time may be used as another strategy. This plan provides two instructional sessions a week of 50 minutes each. It requires a minimum of one or two rest periods, especially for those who are physically impaired. At the conclusion of the session, the usual 10 to 15 minutes must be set aside for toilet and wash-up. Teachers working with impaired youngsters in an IEP should decide what the length of sessions will be. Factors other than those already mentioned include scheduling of facilities, availability of specialists, motivation, and attention span.

Contract teaching allows a student to make an agreement with the instructor to complete a designated number of skills, games, or sports within a prescribed period of time. (Actually, the student's total IEP could come under such a contract.) This strategy, though it appears to be unduly confining and formal, is an excellent motivator for those who enjoy a challenge.

Only after close screening of a youngster's *learning style, needs, and strengths* can a strategy be applied. What is each pupil's preferred way of learning? Does he or she respond best to visual, auditory, tactile, or kinesthetic stimuli, or a combination of these? Knowledge of the five learning styles enables an instructor to select the most suitable means—whether by sight, sound, touch, muscle movement, or a combination of these—for learning numerous motor skills. It is important to match the pupil's learning style to physical and motor fitness needs. But the student's strengths are of equal importance. Cardiovascular endurance, calisthenics, and weight-training should be selected, however, only after identifying the learning style. Such a style can be determined through a personal interview, observation, and by analyzing the test results from several physical and motor fitness tests. All impaired youngsters need to be evaluated to discover their strengths and needs; teaching strategies can then be adjusted to the test results.

Key Terms and Concepts

If a program for impaired students is individualized, it must embrace a sufficient variety of skills, games, and sports to serve as "prescriptions." Whether these prescriptive activities are remedial, therapeutic, or rehabilitative, their effectiveness depends on their degree of individualization; designed *for* individuals, they should be taught *to* individuals.

It is not surprising, therefore, that a teacher involved in an individualized education program may sometimes feel overwhelmed by the size and complexity of these daily challenges. Problems seem to multiply: financial stringencies, oversized classes, and tight schedules threaten the success of the program. To complicate matters, instructors soon realize that the recommendations of the evaluation team are often too general to apply to individual pupils. Two handicapped youngsters of the same age, condition, and sex may, despite the team's recommendation that they be instructed in the same activities, have widely different functioning levels. Only after considerable experience with such disparities can teachers begin to feel comfortable with individualized physical education. Translating theory into practice means turning prescriptions into workable tasks. Instructors must train themselves to observe real differences between various degrees of impairment. They must sense positive and negative attitudes toward learning. They must measure and monitor changing performance levels. They must even make allowances for self-concepts and body images that can either make or break a pupil's motivation.

Physical educators should, therefore, have a thorough understanding of the concepts central to an IEP—"focus," "vigorousness," "type," "locomotion," "level," and "approach."

By concentrating the teacher's attention on the most urgent IEP problems first, the instructor begins to set priorities. "Begin at the beginning" is advice that has seldom made more sense. Why are these impaired students assigned IEP's? What are their functioning levels? What can instructors expect to accomplish? What are the youngsters' own expectations and those of their parents? How are these to be met? To answer such questions is to focus immediately on the matters of *instruction*. A pupil who lacks motor ability, but exhibits potential, clearly requires an instructional focus.

Should the instructor concentrate attention on *recreational, competitive, rehabilitative, therapeutic,* or *developmental* aspects? Swimming illustrates the variety of alternative focuses from which the teacher must make a prudent selection: a moderately mentally retarded youngster may flounder about in the pool because of poor coordination and irregular breathing. The focus called for in such a case is obviously *instructional*.

In contrast, a mildly retarded youngster may already stroke and kick with such confidence that the teacher can focus on *recreational* benefits. A partially blind teenager vigorous enough for advanced swimming lessons may be bored by anything short of the *competitive* focus. But a workout at the pool may also be *rehabilitative, therapeutic,* or *developmental*. Allowing for the fact that more than one focus is possible, each provides a different means of making progress.

Melinda, a bright girl of 12 with severe burns on her arms and legs, does *rehabilitative* swimming to restore function to her muscles and tendons. On the advice of a physician and of an evaluation team, Cindy, a mild cerebral palsied 10-year-old, swims for primarily *therapeutic* reasons while receiving additional physical therapy. Her strength and coordination must be improved if she is to reach her maximum potential. For Ray, born a thalidomide baby without arms, swimming three times a week is a *developmental activity*. Now 12, he has progressed by stages toward greater skill and endurance. Vigorous and sequential instruction has given him a better use of his torso and legs.

Early measurement of exercise tolerance is important. Until the *vigor* of each impaired child has been evaluated, strenuous activities should be avoided. It should be emphasized that the wide range of performance among those who have been labelled with the same impairment serves as a warning: whether trainable mentally retarded or partially deaf, all youngsters should be tested promptly and accurately for vigor.

Pupil responses to a vigorous exercise such as swimming fall into five categories. Each of these serves as a guideline for individualized pool activities:

1. *Unrestricted.* Pupils who fit this description can swim several laps without excessive fatigue.
2. *Mild.* These swimmers show fatigue after three or four laps.
3. *Moderate.* Such pupils are capable of a lap or two but seldom more.
4. *Active.* A misleading term for the uninitiated. Youngsters in this category are restricted to the shallow end of the pool where they may frolic in the water.
5. *Passive.* Because they have handicapping conditions and lack even the minimal vigor of the active group, these pupils merely sit or stand at the shallow end of the pool and are always under close supervision.

"What *type* of activity should I try to teach this handicapped youngster?" "Type," in this context, refers simply to certain qualities that distinguish a number of activities as an identifiable class. So many skills, games, sports, and dances are now easily available that physical educators appreciate a systematic method of selection. PL 94-142, within its definition of physical education, classifies activities as follows:

- Physical and motor fitness.
- Fundamental motor skills and patterns.
- Skills in aquatics, dance, individual and group games, and sports including intramurals and lifetime sports.

A more comprehensive listing for grouping activities appears on pages 101 to 102.

Exactly *how* does a nonambulatory child move about, or cover a given area? Instructors must know the locomotor patterns of individual pupils. Willie, who is in a wheelchair, and Betty, who is in braces, may, with the instructor's encouragement, be persuaded to crawl and creep on the gym floor. Can their willingness to try this be channeled into simple races and tunnel games? Using wheelchairs or gym scooters, such youngsters may even progress to dashes, tag games, and relay races. A few may undertake adapted basketball, floor hockey, street hockey, even square dancing. Some more coordinated youngsters who are not confined to wheelchairs have learned roller skating, ice skating, and even skiing. The ingenuity of teachers in adapting unusual locomotor patterns to ordinary games and sports seems to have no limits. Through their efforts, many impaired children are truly "recreated."

Careful observation of a child's play relationships yields important clues to the *social level* at which he or she should start. Is Jerry, who has cerebral palsy, capable of forming outgoing social relationships? What will bring him out of himself and move him out among his peers? Bobby, who is partially deaf, and Brenda, who has a deformed left arm, enjoy playing in a miniature replica of a community set up in the corner of the multipurpose room. While he imagines himself playing on the tiny baseball diamond, she is intrigued by the small-scale fire station and trucks. Yet they are barely conscious of each other's presence. A third level, *paired* or *coupled* relationship, marks the transition between individual autonomy and *group* interaction. In its most elementary form, such pairings (at a gymnasium multipurpose room, pool, or playground) mark the beginning of the social interaction and the prospect of both children eventually forming with groups. Only through *group activities* will their personal needs be subordinated to common interests. The introverted and socially inept youngster who is shunted aside by impairments begins at last to play dodge ball or participate in other group activities.

Dramatic progress is not the lot of every handicapped child; for many, the social and physical gains are barely perceptible. But the teacher's constant awareness of the levels of social interaction is at the heart of effective individualization.

An *approach* is preplanned, organized in specific categories, and ready to be taught without any adjustments. "What specific skills should I begin to teach," the instructor asks, "and which activities can I expect each of my students to complete?" No ready answers are possible since progress is unpredictable, sometimes disappointing. However, approach to any individual's problems starts with five basic facts: (1) age, (2) past experiences, (3) impairment, (4) developmental stage, and (5) present functioning level. Only after having made this preliminary "approach" can a teacher begin to work out teaching methods and strategies.

Children, including those who are impaired, need to develop basic skills and then proceed to low organized activities, and if able, progress to specific lead-up games followed by more highly organized games and team sports. Although, because of physical impairment, a 15-year-old with cerebral palsy may be restricted to an *adapted* class where she takes part in only *modified* games and sports, another 15-year-old pupil who is trainable mentally retarded can do much better by playing games and sports so well that she should be transferred to the regular program.

What advantages lie in the preplanning and categorizing associated with approaches? First, an approach can individualize an activity. Second, anything designed to satisfy a youngster's individual needs provides better motivation than a hit-or-miss general prescription. Finally, superior motivation means fuller participation, which in turn means greater progress.

Follow-Up and Carry Over

What opportunities for physical activities does the average community extend to its handicapped citizens, particularly to those impaired school children who would benefit from some form of *follow-up* on their formal physical education school classes? As long as taxable resources are commensurate with the public's growing concern for human rights, efforts should be made to finance programs that encourage impaired youngsters to join their classmates in expanded games and sports programs, whether these occur before or after regular school hours, during recesses, on weekends, or through the summer. With the accelerated recruitment of teaching assistants, student teachers, and volunteers in physical education, a dramatic change in the concept of *follow-up* seems imminent. Nor will the change be merely in *numbers* of participants; the quality of instruction has also been affected. Concern for the leisure activities of the handicapped is now widespread, and compassion for their boredom, frustration, and relative inertia has grown. Closer, more imaginative supervision, a more scientific application of proven teaching methods, and a wide assortment of activities—all these contribute to both quantitative and qualitative changes on the educational scene. The skills, games, and sports introduced in recent years emphasize a *continuity* between the student's present and future life. Class activities *carry over* into later life; social skills and a sense of well-being persist into adulthood; the games and sports learned early bear fruit later in life. Increasingly, junior and senior high school authorities put intramurals and interscholastic sports within the reach of the not so fortunate student whose skill, strength, and coordination have long been underestimated.

Increasingly, too, handicapped students in all the grades are systematically observed for signs of improvement in their motor abilities. The performances of some youngsters rise sharply as their participation in follow-up programs increases. Others, because of their impairments, experience slumps, doldrums, backsliding. A third group reaches a learning plateau from which the individuals can't easily budge. Further analysis of ends and means depends on what kinds of questions are asked and how the answers are put to practical use. Has the student been encouraged to take full advantage of the skills acquired during the school hours? If not, why not? Which games or styles of play are best, and which are to be avoided? Is the child competitive or noncompetitive? Does he or she regard group activities more, or less, congenial than games and sports involving "one on one?" Should impaired adolescents, whose motor skills exceed their muscular strength, be guided toward games of skill or toward those that build strength? Most important, perhaps, is the question of *carry-over:* do the physical activities learned in class carry over and, reinforced regularly through *follow-up* programs, finally carry over to mature behavior patterns?

Only through extended contacts with children beyond the physical education setting can most of the above concerns be constructively directed. To bring about effective change, instructors should do their part in informing school board members and city officials of the benefits of follow-up and carry-over whenever the impaired are involved.

At the end of the school day, with time on their hands, where in the community can handicapped students find recreation programs? Facilities are far more available than would appear. Among others are the Y.M.C.A.'s, the Y.W.C.A.'s, Boy Scouts and Girl Scouts, Special Olympics, church organizations and service clubs (Elks, Kiwanis, Lions, Moose, Rotary) and numerous community parks and recreation departments. Today, a growing number of recreators have had experience with the impaired population or are being trained for this specialty. Physical educators should be concerned enough to go out into the community on informal visitations to see how well children have followed up on class instruction. A good working relationship with recreators in the community is imperative with personal visits because it helps to assure better rapport.

During these visitations, the teacher can talk about the pupil's IEP, physical and motor fitness, and home life. The instructor also may observe firsthand how the youngster performs and interacts outside of school. In sum, these visitations can become a valuable information resource for the instructor and a good way to follow up in the joint effort of teachers and recreators.

CHAPTER 6

The Mainstreamed Program

Some impaired children who have special needs are able to succeed in mainstreamed or regular physical education classes. They are allowed to remain as long as they can "meet the challenge," which denotes sufficient skill, strength, and emotional and mental abilities to participate with regular pupils in most of the games, sports, and other activities routinely assigned. "Meeting the challenge" thus suggests the student's ability to cope—to deal with and to overcome at least some problems and difficulties. It does *not*, however, imply an ability to maintain a contest or meet a challenge on even terms of success.

Objectives

A realistic set of objectives takes three different instructional areas into account— the program itself, the instructor, and the pupil. Each teacher is responsible for asking, "Is the regular or mainstreamed program right for this particular handicapped child?" Approaching the problem from the other direction, the teacher should ask, "Is this child right for the program?" Most difficult of all to answer is the question, "Am I, as a teacher, knowledgeable and devoted enough to help youngsters at least part of the way toward the program's stated objectives?" To this end, teachers should, first of all, familiarize themselves with concepts and terms pertaining to students who are impaired. Second, they should seek actual experience with the nature and needs of the impaired. Third, they should ask themselves whether, by temperament or background, they *can* work with youngsters who are different from the "regular" class members.

After analysis of test data (including physical, mental, and emotional), a teacher should be ready to define and develop program objectives. Mainstreamed program objectives fall into four major categories:

Physical and Motor Fitness

The development of:

a. Gross motor skills and movements.
b. Physical fitness values.
c. Game and sport skills.
d. Neuromuscular and kinesthetic awareness.
e. Confidence and competence in performing activities.
f. Rhythm, poise, grace, coordination, balance, and reaction time.

Social Adjustment

An appreciation of:

a. Social interactions in a group situation.
b. Acceptable personality traits of others.
c. Aesthetic and creative values.
d. Achievement and success in oneself and others.
e. A positive social identity.
f. Socially acceptable emotion and tension outlets.

Emotional Adjustment

An appreciation of:

a. The right personal attitude toward others.
b. One's body-image and self-concept.
c. The benefits of emotional maturity.
d. Leisure time as a means of emotional stability.

Cognitive Skills

An understanding of:

a. The physiological effects of exercise upon the body.
b. Basic body mechanics of human movement.
c. Rules, strategies, and the knowledge of games and sports.

Guidelines for Programming

Guidelines for the mainstreamed or regular physical education programs include placement, grouping, curriculum, and motivation. With reference to *placement*, one should distinguish between those students with special physical and motor needs and those who need only accommodations. It is well to avoid uniformity whenever it ignores individual needs. When youngsters with special physical and motor needs are mainstreamed, instructors should avoid having to slow down the others.

In *grouping*, the teacher should avoid holding back the entire class for the benefit of one or two handicapped members. Instructors should weigh the *pros* and *cons* of the competitive sports. Although competitive sports usually accelerate development, they often ignore the individual's interests and abilities. Students should demonstrate ability to perform sequences of related movements before attempting complex activities. The teacher should observe their skills in both locomotor and nonlocomotor movements and judge their performance as individuals, as couples, and as members of a team.

In developing the mainstreamed *curriculum*, the teacher should consider chronological ages since older pupils differ from younger pupils in their physical and social needs. It is important to bear in mind that neither the rules of a game, nor the style and pace of play are carved in stone. "Flexibility" and "fun" should be watchwords to remember. Activities should be selected that appeal to the personal, social, emotional, and physical interests of students.

Good programming calls for instructors to be creative enough to challenge outdated ideas; to know about community resources that might vary and enrich the program; to develop a repertory of alternatives when the weather dictates that classes be held indoors; and to secure additional education on integrating the impaired in the mainstreamed class through conferences, workshops, and in-service training.

Guidelines for *motivation* include giving impaired children a voice in the process of determining ways in which adaptations and accommodations can be made and providing impaired students positive role-models on which to pattern their movements and behavior. Abilities, not disabilities should be emphasized, by selecting activities that bring success and avoid failure.

Class Size and Composition

While handicapped students are being assimilated into a regular physical activity class, no ready-made formula dictates the cutoff point. Each class has its unique problems. However, a ratio of six to eight nonimpaired students to each impaired student in a class of 20 to 25 is possible. If the result is unmanageable, the number of impaired should be reduced.

Mental age, chronological age, motor ability, cognitive skill, and both social and emotional stability all figure in decisions on class size and placement; on-the-scene observations are also helpful.

Mainstreaming may not run smoothly from the start. An instructor should be prepared for some rough going in the first meetings of any mainstreamed class. Glaring differences between the "regulars" and the "impaired," obvious discrepancies between the handicapped child's reported potential and what the teacher actually sees, may be frustrating. Fortunately, steps can be taken to soften the blow. The more experienced teachers of mainstreamed classes say that the early briefing sessions with regular students in advance of the arrival of their impaired classmates is highly effective. It is here that instructors can present the problem as an educational opportunity, thus allaying any doubts that linger in young minds about the philosophy, methods, and objectives of the federal mandate. Frankness from the start will hurt no one. Statements that are direct, brief, unsentimental, and free from moralizing work best. The benefits of mainstreaming to the average boy or girl will be born out when time is spent in physical activities with the impaired. School children across the nation are beginning to see that mainstreaming can work—a realization that in itself has immeasurable educational value.

Safety Measures

The elimination of hazards in facilities, equipment, and procedures is important; but instructors should also regularly question their own procedures and constantly point out hazards to their pupils. The following safety measures to be taken at the planning stage should be applied to facilities, equipment, procedures, and instruction:

1. Is the program adequately housed? Do gyms and classrooms have ample space for all participants?
2. Has the equipment been safety-checked at each session?
3. Are play areas cleared of hazards? Has sufficient space been provided outside the boundaries?
4. Have activities been selected that are suitable for performance in the available area?
5. Do the activities match the potential functioning levels of everyone in the mainstreamed class?
6. Have all damaged or defective items of equipment been repaired or placed out of reach?
7. Are children prohibited from performing on equipment that they are not sure how to use?
8. Have specific safety rules been established and conspicuously displayed?
9. Are instructors *prepared* for accidents at any time during the activity period?

10. Are teachers competent in administering first aid?

11. Is the correct and safe use of all gym equipment grasped by everyone in the mainstreamed class?

12. Are eyeglass protectors provided for pupils who need them? These may be worn when playing basketball, softball, volleyball, and floor hockey. Do pupils with contact lenses understand their care and attention?

13. Does the instructor know how and when to spot fatigue?

14. Have students been warned about unnecessary roughness?

The legal responsibilities of an instructor or recreator acting in place of a parent (*in loco parentis*) are subject to various interpretations by the courts. To be brief, the law regards as reasonable and prudent those who "anticipate danger and accidents." Therefore, negligence must be determined as the direct cause of an injury before legal proceedings can be started. When a teacher acts negligently, he or she may be sued for damages.

Facilities

Adequate space is needed for mainstreaming that meets both quantitative and qualitative specifications.

Outdoor facilities for a typical elementary school should have a minimum of five acres of ground plus one additional acre for every one hundred pupils. This means that in a 500-pupil school there should be at least ten acres of land. Playground surfaces range from all-weather, safety matting (to cover concrete or asphalt) to grass and wood chips for certain sections. Grounds should be relatively smooth, well drained, and well landscaped. It should be obvious that surfaces are of critical importance in accident prevention, especially for pupils whose coordination and reflexes are below par. Nor should planners ignore the function of circles and lines when organizing classes. Painted on hard-top surfaces or on safety matting, such boundaries are surprisingly effective. If the outdoor area is near a street, adequate fencing is mandatory. Frequent inspection of playground areas for litter, hard objects, and slippery surfaces is one way to avoid charges of negligence.

At the elementary school level, indoor facilities should include a gymnasium or a large multipurpose room; a swimming pool, indoor or outdoor, obviously enhances any program. Since few school systems can boast all of these, most instructors must learn to improvise.

Outdoor facilities for a typical junior high school will vary from a minimum of 15 to 25 acres; a senior high school needs a minimum of 25 to 30 acres. School enrollment and the extent of the program will determine the need for additional land.

Part of the play area should be hard-topped or paved in order that it may be used during times when regular playing fields are not useable. This area will provide for activities such as basketball, volleyball, paddle tennis, shuffleboard, dancing, and roller skating. If tennis courts are provided, it is recommended that they be separate from the hard-topped areas.

The fields should be marked for various seasonal sports: football, soccer, field hockey, lacrosse, speedball, track and field events, softball, and baseball.

Indoor facilities at the secondary school levels include a gymnasium (regulation junior high school size or high school size), and multipurpose rooms including a dance studio, a weight-training room, and a wrestling room. In addition, the facility should include dressing rooms, shower and drying rooms, team rooms, storage rooms, training rooms, and offices. A swimming pool is a welcome addition to any mainstreamed program. It should be a requirement in any school physical plant. The accessibility of a gymnasium, pool, or multipurpose room is based on a number of criteria:

Are toilets in the gymnasium locker rooms designed to accommodate wheelchairs? Are the wash basins, mirrors, towel racks, and drinking fountains at the proper height to accommodate those in wheelchairs?

Has at least one shower been designed for wheelchair students?

Are the aisles in the locker room wide enough for the free movement of wheelchairs? Are the floors of all locker rooms of the nonskid type? Are they safe for pupils on crutches as well as for those with braces?

Is the traffic pattern controlled throughout the facility? Are corridors sufficiently wide to accommodate the impaired?

Are signs and markings either in Braille or in raised letters? Are audio-cassettes or other sound-warnings available to assist the blind? Have lights or alternative signals and warnings been installed for the hearing-impaired?

Do regulation ramps lead into the pool building and into the water at poolside? Is there a lift in the pool? Although architectural barriers cannot always be eliminated without great expense, school boards should be alerted to all structural deficiencies and make arrangements to correct them.

As mainstreaming broadens, all sorts of facilities need to be used such as community facilities including municipal or service-club pools, tennis courts, playing fields, gymnasia and bowling alleys.

Equipment

The term "equipment" refers to such permanent instructional apparatus as sports standards, goals, mats, gym scooters, and the like. These have longevity, needing occasional repair or replacement. In the same category are parallel bars, balance beams, side horses, and rings.

Although the equipment listed is designed for regular students, much of it may be used effectively by the impaired. A well-planned, well-financed program will include these items:

Balance Beam
Balance Boards
Basketball Goals (portable)
Benches
Bicycle (stationary)
Cargo Net
Climbing Ropes
Gym Scooters
High Jump Standards
Horizontal Bar
Horizontal Ladder
Hurdles (adjustable)
Mirror (full length)
Net Standards (adjustable)
Parachute
Parallel Bars
Pitch Back Net

Record Player
Scales
Shoulder Wheel
Shuffleboard Set
Side Horse
Soccer Goals (portable)
Stall Bars
Stegel (Lind Climber)
Stilts
Swedish Box
Tape Player
Testing Equipment
Tetherball Set
Trampoline
Tumbling Mats (assorted)
Weight Training (machine)
Weight Training (traditional)

Playground equipment for both regular and impaired pupils includes many traditional as well as improvised items. All outdoor apparatus should be carefully selected for both safety and pedagogical value.

Backboards for basketball
Backstop for softball
Barrels
Benches
Cargo Net
Climbing Ladder
Horizontal Bars
Horizontal Ladder
Jungle Gym
Low Balance Beam
Planks

Rope Ladder
Sand Boxes (locate in shade)
Slanting Ladder
Slides
Standards for volleyball and tetherball
Sturdy Boxes
Swings
Tables
Tires mounted in the ground
Tires suspended from ropes
Tunnels

Supplies

"Supplies" refer to expendables such as balls, bats, hoops, wands, and nets. These must usually be replaced over a relatively short period of time. The following list includes the number of units recommended for a regular or mainstreamed class of from 20 to 25 pupils, 10 to 15% of whom are impaired.

Balls, audible (2)
Balls, plastic (18)

Balls, Hoppity-hop (18)
Bamboo Poles, 14″ (4)

Barrels (2)
Basketball, junior (6)
Basketball, regular (6)
Bases, indoor (1 set)
Bases, outdoor (1 set)
Batons (6-8)
Batting Helmets, assorted sizes (4)
Batting Tee (2)
Beach Balls, large (18)
Bean Bags (24)
Blocks, wooden (12)
Bowling Pins (10)
Boxes of various sizes (8)
Cageballs (1)
Clothesline Rope, assorted
Colored Masking and Plastic Tape
Dartboard & Darts (2 sets)
Deck Tennis Rings (4)
Dowels (12-18)
Fielder's Gloves, assorted (12)
Footballs, junior (4)
Hockey Set, plastic (6)
Hoops, plastic (18)
Indian Clubs (6)
Individual Jump Ropes (18)
Jar Rings, rubber (24)
Kickboards (6)

Kicking Tees (2)
Long Jump Ropes (6)
Magic Ropes (12)
Mask, Catcher's (2)
Measuring Tapes, 50' (1)
Paddles, wooden (6-8)
Playground Balls, 5" (18)
Playground Balls, 8½" (18)
Playground Balls, 10" (18)
Polyethylene Play Devices (cubes, blocks, roll-a-sphere)
Protector, chest (2)
Records, tapes, assorted
Rhythm Sticks (kit)
Rubber Innertubes, assorted (4-6)
Shuttlecocks, hand (6)
Soccer Balls (6)
Softballs (6)
Soft-Soft Balls (6)
Softball Bats (4)
Sponge Balls, large (18)
Stop Watches (2)
Tire and Tubes (6)
Traffic Cone Markers (12)
Volleyballs (6)
Volleyball Nets (2)
Wands, 2-4' (18)

A few examples of adapted devices include the following items: a bowling-ball pusher, a badminton racquet (attached directly to an amputee's prosthesis), a badminton serving tray for an amputee, a bihandled table tennis paddle, a bow sling for archery, a bow stringer for wheelchair archers, an adjustable tripod for crossbow archery, and an ankle stablizer for skating. Some of these are homemade, some improvised from materials at hand, while others may be purchased ready-made.

ACTIVITIES

Activities should be selected and scheduled in order of difficulty with specific activities designed for perceptual-motor, physical fitness, social and emotional development.

Organization Activities

Medical examinations
Dressing and showering procedures
Formations, spacing
Safety procedures.

Movement Experiences

Body part identification

Movement exploration

Locomotor movements

Non-locomotor movements

Manipulation activities

Creative rhythms

Mimetics

Sport mimetics

Gymnastics

Tumbling

Apparatus

Pyramid building

Balancing

Stunts and Self-Testing Activities

Individual

Partner

Group

Physical Fitness Activities

Warm-up

Weight training exercises

Obstacle course

Relaxation

Ball Activities

Ball skills
Ball games
Lead-up games
Individual/couple sports
Team sports

Run and Tag Games

Relays

With and without equipment

Swimming and Diving

Dance

Singing games
Folk dancing
Square dancing
Social dancing
Popular fad dancing

Miscellaneous Activities

Parachute
Playground
Rope
Tire and tube
Hoops and wands
Cargo net
Classroom and limited space

PLANNING

From the list of activities, teachers should develop and formulate the daily, weekly, monthly, and seasonal programs.

Daily Planning

The time devoted to an activity varies with the type and severity of the student's impairment. When regular and impaired pupils are scheduled in the same class, coordination problems arise. A clear-cut plan for the day is essential; activities must be selected to involve everybody. The following plans are suggested as guides to the instruction of pupils.

SAMPLE DAILY LESSON PLAN (YOUNGER PUPILS)

Change Period

1. Change to sneakers (if available)
2. Change to gym suits (if available)

Warm-Up Period—select one type:

1. Walking, running, skipping, etc. (locomotor).
2. Stretching, twisting, bending, etc. (nonlocomotor).
3. Mimetics: animals, toys, others.
4. Calisthenics.
5. Free play.

Teaching Activity—select one type:

1. Identification of body parts.
2. Body, space, and balance awareness activities.
3. Directionality, laterality, and verticality activities.
4. Locomotor and nonlocomotor activities.
5. Manipulation activities.
6. Movement exploration.
7. Ball skills.
8. Games (ball, relay, tag).
9. Mirror activities.
10. Rhythms.
11. Dances.
12. Parachute or cargo net activities.
13. Tire and tube activities.
14. Apparatus, tumbling, and stunts.

Review Activity—an activity that has been previously taught to help pupils relearn and have fun—select one type:

1. Movement exploration.
2. Games
3. Rhythms.
4. Dance.
5. Apparatus, tumbling, or stunts.
6. Free play.

Change and Wash-Up Period

1. Change clothes.
2. Lavatory, wash-up, drinks.

NOTE: Time allowances for various parts of the daily lesson should be flexible. Instructors can judge how long a given activity should continue by observing class-response and motivation or, as in one-to-one instruction, individual attitudes.

SAMPLE DAILY LESSON PLAN (OLDER PUPILS)

Change Period

1. Change to sneakers (if available)
2. Change to gym suits (if available).

Warm-Up Period—select one type:

1. Locomotor movements.
2. Nonlocomotor movements.
3. Calisthenics.
4. Sport mimetics.
5. Free Play.

Skills and Technique Period—select one type:

1. Body, space, and balance awareness activities.
2. Lead-up skills and games.
3. Individual or partner activities.
4. Apparatus, tumbling, and stunts.

5. Dance movements, steps and patterns.
6. Swimming activities.
7. Obstacle course.

Lead-Up Game, Game, Dance, or Continuing Activity—select one type.

1. Individual or group activities.
2. Apparatus, tumbling, and stunts.
3. Dances.
4. Swimming activities.
5. Team sports.
6. Obstacle course.

Change and Wash-Up Period

1. Showers, if possible.
2. Change clothes.
3. Lavatory, wash-up, drinks.

Seasonal

The seasons of the year lend themselves to planning in the activity program. Although three seasons of the year are considered, it may be necessary in some parts of the country to have two winter or indoor seasons in order to facilitate planning, while in other parts of the country, all planning should be for out-of-door participation. Each of the seasons can be divided into nine-week blocks: a fall season of nine weeks, two winter or indoor seasons of nine weeks each, and a spring season of nine weeks. This type of planning is predicated on a total year's program of 36 weeks.

Planning For Leisure Time Activities

The question is frequently asked, "How do impaired students spend their leisure hours outside of their mainstreamed classes?" Activities for them may be well planned during the school day and during extra classes after school, but what happens to pupils during evenings, weekends, and vacation periods?

Parents have a role in encouraging other families to join in supervised neighborhood recreation. Some parents who have background may also teach activities to the group. However, it is primarily the recreator who should provide the participants with meaningful activities. In accordance with PL 94-142 and Section 504, recreation departments have an obligation to provide services to their handicapped citizenry. A working relationship with the school, knowledge of medical history, handicapping conditions, ability levels of each participant, and a familiarity

Sample Seasonal and Daily Plan (younger pupils) (ages 6–12)

	Monday	Tuesday	Wednesday	Thursday	Friday
Fall Activity Warm-up	Running and hopping (locomotor)	Bending and stretching (nonlocomotor)	Mimetics	Teach proper use of play-ground equip-ment (emphasize safety)	Pupils may select the activities they wish to play
Teaching activity	Identification of body parts, body space, and balance awareness activities	Directionality, laterality, and verticality activities	Ball skills, (roll, toss, throw, catch) circle ball		
Review activity	Identification of body parts, body, space, and balance awareness activities	Directionality, laterality, and verticality activities	Continue circle ball		

Winter				
Activity				
Warm-up	Skipping and galloping (locomotor)	Twisting and turning, rising and falling (non-locomotor)	Free play	Free exercises to music
Teaching activity	Movement exploration and relays without equipment	Parachute activities	Tumbling and stunts	Balance beam
Review activity	Continue relays	Continue parachute activities	Tumbling and stunts	Balance beam
Spring				
Activity				
Warm-up	Running and leaping (locomotor)	Running in place	Free exercises to music	Mimetics
Teaching activity	Kicking skills and kickball (game)	Relays with equipment	Long rope and individual rope jumping	Circle dodge ball
Review activity	Continue kickball	Continue relays	Long rope and individual jumping	Continue circle dodge ball

(For Winter warm-up group and Spring warm-up group, the final column reads: "Pupils may select the activities they wish to play")

Note. A. It may be necessary to spend several periods when teaching some of the activities.

B. Individualized and group instruction should be used.

Sample Seasonal and Daily Plan (older pupils) (ages 13–18)

Fall Activity	Monday	Tuesday	Wednesday	Thursday	Friday
Warm-up	Free exercises	Locomotor and non-locomotor activities	Free exercises	Free play	Choice of activities
Skills and techniques	Football skills field hockey skills	Soccer skills	Football skills	Dribbling, shooting, and passing (floor/street hockey)	
Lead-up game/game	Flag football (B) Field hockey (G)	Soccer B/G	Flag football (B) Field hockey (G)	Floor/street hockey B/G	

Winter *activity*					
Warm-up	Basketball mimetics	Free exercises	Free play	Locomotor and nonlocomotor	Choice of activities
Skills and techniques	Basketball skills	Stunts—crab, seal, and frog forward and backward rolls	Sideline basketball	Dance movements, steps, and patterns	
Lead-up game/game Dance	Basketball	Balance beam— walk forward and walk backward			
Spring *Activity*					
Warm-up	Calisthenics	Relays	Stretching exercises	Jogging	Choice of activities
Skills and techniques	Softball skills	Horseshoes, quoits, shuffleboard	300-yard run relays	Pupils select activities they wish to play	
Lead-up game/game Dance	Softball	Badminton, tennis			

Note. A. With older students, emphasis on individual and couple sports. B. (B) boys, (G) girls.

with the type of activities offered at school are the essential factors needed by the recreation leader. Because recreation is voluntary in nature, the mainstreamed child should, even after school, find a new sense of belonging, delight, and achievement.

In most cases, the leisure time activity program offered by a recreation department should be a carry-over from the school instructional physical education classes. Although this guideline is important, pupils who enter a recreation program should also be given opportunities to learn new activities and to be free to choose those they wish to play.

Residential Field Experiences

Because of mainstreaming, integrated camping is a growing phenomenon. Whether daytime or residential, private, agency, or city-sponsored, these "field experi-

An Adventure Task—Over the Wall   With helping hands and on a safety belay rope, a young-ster, ordinarily confined to a wheelchair, can experience success in an "Outward Bound" type activity.

(b)

ences'' bind together the academic life and the outdoor life. What a youngster has learned at the school, gym, pool, or playfield is now connected with a deeper, more exciting and challenging existence.

Residential field experiences that last from two or three days to a week or more aid the socialization process. When living together in the same tent or cabin, everyone gets to know everybody else; friendships ripen and identities emerge. Usually, the ratio of the regular to impaired campers is approximately that of the typical mainstreamed class, or, 10 to 15 percent.

Colleges and universities affilitated with school systems usually sponsor and administer these projects. They, in cooperation with school personnel, plan programs, engage the staff, and evaluate the project. The school sector has the responsibility for teaching the pre and post phases of the program. If no college or university can affiliate, the school personnel then assumes all responsibility for running the residential field experience.

A glance at a fifth or sixth grade curriculum for a typical residential field experience reveals a kaleidoscope of offerings. Reading, music, arts and crafts, environmental studies and natural sciences, plus social interaction through outdoor activities are features of the program. The school's academic program should merge with the field experience. The process should require previous classroom preparation at school followed by supplementary activities after the residential field experience.

Staff recruitment is handled in one or two ways. For the trainee who will serve as an assistant or counselor, programs usually depend on undergraduate or graduate students in nearby colleges and universities who are preparing for degrees in physical education or recreation. An alternative is to recruit capable volunteers.

The residential field experience program centers on noncompetitive activities for groups of 4 to 8 campers in living and learning settings; modified "outward bound" concepts and skills woven into the entire program; an interdisciplinary problem-solving approach to environmental studies; the performance of drama, art, and reading episodes that express program themes.

The goals of a residential field experience may be summarized as follows:

- To provide personal enrichment and an improved self-image that will challenge pupils to interact in problem-solving experiences.
- To engage the services of college students majoring in physical education, special education or recreation, for the purpose of promoting interdisciplinary learning experiences among the impaired.
- To promote an atmosphere whereby impaired pupils can work toward common goals, personal or social, physical or intellectual.
- To promote a closer understanding of the balance of the human and natural environment through a study of the out-of-doors.

CHAPTER 7

The Adapted Program and Adapted Activities

While theoretically and ideally it would be "best" to have all children and adults in a "mainstreamed" program, realistically and practically such a situation is not possible or advisable. For some impaired persons, it may be possible to participate part of the time in the regular or mainstreamed physical education class and part of the time in the adapted class. The needs of others will demand participation *only* in the adapted class. The term "adapted class" in this context, therefore, implies the segregation of students with impairments, who may or may not have similar handicapping conditions.

The major aims of the adapted program are to assist each student in acquiring motor skills, physical fitness and acceptable social-emotional traits. These aims may be met through the following objectives:

1. To improve motor ability.
2. To improve fitness.
3. To improve body mechanics.
4. When possible, to alleviate or reduce handicapping conditions.
5. To learn a variety of skills, games, sports, and dances.
6. To develop acceptable social traits.
7. To develop acceptable emotional traits.
8. To develop a positive self-concept.
9. To develop a positive body-image.
10. To promote a better understanding of impairments.

113

Relaxation   A class of 12 boys and girls with physical impairments enjoy a moment or two after "racing" by their different methods of travel.

11.   To use leisure time more constructively.
12.   To emphasize abilities.

Class Composition and Size

Adapted classes are seldom homogeneous with respect to physical, mental, social, emotional or functional impairments, or any combination of these. Since each student has different needs, interests, and potential, these should be recognized in order to build upon existing abilities and to reduce deficiencies. There are other accommodations that can facilitate more flexible programming for these youngsters. Despite a lack of homogeneity in an adapted class, the teacher is expected to accommodate each student.

The size of an adapted class ranges from 6 to 12 students. The kind and degree of impairment, the availability of teacher aides, facilities, equipment, the instructor's background—all affect decisions about class composition and size. Adapted classes are usually coeducational except for contact sports.

Setting Up The Schedule

Sessions should meet once or twice a day, for from 20 to 45 minutes depending on ages, grades, and physical conditions of students. Additional classes after school hours may be planned to meet special needs, or by popular demand. Adapted physical activities classes should be incorporated into the regular school day like any other subject in the school's curriculum. Since the impaired pupil can become restless from sitting, like anyone else, teachers should be alert to the need for a change of pace with a shift from desk work to movement activities. If the facilities are scheduled to the hilt, instructors should make use of the classroom itself or any other available area. In spite of space limitations, classrooms can be adapted to allow for a number of different physical activities.

Safety Tips

The safety of each student in an adapted program demands effective and enforced policies. Suggested below are some basic safety precautions to be observed before, during, or after sessions:

1. Provide deaf pupils with colored T-shirts or vests so that their classmates will know they cannot respond to auditory signals.
2. Be sure that wheelchairs have no broken or exposed spokes, no unprotected or sharp edges, and locking mechanisms that work.
3. Remove all gymnastic equipment that is not in use.
4. Select low-risk activities. A thorough familiarity with each activity is imperative if risks are to be minimized. Anticipate the problems in each phase of the game or sport, especially when moments of congestion or accelerated speed increase risk.

(a)

Parachuting A group activity emphasizing cooperation and physical activity for different ages and different mental and physical abilities.

(b)

5. Do not allow students to perform on equipment that has not been in-
    spected by the instructor.
6. Clear all debris, obstacles, and barriers from outdoor areas before ses-
    sions start.
7. Move tables, desks, and chairs to the side to allow enough free space for
    activities. Be aware of projecting corners and unmovable equipment.
8. Show pupils in wheelchairs how to avoid colliding with each other;
    practice starts, stops, sharp turns, and reversing directions.
9. Discuss with the class members the need for understanding the impair-
    ments of others.
10. Instill in students a sense of responsibility for their own safety as well as
    that of others.
11. Do not compel participation by those who fear injury. Introduce them
    first to activities that are safe enough to build confidence.
12. Safety depends on the instructor.

ADAPTED ACTIVITIES

An adapted physical activity is any type of skill, game, sport, or dance that has been
modified or adjusted to fit functioning levels. Instructors should look upon an
adapted activity as the medium through which objectives can be met. Caution
should be exercised to ensure that an activity not be so modified, or its challenges so
diminished, that its benefits are destroyed. Adapted activities may be used in any of
the programs: (1) mainstreamed, (2) dual, that is, mainstreamed and adapted, or (3)
adapted only.

Adaptations

No set procedures exist for adapting activities. The following guidelines may prove useful in making adaptations.*

Adaptations should be within a student's ability range. An adaptation should assist a student to participate successfully in planned activities within his or her ability range. It may be necessary to modify further or eliminate an adaptation as a student's skill increases, to encourage continued progress in student development.

Adaptations should allow a student to participate within guidelines established by his or her physician. Adaptations must be made that encourage a student to stay within activity limitations established by the physician, while at the same time allowing the student freedom to participate within his or her ability. As a student uses an adaptation, attention must be given to possibilities of new problems being created. Since aggravation of other existing conditions is a possibility, frequent reevaluation of an adaptation as used by a specific student is necessary; appropriate adjustments are made when necessary.

A student should participate in the development of an adaptation and be positive toward its use. Cooperation between teacher and student is necessary for the development of a successful adaptation. The student and teacher must study a problem together to create a successful adaptation that overcomes a student's specific limitations. Ongoing appraisal regarding an adaptation's use is necessary for continued student acceptance.

Adaptations should be constructed safely. In planning and constructing a device adaptation, student safety must be uppermost in a teacher's mind. An adaptation should encourage student participation yet be safe for the user as well as other students who participate.

Adaptations should be made in activities appropriate to the student's age and interests. Each student should have opportunities to develop and use his or her abilities and capitalize on personal interests. Since participation with nondisabled peers is a common desire, adaptations should be *planned to encourage and allow this type* participation.

The sections that follow consist of suggestions for adaptations applicable to a variety of skills, games, and sports.

LOCOMOTOR

- Allow pupils to substitute wheelchair movements for running and other locomotor movements.

*Jim Cowart, "Teacher-Made Adapted Devices for Archery, Badminton, and Table Tennis," *Practical Pointers*, American Alliances for Health, Physical Education, and Recreation, Washington, D.C., Vol. 1, No. 13, May, 1978, p.3.

Scooters   Ball activities may be combined with gym scooters to create a "new" game.

- Alternative modes of locomotion should constantly be explored such as crawling on air mattresses or mats and using gym scooters.
- Varying the *speed* of the activity makes it practicable for a broad segment of handicaps.
- Holding the hand of a nonsighted classmate provides guidance and direction for movement activities.

THROWING, CATCHING, AND BATTING

- Attach elastic or string to balls for each retrieval.
- As a substitute for the finger-release involved in tossing or throwing a ball, bandage a small plastic cup or container to the child's clasped hand so that a simple arm-swing will automatically put the ball in flight.
- Pupils who are unable to toss or throw can usually be taught to drop a ball or object at a target marked on the floor.
- Trapping a ball or object in the lap is, for many, an acceptable alternative to catching in the hands.
- A small plastic container or basket can be placed on the lap or in between the legs to catch the ball.
- Use a batting tee instead of "pitching."
- Experiment with a table for teaching how to catch or bat a ball. Roll the ball along the table, catching it in a paper bag, or waste basket, or letting it go

through the arms; in batting, hit the ball along the table. Use a light bat of plastic, a paper tube, or the hand.

INDIVIDUAL, PARTNER, AND SMALL GROUP ACTIVITIES

Jumprope:

Ropes may be placed on the floor or ground forming geometric figures. Youngsters then attempt to fit their bodies inside the rope figures.

Pupils may create their own jumprope steps, patterns, and routines.

Children unable to be "jumpers" may be "turners."

Those unable to be "turners" by themselves can be assisted with their hand grips and arm movements.

Hopscotch

Tossing objects into the marked spaces may be changed to pushing objects or kicking them.

Larger objects should be available.

The size of the spaces may be increased.

Jump Rope To develop coordination, group or individual rope jumping may be used.

Numbers, letters, words, or colors may be placed in the spaces for learning purposes.

Pupils unable to jump or hop may be allowed to toss an object while another pupil performs the movements.

Children may crawl or creep into the spaces without tossing the object.

Those with braces or walking devices may maneuver through the spaces and patterns instead of jumping or hopping through them.

Only through verbal instruction or auditory signals on distance or direction can hopscotch for the blind be practicable.

Wands

Body positions may be changed to sitting, kneeling, or lying (prone or supine).

Letters, numbers, and words can be formed by making gestures in the air.

If a wand cannot be held, bandage or strap it to the hand and wrist as if it were in a grip position.

Wands may be placed on the floor or ground; pupils may crawl, creep, or walk around them, straddle them or jump back and forth over them.

Wands may be held at the ends, and various exercises may be performed while pupils assume different positions.

A board 1 in. × 4 in. × 12 in. may be placed across a wooden wand for a balancing activity.

Bowling

Body position may be changed to sitting.

Distance from the foul line to the pins may be shortened.

Ball may be held with two hands and released between the legs down a shoot or trough.

The number of rolls to knock down the pins may be increased.

Pins painted bright colors or numbered enhance attention.

Ball may be released from the lap or tray while student is in a sitting position.

Children may use an adapted ball pusher.

In the gymnasium as well as in bowling lanes, blind pupils may use ramps.

For a totally blind youngster, directions can be made clearer by locating steady sounds: tapping the floor, striking two metal objects at floor-level or bouncing a basketball.

Variety   A variety of activities, including bowling, which helps to develop skills and achievement, should be conducted during the play period.

Tires and Tubes

Paint tires bright colors for excitement.

Several tires may be placed in an upright position halfway in the ground or in concrete so that youngsters may crawl through or balance on top of them.

For a tug-of-war, body position may be changed.

Tubes may be placed in a circle; pupils may sit inside the tubes, hold hands, and sing a song.

Large tubes may be used as springboards.

Use car inner tubes cut into bands for isokinetic activities. Bicycle inner tubes can be used for the same purpose. Movements of hands, arms, feet, and legs are possible in unlimited combinations.

Beanbags

Change the materials and colors of beanbags. Number or letter them. Sew or glue pictures of clowns, birds, and animals on them.

Attach strings or elastics to beanbags so that wheelchair pupils can retrieve them.

Beanbag Toss   A quiet game in which skills and success may be developed.

Have students use various body parts for different types of relays: relays with bags on heads, bags pinched between knees.

Hoops

Hoops placed flat on the floor or ground challenge children to fit their bodies inside.

Have pupils twirl hoops in various body positions—sitting, kneeling, lying on back or stomach. Music helps.

Hoops may be twirled around both arms or both legs.

Encourage children to start by learning to creep, crawl, or walk as close as possible beside, inside, and around hoops without touching them.

Place hoops on the floor or ground in pairs, or alternating left and right; invite pupils to walk, run, hop, or jump in and out of them.

Hoops that are hung vertically serve as targets through which objects can be tossed or thrown.

Challenge students to balance hoops on four fingers, then three, two, and only one.

Hoops may be rolled over various types of large geometric figures: circles, ovals, and figure-eights.

Cargo Nets

For climbing, substitute stretching, swinging, or balancing.

The speed and height of climbing may be increased or decreased.

While hanging on the net, pupils may make different body shapes and movements or perform a "tug-of-war."

Obstacle Courses

Various locomotor movement may be used in the obstacle courses.

The types of obstacles and barriers may be changed as to sizes, shapes, colors, and height.

A time limit may be set for completing the course.

Obstacle courses for wheelchair students may be improvised from materials and objects at hand.

OTHER RELATED ACTIVITIES FOR INDIVIDUALS, PARTNERS, AND SMALL GROUPS

Horseshoes, shuffleboard, and similar games may be played either sitting or standing. The number of points necessary to determine a winner may be decreased or increased, depending on the endurance of the participants.

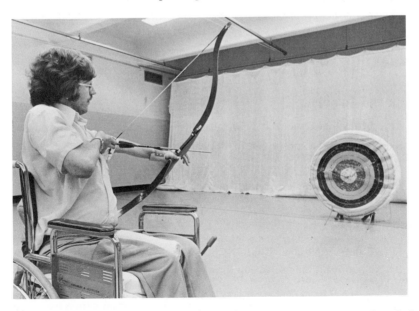

Archery   An indoor or outdoor activity for all ages; safety must be closely observed, particularly in this sport.

Golf   Chipping to the "green," over a "sand trap" (walkway).

Portable walls, without a ceiling, may be used for adapting handball and racquetball.

Students with braces or crutches as well as amputees with one leg or one arm can play selected activities such as golf, archery, or badminton, as long as proper adjustments are made. (In some cases, these modifications may not be necessary.)

GYMNASTICS AND APPARATUS

Stunts and Tumbling

Less difficult movements may be substituted for the originally designed stunts.

Side rolls may be substituted for forward or backward rolls.

Regular stunts may be replaced by "creative" stunts.

In some cases, simple pyramids may be built.

Climbing Ropes

Length may be shortened in order to reduce the climbing distance.

Before pupils lift themselves up from their wheelchairs, make certain the chair is locked.

Holding the body's weight off the floor or wheelchair on a time basis may be substituted for climbing the rope.

Climbing Ropes   Rope climbing and swinging are worthwhile activities for developing strength.

Balance Beam

For those who use walkers or wear braces, a maneuver along a floor line is a sufficient beginning. They may later progress to the regular balance beam.

A 2 in. × 8 in. × 10 in. plank placed between two low chairs or benches may serve as a balance beam.

Although slowness should be enforced at the outset, the tempo of movements may later be accelerated.

Vaulting Boxes

Wooden or plastic boxes of various heights are satisfactory substitutes for the regular vaulting box.

Falling off the box onto several layers of mats is, for many children, the equivalent of actual jumping.

Trampoline

For blind youngsters, a bell or light pieces of metal (keys) can be hung under the center of the bed as an auditory guide when performing.

A box mat may be substituted for the trampoline.

Youngsters with neuromuscular or orthopedic impairments should, after explanations and demonstrations, be helped onto the trampoline from their wheelchairs. Vertical movements from a sitting position are introduced first. Then, while thrusting the hips forward and the chest upward simultaneously, they swing their arms upward to gain maximum height. In the prone position, they use hands and arms to establish a rocking action by pushing their upper bodies off the bed. In the supine position, their forearms and elbows are used to activate the upper body in establishing a rhythmical bounce pattern.

Horizontal Ladders

The ladder may be lowered to accommodate those who lack upper body strength.

Hanging and swinging within a time limit is an acceptable approach to traveling.

TEAM SPORTS

Basketball*

Baskets may be lowered, court dimensions reduced, and playing time adjusted.

Various sizes of balls make the game possible to more children.

Some armless students may be taught to use their feet for basket shooting.

Tapping loudly on the rim of the basket, ringing a small bell, or providing a sounding device (portable radio or portable loudspeaker) behind the backboard—any of these will enliven the shooting for blind students.

Football

Different types and sizes of balls may be used, but rubber, sponge, or plastic are preferred.

The dimensions of the field may be reduced, and playing time may be shortened.

"Tackling" should be done by *tag* or *flag*, not by regular tackling.

Line blocking may be changed to pushing. Downfield blocking may be banned.

Running may be eliminated and only passing allowed.

The point after touchdown as well as field goal attempts may be used or eliminated.

Wheelchair students often serve effectively as centers.

*Information and rules relating to wheelchair basketball are available from Benjamin H. Lipton, National Wheelchair Athletic Association, 40-24 62nd St., Woodside, NY 11377.

Basketball   Not necessarily to develop N.B.A.ers, but for fun and skill for those in wheelchairs or with mental impairments.

Floor or Street Hockey

The dimensions of the playing area should be commensurate with the number of players on a team and the space available.

The tempo of the game may be slowed down simply by changing the locomotion from running to walking.

The goals may be widened, and playing time reduced.

Hockey   With sticks or crutches, pucks or balls, in wheelchairs, walkers, or with canes, hockey can be played.

Plastic balls of various sizes are good substitutes for pucks.

Instead of using sticks, students may kick the puck or ball.

Armless pupils often play the goalie position and use their legs and feet to block shots.

To prevent pucks or plastic balls from going out of bounds, small wooden benches or plastic boxes may be used on the boundary lines.

Pupils with a limited handgrip but with a fair degree of arm movement can manipulate hockey sticks that are bandaged or strapped to the dominant hand.

Wheelchair students or those with insufficient leg mobility may fill in the goalie position quite creditably.

Youngsters who wear braces or who have walking devices should be instructed in balancing themselves before attempting to hit a puck or ball.

Crutches may be used in place of the hockey stick.

Soccer

The playing area and goal may be reduced in size, the periods shortened, and the pace slowed to walking.

Running kicks may be changed to stationary kicks.

Mike Whether one uses one's head or feet, sports play an important role in a person's life.

(b)

Wooden, plastic, or fiberglass boxes or benches, or other types of barriers, may be placed around the playing area to help keep the ball in play.

Different sized playground balls may be substituted for a regular soccer ball.

The number of players on a team may be safely increased to speed up the pace.

For students who are unable to either run or kick, rules should be relaxed to allow tossing the ball.

Wheelchair pupils may be designated as goalies, and chairs may be used for blocking the ball.

Softball

The distance from the pitcher's area to home plate, as well as the distance between bases, may be decreased.

The use of batting tees gives the impaired a sense of confidence and success.

The number of defensive players may be increased so as to decrease the individual's field coverage.

Called balls and strikes may be omitted, and batters may be allowed five or more attempts to hit the ball.

If a student is capable of batting but cannot run, a ''designated base runner'' may be allowed.

Softball   While one holds the ball on the tee, the other hits for a home run.

Pupils without arms learn, with proper instruction, how to pitch or throw the ball with their feet.

Volleyball

Increase or decrease the dimensions of the court and the height of the net to suit the number and abilities of players.

Some youngsters may only be able to manage by catching the ball before throwing it back over the net.

Similarly, in serving, the ball may be either tossed or thrown rather than struck.

Allow the ball to bounce on the floor one or more times before it is hit or thrown back over the net.

Instead of staying in the designated service area, the server may move up closer to the net.

To get the ball over the net, servers may be allowed a predetermined number of "tries." The same policy may apply to volleying.

Blind pupils may be designated exclusively as servers and thus become effective players.

The game may be played while in a stationary standing or sitting positions.

When beginning a unit on volleyball, progress from balloons to beach balls to plastic balls to partially deflated playground balls to regular-sized balls.

Track Events

Distances may be decreased, running lanes widened, and types of locomotion varied.

For dashes, use gym scooters; for baton exchanges, use touching hands; for relay races, use regular or air mattresses on which pupils may crawl or creep.

If hurdles are not available, corrugated, wooden, or plastic boxes may be used. Conventional hurdles should be lowered.

Jumping   Fun, but with a helping hand should the jumper fall backwards.

Field Events

A raised (1/8 in.) starting line makes the standing long jump practicable for the blind.

Use a wider take-off board than the standard size.

Show blind youngsters how to pace-off and "feel" the distance from the ground to the crossbar. Examples include the high jump and running long jump.

For many pupils, a shorter runway makes the running long jump much easier.

Crossbars of string or rope help to insure safety.

Softballs may be substituted for the usual four-or-six pound metal shot puts.

DANCE

Creative Movements

It should be understood that "creative" means what it says: any shape or form that is transposed from mental creation to physical formation is correct and acceptable.

By listening carefully, impaired students will get the "feel" of the music that can motivate them to explore their surroundings and to create movements while the body is in motion.

Swaying, swinging, sliding, balancing, and wheeling should be openly admired, not corrected.

Personal dance movements—swinging from side to side, clapping hands, and moving the head are praiseworthy forms of expression.

Rhythms

The tempo may be slowed down, locomotion varied, and body position changed from standing to sitting to lying.

Allow pupils to use any type of bodily movements to interpret rhythm, tempo, and phrasing.

When students cannot get the rhythm of their musical accompaniment by tapping their feet or by clapping their hands, or snapping their fingers, they should be encouraged to mark time any way they can.

When the record player is on a wooden floor and the volume increased, nonhearing students in their bare feet can often pick up vibrations through their toes or soles. Fingers and palms are likewise sensitive receptors.

Do-Si-Do   Boys and girls with special needs enjoy dancing.

Folk

Use square, line, or round dances with the orthopedically impaired that involve few complicated step patterns.

A reduced record speed enables pupils to walk through a dance pattern before undertaking a faster tempo.

If impaired pupils cannot perform movements in a "do-si-do," allow the nonimpaired partner to substitute.

Youngsters with walkers may use one hand or no hands while their nonhandicapped partners dance around them.

If both dancers use walking devices, they may form a pivot for circular movements by touching or locking their devices.

Crutches or walkers are a means of raising the body while steadying it for freer movements.

For "honor your partner," those who are unable to bend at the waist may simply nod their heads.

For "promenade," some may have to place one hand on the shoulder of their nonimpaired partners.

For "allemande left and right," wheelchair pupils can replace offering hands with wheeling to a specific spot. These pupils may also wheel around in a circle, eliminating hand movements.

For the mentally retarded, colored ribbons, crepe paper or elastic bands on the wrist indicate direction ("allemande left and right" becomes "allemande red and green").

Social

Free movements of social dancing are enjoyed by some cerebral palsy youths or youths with poor coordination because they may reduce the possibility of spasms.

Mark the floor so that students may learn where to step.

Dance steps may first be taught in a stationary position without music.

FITNESS

Through exercise, the range of motion is likely to increase within the student's limitations.

A sitting press can replace a standing press.

Flexibility   An important component for all.

Push-ups in the horizontal position may be attempted at angles off the vertical; knees may remain in contact with the floor when doing push-ups.

Weights may be reduced or eliminated in both free and weight-training exercises.

Time-extensions make interval training more practical for the impaired.

For interval training, a treadmill or a stationary bicycle may be used; running may be substituted by walking.

The number of stations in circuit training may be decreased, increased, or changed to meet the needs of the impaired.

OUTDOOR ACTIVITIES

The buddy system may be utilized on hikes or when moving from one activity to the next.

Pathways can be widened, cleared of obstacles, and in some cases hard-topped, for wheelchair participants.

See Saw   Simple activities on homemade equipment often provide hours of interest and fun to persons who are retarded or otherwise handicapped.

Spaces cut in picnic tables will allow wheelchair students or campers to draw up to the table comfortably.

Ropes with clips, hung from trees or uprights, may be attached to wheelchairs to provide swings.

Pontoon boats, designed to accommodate several wheelchairs, provide experiences on the water not easily attained in other craft.

Metal detectors may be used to differentiate between rocks and materials; these are helpful to all, but particularly to blind students.

Records or tapes that contain bird sounds along with a commentary on colors, habitats, and the like are helpful for blind campers.

With proper instruction, small saws may be substituted for axes.

Poles with miniature skis attached to the ends are now universally accepted for leg amputee skiers.

Toboggans and sleds should be equipped with strong railings of rope or wood.

Demountable safety seats of plastic are now available for toboggans and sleds.

Three

INSTRUCTING IMPAIRED YOUTH

8

The Team Approach

Within the last decade, growing public concern for the handicapped has opened up exciting educational prospects. States, counties, cities, towns, and numerous agencies, both federal and state, have started rehabilitation programs that are unprecedented for size and expertise. Of special benefit to impaired youth are the redesigned curricula initiated by numerous elementary and secondary schools. Universities, too, are developing undergraduate and graduate programs in adapted physical education in this segment of the American life.

The best way to provide services to impaired youth is, nevertheless, a major problem for today's educator. Until now this task has been complicated by trial and error, fragmented efforts, and vague objectives. What has emerged from a period of groping is the conviction that empathy and knowledge must be pooled to have an effective program. A team appraoch makes possible the interplay of specialists working toward a single goal. It becomes increasingly clear that centralized staffing lies in the creation of a local supporting unit, or team. Such coordinated support has three functions: training—imposing disciplines and drills to reach clearly defined objectives; instruction—communicating a body of knowledge; and service—lending continued assistance after training and instruction. These three functions, when properly defined, assigned, and applied, call for the joint efforts of the following professionals and persons. The following listing of personnel by position is an arbitrary one that relates to the physical education teacher and others on the "team."

The *School Administrator* provides educational leadership for all programs and initiates plans for specialized facilities, equipment, and supplies. His or her administrative duties include calling and conducting teachers' meetings as well as making arrangements for the transportation of pupils with special needs. Problems of adjustment between pupil and teacher, and other professionals, are adjudicated by the administrator.

The *Physical Educator or Teacher,* preferably a specialist in adapted physical education with instructional methods and techniques for the impaired, advises, supervises, and teaches both the pupils and the teachers. There should be close cooperation between the classroom and physical education teachers. The adapted physical education teacher should have knowledge of the physical, mental, and psychological characteristics of children with impairments. Some impaired students can be integrated into classes with regular pupils while others must be placed in the adapted physical education classes.

The *Classroom Teacher,* in addition to offering academic instruction to students, serves the role of a "human-service" agent. Because of mainstreaming, he or she is in daily contact with impaired youngsters. This teacher is often called upon to conduct physical activities programs and, therefore, needs training in adapted physical education and in special education.

The *Special Education Teacher* is prepared to offer direct academic instruction to handicapped youth. He or she also acts in the capacity of consultant to the regular classroom teachers and to the physical educator. Since these teachers are often called upon to conduct physical activities programs, they should gain some knowledge of adapted physical education.

The *Teacher Aide/Volunteer* fills the role of assistant to the teacher. Having usually completed a professional training program, the aide may be either a paid "paraprofessional" or a volunteer.

Although teacher aides are usually under the supervision of the teacher, they may be given considerable latitude, including some teaching responsibilities. Their duties are often clerical as well as instructional. They prepare and maintain materials, bulletin boards, and displays; they operate audio-visual equipment and keep daily attendance records; they help prepare supplies and equipment, duplicate materials, and maintain pupils' records.

Impaired children like the personal attention a teacher aide can give. Some of the children need assistance in dressing, going to the bathroom, getting around the classroom, around the school, and in and out of buses, duties to be performed by the aides or volunteers.

The *Physician* makes examinations and provides professional services to school children who have impairments. In certain cases, the physician discusses the pupil's impairments and health needs with the teacher and parents. When needed, medical advice regarding the type and amount of physical activity in which a pupil can participate should be offered to the teacher or physical educator.

The *Nurse* works closely with the physician, teachers, pupils, and parents. Duties of the nurse include assisting in medical examinations, administering health, posture, general hearing and vision tests, keeping health records, making referrals to the doctor, administering first aid, and checking on the general health of the pupils.

The *Psychologist* administers intelligence tests and other evaluative psychological instruments to pupils and interprets the results. The psychologist counsels impaired pupils with behavioral problems, especially those with emotional problems, and discusses possible plans and procedures with teachers and other interested personnel.

The *Physical Therapist* works under the direction of the doctor, using selected physical modalities, prescribing and giving exercises, and recommending methods for developing overall muscle strength and coordination. The classroom teacher and the physical education teacher are given advice by the physical therapist concerning the pupil's impairments and their correction or maintenance.

The *Occupational Therapist* provides services affecting change through pupil involvement in purposeful everyday sensory-motor integrative activities. These help the pupil to learn and improve activities of daily living such as feeding, dressing, and toileting. The therapist helps to develop personal independence, whether in eating, in work, or in physical activity, in a creative and constructive manner.

The *Speech Therapist* consults with the teacher on the improvement of oral skills. Personal instruction and therapy are given to pupils with significant speech problems. Working with school administrators, the speech therapist develops communication programs for the school system or for institutions and resident facilities.

The *Hearing Therapist* (audiologist) identifies auditory losses by means of precision tests, and then consults with the classroom teacher to develop corrective programs for children who are either partially or totally deaf.

The *Recreation Therapist* provides recreational and leisure-time activities for impaired boys and girls, usually in community or private social agencies. Leisure-time activities are also offered to impaired populations in residential schools and hospitals. Play therapy is a keystone in the treatment of impaired children used by the recreation therapist. It includes three kinds of activities: *psychomotor*—games and sports, especially swimming; *sensory*—concerts, plays, and dance performances; and *cognitive*—reading for pleasure and attending lectures.

The *Social Worker* serves as an interactor for the impaired student, the family, and friends. The social worker helps impaired students to adjust and cope with the pressures of school and community life. The social worker serves as liaison or referring agent of the impaired to systems that can provide resources, services, and occupational opportunities.

Parents and Family—mother, father, brothers, sisters, cousins, aunts and uncles are all valuable team members. There is no substitute for those who have lived with impaired children through years of adaptation, struggle, and survival.

Family members can help youngsters develop to the extent of their abilities through the setting of goals that are within realistic limits. Parents and siblings should be encouraged to teach the fundamentals of movement through play activities that are essential to living.

Characteristics of Personnel Working with Impaired Children

Organizational ability, sincerity, patience, kindness, and a sense of humor are premium qualities for team members. Since instruction may sometimes involve extra hours with little, if any, sign of progress, the interested person accepts such challenges and realizes that any degree of progress is rewarding to oneself and one's pupils. Personnel should be convinced that the handicapped can succeed. If leaders and parents believe this, children will respond.

Tasks are immeasurably lightened when pupils have fun. The ability to laugh at oneself is a virtue. A teacher's self-enjoyment can have a positive effect on pupils. Laughter may not move mountains but, used properly, it can raise hopes, remove inhibitions, and spur effort. Teachers or therapists with a genuine commitment—those who love their work as play, those who understand impairments, and above all, those who delight in helping students achieve, no matter what the odds—will usually win the affection and respect of the handicapped child. The relationships established through shared physical activities are part of a larger educational process in which all children, whether normal or impaired, have a chance to prove and improve their capabilities.

The cooperative effort of professionals and lay persons with technical drive, grasp, and vision are necessary to better the physical, mental, and emotional well-being of impaired students. Following are examples of the effectiveness of teamwork in action.

Sue, an eight-year-old with spina bifida and a hearing problem, is in a wheelchair, though she can maneuver with the aid of braces. She has been taking private tutorial lessons for two years, but now her parents have decided it would be best to send her to a public school. Intelligent, physically undeveloped and withdrawn, Sue needs exercise, motor-skill training, and socialization with her peers. Her parents have taken Sue to school several times to visit the class that she will be entering in the fall, to acquaint her with the pupils and teacher.

The physical education teacher conducts the physical activities program. After reviewing Sue's medical records, the teacher thought it best to request help from the adapted physical education teacher for the total school system, who had taught impaired youngsters in the past. A beanbag toss at various-sized targets was suggested. The physical therapist gave Sue exercises three times a week, both from sitting and standing positions. The occupational therapist taught her how to put on and take off her braces. The hearing therapist, who has run auditory tests on Sue, consulted with the teacher on seating and ambient noise. The school nurse visited her on occasion for a friendly conversation and to answer any health questions she might have.

All of the team members kept records of Sue's progress. Her parents came to visit her at school once every month or two to observe the individualized program. It was their judgment that the team effort made a positive difference in Sue's well-being and in prospects for her to live a full and useful life.

Ten-year-old *Terry* has cerebral palsy and mental retardation, one of several forms of "multiple" impairments. Having just moved into the city, his parents wanted him to attend a special class. In a conference with the school principal, special education teacher, and nurse, Terry's medical and academic records were reviewed.

Terry's special education teacher was a warm and understanding person, who instructed him in the classroom and conducted the physical activities program with the help of the adapted physical education specialist.

The family physician examined Terry once a year; a psychologist administered intelligence tests and counseled him periodically. The school employed physical, occupational, and speech therapists. These specialists rendered their services to Terry weekly and the nurse saw to it that Terry received his medications on a regular basis.

The team approach was helpful for this handicapped boy. If such services were unavailable to him, Terry would be shortchanged.

CHAPTER 9

Tactics for Instruction

The strategy of an instructor may be defined as that of employing resources to give maximum support to any adopted policy. The term *tactics,* however, has a more specific application: "the art or skill of employing available means to accomplish an end."

Teachers of the handicapped have, with relative ease, adapted generalized learning models to their own needs. What are the best tactics for teaching impaired pupils in physical activities programs? The answers lie in consideration of seven stages or steps:

Assessment of the potential of the impaired learner for adapted physical activities is important in planning an individualized program. The results of the medical examination should be studied for data on the students' abilities, their basic physical strength, and their degree of tolerance for physical activity.

Ralph, a thirteen-year-old muscular dystrophy student, had been given a medical examination before entering school. It revealed that he had fair muscular strength and motor coordination and could tolerate certain types of activities. The pupil evaluation team, which included his adapted physical education teacher, recommended a program that focused upon calisthenics, a limited amount of weight training, and swimming.

The developmental status of the pupil can provide clues to specific sequences of activities. Tommy, a nine-year-old emotionally disturbed pupil, was placed in an adapted class. It was obvious that he was not ready, since he refused to play with

146

others in the group games. He chose activities such as push-ups, sit-ups, and jumping rope; he wanted to throw a ball higher and run the 50-yard dash faster than anybody else. The *tactics* for Tommy's particular situation were easy to prescribe but difficult to carry out. In addition to the individualistic activities that were Tommy's exclusive interest, he needed to participate with others.

Over a period of time, Tommy was motivated to join in couple and small-group games, and later with the entire group. The tactics were to explain that he could improve his performance, have fun, become better acquainted with classmates, and learn to be a team player.

Basic skills, appropriate at an earlier age, must be taught to some youngsters before prescribing more complex skills. The program may call for individualized instruction in the simpler skills and encourage group instruction for the more complex skills.

Although Molly, a seven-year-old blind pupil, had never been taught how to jump rope, her teacher started her on the way by having her jump vertically. She joined her classmates, two of whom took turns swinging the long rope for her while calling out "Jump!" whenever the rope was directly overhead. This was followed by teaching her how to swing an individual rope over her head, stepping over it each time it hit the floor after stopping near her feet. The next stage—actual jumping—again required a caller. Molly's swinging and jumping, once she coordinated and synchronized them, formed a complex skill.

Data on self-concept can furnish clues as to whether individuals might or might not be compliant in an adapted physical activity program: hints as to why they might resist involvement in such a program, ideas as to how to motivate such persons, and the events that might be rewarding or punishing to them.

A shy, insecure boy, Vern, was seldom successful academically or socially because his classmates answered before he had courage enough to respond. As the number of failures increased, his self-concept decreased, and he began to doubt his ability to succeed in any situation. As he became less assertive, he failed more frequently, and grew listless and apathetic. Gradually he withdrew from physical activities, yet Vern longed for success in competition. Low self-esteem was sufficient to bar him from actively applying his abilities. Vern's teachers had to reckon with these clues before deciding on the appropriate tactics to return him to participation.

They knew he needed a lot of individual attention. His classroom teacher volunteered to spend extra time with him on his academic subjects. His physical education instructor convinced Vern that he showed promise in physical ability. Selecting activities such as relays, swimming, and lead-up games within Vern's abilities, the instructor rightly foresaw the results. Once his classmates realized that Vern was able and willing to take part in activities, they accepted him as a friend—a status that extended after school and on weekends.

Assessment is fourfold: (1) it measures physical ability and physical limitations; (2) it evaluates mastery of or lack of basic skills; (3) it takes into account personality traits as they accept or reject education; (4) it establishes the means to circumvent resistance.

Training is essential in the individual skills and abilities that comprise a complex psychomotor activity. Impairments impose varying limits on youngsters, who need training to adjust to their particular impairment(s). Students should receive training in the skills that are required to perform the complex of activities that have been planned. Once the basic units of this complex have been mastered, learners can focus their attention on finer points of the activity as a whole.

Motivation of impaired learners is important. Unless teachers can generate a positive and sustained interest among their students, they will merely submit to the program, but not enthusiastically participate in it.

The three most common causes of resistance are fear of depersonalization, fear of pain, and fear of failure. In the first instance, an impaired pupil who responds poorly to treatment may tell a teacher, "There are a lot of things I can do, but you aren't interested in me. You're only interested in what's wrong with me!" Once the student is convinced, however, that the person, and not the impairment, is the real object of concern, the student will usually respond in a positive fashion.

Mark, a Down's Syndrome ten-year-old, attends a special class. Currently involved in a unit on pyramid building, he is afraid of back pains, yet he wants to be positioned at the pyramid base. His teacher needs to motivate Mark. She shifts him to the top where pressure is minimized, convincing him that position would give him opportunities to practice balance and have more fun.

How can a teacher develop interest in a physical activity program? These steps are suggested:

- Impaired pupils must be convinced that they are special persons and that their welfare is of prime concern to the teacher. Often this step requires that the teacher establish a good relationship with pupils before the program starts. Once enrolled, pupils will reinforce their self-image if they receive even a little recognition or praise. To win the support, confidence, and "ear" of a key observer makes all the difference to the students in an adapted or special class.
- Pupils must be convinced that the program developed for them will not be too painful. The student should be consulted to determine when and how he or she feels pain in the execution of an activity.

Communication from teachers to pupil about the exact details of a response to be learned cannot be left to chance. Childish preconceptions, juvenile impulses, and immature willfulness are blocks to learning. Whether verbal or nonverbal, tactics of communication must first be "encoded." The *encoding process* means, first, formulating instructions for performing the activity; second, adapting them to the handicapped pupil; and third, transmitting the resulting message. The act of "encoding" starts with the teacher.

Once the encoded message is transmitted, the pupil is confronted with "decoding" it in the form of a response, or a "feedback." The *decoding process* may be represented in four stages:

1. Either visual or auditory input data, or both, is received by the pupil through sensory pathways, which in turn stimulate the sense of sight or hearing, or both. Students with specific sensory defects—blindness, partial sight, deafness, or partial hearing—are, inevitably, affected at the input or sensory level.
2. The information, once interpreted in the pupil's brain, acquires *meaning*.
3. The meaning of the teacher's message is thereupon *evaluated* by the pupil, who may or may not respond to instructions.
4. If students do respond, they perform to the best of their ability; if not, the teacher must be prepared to *interpret* the pupils' behavior (hesitation, lack of interest, a poorly coordinated response). Having observed and evaluated such difficulties, the teacher then fashions new tactics in the form of a new message better adapted to the immediate circumstances. In short, *decoding* of students' responses leads to the *encoding* of a different set of instructional tactics. Again, for learning to take place, the teacher must accurately interpret the response, or feedback, provided by the student's encoding or decoding behavior.

Feedback plays a major role in communication: it helps the instructor to determine whether the information presented to the pupil is formulated and transmitted appropriately. Irv, a seventeen-year-old educable mentally retarded, attends a vocational technical high school. Whenever the physical education teacher gives verbal instruction, Irv returns puzzled looks or seeks help from classmates. Is the instructor's message too fast, or too complicated? It could be both. His teacher speaks more slowly in simple terms and seems to get better results.

Feedback helps the instructor to determine whether the student's interpretation of the data is accurate. A ten-year-old neurologically impaired, Jean, attends a special class. Enrolled in the adapted physical activities program, she is capable of understanding only a few activities such as tossing the beanbag. Her instructor speaks to her in the simplest possible terms, but Jean's tosses are consistently poor. Such feedback has alerted her teacher to the need for a new approach so as to avoid further stress. Instead of tossing the beanbag, it is handed or passed from the right hand to the left hand and then to other members of the group. Later, tossing is added from short to longer distances.

When encoding information is appropriate, feedback tends to give the subject more confidence. Jerry, an obese ten-year-old, who is in a regular physical activities program, is burdened and embarrassed by his weight. The classroom teacher, who prides herself on her ability to teach physical education, rates the boy's overall performance "below average." Although smart enough, Jerry has a severe weight problem that the teacher and Jerry's mother have jointly confronted with a weight-reduction program. By pointing out the appearance and skill of his classmates, they have impressed upon Jerry the importance of avoiding between-meal snacks, desserts, and candy. They also urged him to continue physical education classes, made much of even the smallest weight loss, and encouraged him to keep active during after-school hours. In the months that followed, Jerry began to lose weight and was able to perform without strain or discomfort.

Continuous and close rapport between teacher and pupil is essential. To be certain of the pupil's "readiness state"—mentally, physically, and emotionally—instructors should satisfy themselves on several points: What effect does the impairment have on learning ability? Is the acquisition of motor skills the main objective or does cognitive information have priority? Should a time limit be placed on learning a given physical activity? What is the quality and extent of the responses and feedback? Having viewed and analyzed the pupil's performance, the instructor should explain to the student what response is appropriate. This explanation should be accompanied with a series of suggestions aimed at each student's individual needs. The procedures should be described slowly and simply. Only the instructor who is flexible, imaginative, cheerful, and genuinely involved will make progress.

Reinforcement is defined as the strengthening of the relationship between a stimulus and a response. In most instances, responses are complex and consist of many subresponses. Subresponses can be reinforced as each one occurs (supporting response) and as they combine to form an integrated whole (terminal response). In both cases, reinforcement enhances learning.

Supporting reinforcement leads, first of all, to the correct positioning, or shaping, of each subresponse in a compound skill or activity and, second, to the knitting together of the same movements as a continuous whole ("chaining"). Involved in this process are both positive (reward) and negative (disapproval) reinforcement. Positive reinforcement accomplishes two things: it indicates approval at a given stage in the sequence and it identifies the correct shape of each subresponse. Although such strengthening usually comes from the teacher, it may also originate with the pupil's classmates. In group instruction, positive reinforcement may take the form of *verbal* approval ("good going," "nice work," "well done") or *nonverbal,* (nods of the head and reassuring winks). Ideally, a student who "gets the feel" of a correctly executed skill or activity will find reward in personal satisfaction.

Negative reinforcers are designed to correct inaccurate responses. Like their positive counterparts, they may be either *verbal* ("not so good," "try again," "you can do better than that") or *nonverbal* (head shakes, frowns). Supporting negative reinforcement is intended to teach the student what not to do—the responses to be avoided. Although easily misinterpreted as punishment, negative reinforcers are legimate tactics as long as they are promptly followed by instruction. Strong verbal disapproval should be avoided lest the pupil feels embarrassed, or feels punished. The instructor needs to make the learner feel that an inaccurate response is simply something to be improved. Objectivity, frankness, and close observation—these are essential. An extroverted youngster responds more positively to public correction than does an introvert, who understandably appreciates remarks that are tactfully expressed and made in private. In fact, withholding comment altogether and simply asking the student to repeat the subresponse may be more effective. If, however, the movement is unacceptable, it should be identified and practiced.

Since *supporting reinforcement* is fractional in nature, it should be given immediately after each subresponse. Too great a time interval between the response and the reinforcement breaks the ''chain.'' If intervening behavior between the response and the reinforcement is allowed, the pupil will mistake the incorrect response for the correct one. To illustrate: a child being taught to kneel is instructed to put the right knee down, at which moment this response is reinforced by the instructor. If, during the short waiting period, the child happens to lift the right knee, the instructor may inadvertently reinforce this latest response, which is not an integral part of the training series.

The trial limits for learning a particular skill or activity cannot be predetermined: there may be a multitude of responses, and learning may take weeks, months, or even years. It is the teacher's duty to reinforce each subresponse until it is learned. Then, he or she should proceed to the next subresponse and reinforcement. This process should continue until all the subresponses included in the skill are learned. After a period of time, only verbal cues may be necessary.

Each subresponse is linked (chained) with another as part of a total skill or activity that is both continuous and whole. By reinforcing the first response, therefore, the instructor automatically reinforces the next.

Early in the learning series, supporting positive and negative reinforcement should be provided on a regular basis. As the skill or activity begins to develop so that the pupil seems capable of independent practice, the teacher should ease up on the reinforcements until eventually they are omitted entirely.

Terminal reinforcement is delivered following the execution of the entire compound chain of responses, not after any particular one. It may be either immediate or deferred; the form it takes depends on the student's personal needs. *Immediate* reinforcers for some pupils may be abstract or verbal (personal praise and recognition); for others, they may be concrete or material (candy, cookies, or fruit). *Deferred* reinforcers, on the other hand, are usually symbolic—grades, stars on a chart, or special privileges.

Practice leads eventually to the ''autonomous'' phase of a skill, in which errors are reduced to a negligible degree. Such autonomy combines speed and accuracy with freedom from either stress or distraction. Complete mastery, though seldom reached by the handicapped, is obviously beneficial to them both physically and psychologically. Through practice, an impaired person can *overlearn* a skill to the point of proficiency that is almost autonomous. Thereafter, pupils can design their own therapy rather than rely on an instructor. They become independent enough to cope with their disabilities. Overlearning thus produces solid physical and psychological gains, among others, and resistance to the very stress and fatigue with which overlearning is at first associated.

A problem basic to the autonomous phase of skill execution is the *scheduling* of practice periods for maximum therapeutic and educational gain. Periods that are too brief or too widely spaced apart will seldom improve physical status or learning efficiency. On the other hand, long periods often tax the strength and endurance of the impaired, weakening their motivation. Similarly, monotonously repetitious movement patterns consume class time that might be better devoted to learning lifetime skills and activities.

Some practical guidelines are suggested for use in planning the number and length of practice periods:

The nature of the task should determine to some extent the length of a practice period. If the skill is fairly simple and unitary, it can be practiced repeatedly during a single session. In complex tasks requiring coordinated movements, practice might necessarily be extended over several sessions.

During rest periods within a given practice session, or in the intervals between sessions, learners can practice tasks they have already learned in preparation for tasks they are beginning to learn. Of course, fatigue becomes a major concern when the skills involve gross body movement.

Provisions should be made for students to practice on their own time and after school hours on schedules they develop with the instructor. Most complex physical and manipulatory skills require practice beyond that provided by formal instruction.

Massed practice (provides little or no interruption for rest) is advisable when a new skill is to be learned. Distributed practice (allows for rest periods or intervals of days between practices) will be more effective in the long range learning of skills. The teacher should provide periods of both massed practice and distributed practice in teaching activities.

Mental practice may be defined as repeating by recounting in memory an already performed sequence of skills. It is a means of reviewing previous performance and of planning the next trials; it is a means of planning the order of movements in simple skills; it reduces the amount of extinction in the next performance, and it preserves a mental set for a quicker start at the next practice session. It is felt that mental practice is important at the proficiency level for maintaining awareness of feedback and for adapting to cues.

The *transfer* of a skill—carrying it over to another activity or milieu—is a sign of growth. The movement of the arm in throwing overhand involves muscles and responses essential to serving a tennis ball. Teachers should be on the alert for the positive transfer of a learned skill to the pupil's everyday life. Once skills have been learned in class, they are transferred and used in intramural and recreation programs. The instructor should encourage students to believe that the learning of basic skills, movements and patterns leads to games and sports.

10

Teaching Approaches and Suggestions

The various instructional procedures that teachers have at their disposal may be referred to as *approaches*. In this chapter such approaches assume a variety of forms; they may be methods, techniques, or suggestions. Once apprentice teachers learn terminology and begin to relate instructional means to instructional ends, they gain new perspectives on each part of their day-to-day work as it relates to the total physical activities program.

The term *method* will be used in this chapter to mean any general, organized, or systematic instructional procedure. A method can fall into one of three categories: *direct* ("traditional" or "teacher-centered"); *indirect* ("problem-solving" or "pupil-centered"); or a combination of both teacher-initiative and pupil-responsibility.

The term *technique,* on the other hand, usually refers to detailed and specific instructional procedures. Presented in small units, these techniques are the teacher's points of contact with the pupil in presenting any skill or activity. They differ from methods in being more immediate, more sensory, and therefore more receptive to pupil feedback. Such receptivity makes possible more individualized adjustments to learning difficulties. Any of the numerous *techniques* available to teachers can be applied to any of the *methods,* whether direct or indirect. Techniques, in short, are numerous, varied and highly adaptable. Two categories of techniques will be treated: sports instruction and task-analysis. Extensive treatment of teaching techniques in sports and all other physical activities are available through publications*, which organize them by categories: locomotor and nonlocomotor; relays; rhythms and dance; games of low organization; stunts, tumbling, and apparatus; individual, couple, and small group activities; physical fitness, and outdoor experiences and camping.

METHODS

Five teaching methods are recognized by theorists and practitioners. The first four, *verbal, visual, kinesthetic,* and *tactile* may be considered *direct* approaches that are primarily teacher-centered, authoritative, and one-way. The direct methods minimize pupil feedback.

A fifth method, known as *movement-exploration,* may be classified as "two-way," and maximizes pupil feedback and interplay. In actual practice, these five theoretically distinct methods of teaching physical activities frequently overlap. They merge in the hands of resourceful teachers who welcome problem-solving.

Verbal

The *verbal* method involves the use of primarily spoken words to convey the desired pupil-response. Two advantages of this approach are self-evident: first, it permits a quick and direct "laying-out" of instructions; second, it provides a ready identification of each component together with descriptions of both "internal" and "external" cues. For example, a classroom teacher has a special group that consists of pupils with cerebral palsy ranging in ages from 12 to 14. Though wheelchair-bound, all six of them have good vision and a fair use of hands. The teacher, familiar with wheelchairs, gives detailed instructions on their use in an obstacle course. For most wheelchair-bound youngsters, each step in the process is an acquired skill. The teacher explains maneuvering techniques as well as speeding hazards such as misjudging an obstacle and overturning. Having *verbalized* the skills and safety precautions, she assumes, but with a vigilant attitude of wait-and-see, that the course is open to all comers. As things get underway, she is there offering verbal assistance whenever it is needed. Only two students perform satisfactorily; four repeatedly lose control. Having foreseen trouble, the instructor proceeds with more detailed verbalization: she tells the four who failed not to slouch over, to sit in the center of the chair, to focus on some line or lines she designates for direction. She explains what to do on the verge of tipping over. "When you feel

*George Sullivan, *Better Sports Series*, New York, Dodd, Mead.
Goodyear Physical Education Activities Series, Santa Monica, Calif., Goodyear Publishing Company.
Physical Education Activities Series, Dubuque, Iowa, William C. Brown Company.
Sports Illustrated Library, N.Y., J. B. Lippincott Company.

your muscles tighten on the right or left side," she tells them, "try to pull yourself back to the middle of your chair and sit up as straight as you can."

In presenting *verbal* methods exclusively, the teacher must, however, exercise caution. Regardless of the mental ages of the pupils, she must speak as simply, directly, and unambiguously as possible. The teacher's vocabulary must be free of abstractions, with sentence structure uninvolved. As long as instructions contain concrete terms, clear imagery, and the saving grace of humor and imagination, teachers can hold even those listeners with short attention spans.

Visual

In using a *visual* method (in contrast to one that is verbal), the skill or activity is demonstrated so that students can see what the "model" to be learned looks like. Sometimes no translation into words is necessary. For the retarded child who is slow in understanding images from words, a *visual* approach is essential.

Besides live demonstrations, many other means of visualizing a model of a skill or activity are now available. Instructional media of various kinds have supplemented and, in some cases, replaced actual performance. The available visual aids form a lengthy list; they include films, filmstrips, loop films, slides, photo enlargements, posters, and diagrams. Most widely used, perhaps, is the combination of two visual approaches, which may be illustrated by the following use of both film and videotape.

Having viewed a film version of an activity, pupils imitate it while a video camera records their performance. Thereafter, pupils see themselves on a videotape projection and draw comparisons between the "professional" performance and their own. Such a teaching sequence produces mixed results. For some, the original film and the videotape are strong motivators, while for others the gap between the ideal and the real—between the filmed model and their own videotaped efforts—is so great that motivation lessens.

To an instructor who is technically informed, any school or institution equipped with instructional media is a professionally attractive place. Visual aids attract impaired pupils, especially when performances they observe are by other impaired persons. When they realize that the models themselves overcome similar handicaps, they may try harder.

Immediately after a session with visual aids, students should be given every opportunity to practice. For some of the handicapped, repeated showings are necessary. But regardless of frequency, each activity should be projected slowly enough for full absorption. To reinforce the day's lesson, instructors can display pictorial materials on the bulletin board.

Pupils should be encouraged to bring to class pictures clipped from newspapers or magazines that depict a skill or activity to which they aspire. Before beginning the unit on balancing, for example, they can be asked to cut out pictures of other youngsters performing such activities. A diagrammatic presentation of balancing positions drawn or placed in sequence on the chalkboard is also useful.

Today's teacher can also utilize television by coordinating teaching hours with station programs. At home, pupils should be reminded to watch televised professional performances that are directly related to their school work. Therefore, it is up to instructors to keep posted on current offerings through the media, whether public or commercial.

Other printed materials—textbooks, periodicals, pamphlets, and clippings—provide game rules and strategies. Most impaired youth can usually pick up the terminology of the experts in such sports as basketball, soccer, aquatics, or dance with relative ease. Instructional media are not substitutes for the relationship between teachers and their students.

Kinesthetic

After considering the verbal and visual methods, instructors should be aware of the *kinesthetic* method, one that provides sensory data not easily acquired by other means. Kinesthesia is thus defined as "a sense mediated by end organs located in muscles, tendons, and joints and stimulated by bodily movements and tensions." Words, pictures, and demonstration, however vivid, cannot in themselves communicate actual sensations; by means of movement the experience of a physical activity can be induced when verbal and visual means fail. To cite a hypothetical case: a special education class might consist of four multihandicapped children with both cerebral palsy and mental retardation. In learning how to roll sideways, the pupils listen to descriptions of the movements and look at pictures. Yet, if their responses are poor, they need a new approach. The instructor places each youngster at the center of the mat, one at a time; he or she *assists them manually* in rolling over and over to the end of the mat and back. After a period of time, all four pupils, though multihandicapped, have "caught on." Their fears have decreased, and their muscular responses to these unfamiliar positions can be rated "fair." They are able to roll, with occasional assistance, the full length of the mat.

In applying the kinesthetic method, the teacher asks the pupil if he or she is aware of the pulls and tensions on muscles, tendons, and joints. This state of awareness is helpful to learning various positions and movements.

An analysis of teaching trainable mentally retarded children how to throw a ball overhand will illustrate the kinesthetic method. Six pupils are positioned facing their classmates. Each child is asked to hold a ball lightly, moving the fingers around it until the grip feels natural. As fingers tighten around the ball, the pupil should recognize the change from a loose to a firm grip, a sensation involving increased finger pressure as well as tension on the muscles, tendons, and joints. When the elbow of the throwing arm bends, the teacher can point out that tension felt at the elbow is to be expected. Similarly, as the arm swings backward, tension is placed on the shoulder area. The next phase calls for swinging the arm forward close to the ear in an overhand arc; here, too, stresses are on both arm and shoulder. Throwing the ball back and forth to each other, pupils gradually acquire the correct "feel" of the entire sequence.

Two drawbacks to the *kinesthetic* method have been cited by authorities. First, many youngsters lack "body awareness;" taking movement for granted, they have difficulty identifying muscular tensions. Young retarded children, especially, are often incapable of objectifying to this degree. Teachers should repeatedly demonstrate *which* movements produce *which* effects.

A second drawback relates to personnel. The correctness of a response suffers unless the instructor has sufficient time to keep the student's attention on performing acceptably. The *kinesthetic* method, which usually follows *verbal* and *visual* instruction, requires the attention of both teacher and learner. Without such focus, students will find difficulty in performing independently. This means that at least some understanding of how muscles contract and extend in movement is helpful in the performance of a skill or activity. The learner thus becomes familiar with those muscular actions proper to the right movements or "model."

Tactile

The *tactile* method involves the sense of touch as a means of interpreting one's environment and encompasses both kinesthetic (internal) and tactile (external) sensations. These are experienced simultaneously through contacts, pressures, and tensions associated with movements; touch involves feeling, rubbing, and manipulation.

The tactile method is commonly used with the blind and retarded. Teachers of the blind rely heavily on this approach. Similarly, the retarded who have difficulty in conceptualizing are extremely receptive to tactile strategies. Nonimpaired pupils, when given the opportunity, also benefit from them. Teachers who work with the blind combine tactile approaches with verbal approaches; with the retarded, however, all methods should be tried.

An activity that begins in a passive state may gradually become active; instructed at first merely to hold a beanbag, a child may then be asked to move the fingers around it; feel, rub, and manipulate it; and eventually, toss it. The passive, combined with the active tactile method, broadens innumerable skills and activities—crawling, walking, jumping, throwing, and playing with toys.

Movement Exploration

A fifth method, described as *movement exploration,* came to the United States from England, where it had been used extensively in the Primary Schools. Unlike the "direct" methods of teaching described above, *movement exploration* is pupil-centered, not teacher-centered and, therefore, "indirect." Once their teacher sets a particular objective, youngsters are given wide latitude in reaching it. They set their own pace, evolve their own style, and even determine other objectives related to the basic one. Teacher-initiated visual demonstrations and models may be temporarily suspended, as are commands and instruction conventionally associated with the verbal method. To induce *movement exploration,* however, questions and suggestions are often used as starters—to stimulate activities pupils can then build upon, sustain, and evaluate on their own. By taking the initiative, comparing their own movements with those of classmates, and vying with others for speed and coordination, a handicapped child discovers new dimensions in an otherwise restricted area.

To illustrate, a special class of seven to nine-year olds might be asked a question that encourages creative self-expression: "Can you make yourself bigger? Let's see you grow!" The responses range from simple gestures with arms and legs, to novel body positions, to a variety of facial expressions. One boy sticks out his chest or stomach; another pupil "spread-eagles" to form a human "X"; and someone especially energetic takes up more space by running in a rapidly widening circle. Teacher: "And now, can you make yourself smaller, and smaller, and smaller?" Doubling up, crouching, curling in a ball, hiding arms, legs, and head—a number of movements are soon in progress. Teacher: "Show me a new way you've never tried before to get from here to that corner of the gym." Here again, the kind and degree of impairment determines, in each case, the style and speed of the response. Some pupils may have to crawl or creep; others may walk, run, or skip—each with his or her own creative variation—across the gym floor. "And now, see if you can do it backwards or sideways"—a suggestion carried out with considerable amusement, but more important, with ingenuity and new physical adventures. In short, movement exploration enlarges physical experience and instills self-confidence.

As long as the objectives defined by the teacher fall within the mental and physical range of everyone, *movement exploration* has dramatic possibilities. Teachers should know in advance, however, the potential ability of each child. Lead-in questions should be brief, clear, uncluttered by detail and, above all, void of how-to-do-it clues:

"*Can you* find your own space in this room?"

"*How can* you make yourself small? Big?"

"*How would* a rabbit (snail, frog) get from here to there?"

"*Can you* do the same thing backwards? Sideways?"

If, as it sometimes happens, a child can do almost nothing independently, teachers must decide when to intervene. Challenges are not inviting to everyone;

and self-motivation comes hard, both physically and emotionally, for a large segment of the school population. Yet many impaired youth want to try, and will try, to explore new movements and positioning if they are able to. What they do with their bodies positively affects self-attitudes. The once difficult or awkward task grows familiar, coordination improves, new horizons appear.

Teachers of *movement exploration* should evaluate a pupil's movement in a subjective rather than objective manner, impressionistic rather than precisely analytical, informed rather than technical. The evaluation should be individualized, however. Since *all responses are acceptable,* there are no norms and no failures. The teacher's comments should be positive and constructive since they intend to improve an impaired youngster's self-concept and body-image by encouraging the youngster to participate, persevere, and succeed.

Combining Methods

The following examples are intended to illustrate two or more of the five methods, combined to instruct one activity. Few, if any, of the activities would encompass use of all of the methods for teaching a given activity.

A typical lesson that combines verbal, visual, and exploratory methods involves choosing one object from a group placed at the center of the gymnasium floor (hoop, jump rope, beanbag, wand, bat, and ball). The teacher begins: ''What is it you have chosen?'' ''Describe it for me. . . .'' ''Now show me how to use it. . . .'' ''What else can you do with it?'' There is an active response by most of the class. Those who are at a loss, however, look across at their classmates for a cue or are given a hint by the teacher.

Acting out the growth of a flower, plant, or tree stimulates movement exploration in bodily expression. Instructor: Be a flower—first a seed . . . now you are sprouting in the spring air . . . you are growing buds and leaves . . . you are blooming!'' If a pupil hesitates, the instructor resorts to verbal instructions that are reinforced, if necessary, by visual aids. A sequence of sketches or pictures of a flower's life span may prove helpful, and in numerous instances, music spurs creativity. When verbal and visual instructions are deliberately withdrawn, however, the results may be mixed: some pupils, if left to their own initiative, show style and confidence while others are inactive. Teachers should recognize early signs of lagging interest. With the impaired, it should be remembered that desire usually exceeds ability; to impose an exclusively exploratory method on children with mental or physical deficiencies may simply be unrealistic. For children to be taught how to act out the life-process of a flower, no single method will suffice.

In a mainstreamed class of third-graders, for example, there may be two pupils with mild cerebral palsy, a third whose arm has been amputated, and a fourth who is partially deaf. Some means must be found to keep everyone in class active and interested. How does an instructor avoid slighting either the regulars or the impaired? Four suggestions are offered:

1. Tact and ingenuity must go into the selection of an activity that third grade pupils at all levels of ability can fully enjoy.
2. Instructions must be delivered clearly and slowly.
3. Diagrams and demonstrations aid both the handicapped and the "regulars."
4. "Regular" pupils can be recruited to assist with demonstrations.

In a game of circle dodge ball everybody in the mainstreamed class should be given a chance to see just what goes on—where the teams stand, how the ball is put in play, and why the players move as they do. A *combination* of teaching methods, the instructor soon learns, is essential.

After the count-off, each team member is allowed to show how he or she dodges the ball while staying inside the boundaries. A player with mild cerebral palsy may have difficulty in moving; by coaction a regular teammate can help the impaired player avoid the ball. A partially deaf pupil, who frequently loses his balance during the game, is shown how to widen his stance and crouch low for stability. The game of circle dodgeball has thus given the teacher an opportunity to use the verbal, visual, and movement exploratory method as well as the kinesthetic method.

TECHNIQUES

Those who ask "Where should I start?" or "At what point do I switch from methods to techniques?" should defer judgment until they have reviewed the nature and degree of the impairment and the ability, both actual and potential, of the student in question.

For most impaired youngsters, learning how to bat a softball requires a general method of instruction. The stages in this introductory method are roughly these:

"Stand near (or bring the wheelchair close) facing homeplate."

"Grip the handle of the bat tightly with both hands."

"If the bat is too long, then choke it up."

"Always keep the label straight up, facing you."

"Hold the bat high and away from the shoulder."

"Look at the ball on the batting tee."

"Now swing, and see if you can hit it."

"Good! Try again."

The difference between the above *method of* and *techniques for teaching* the same skill or movement is a matter of specificity and precision. An abundance of details are available to pupils who are ready for the complexities of *techniques:*

Stance

Right-handed batter* stands (or sits in a wheelchair) on the left side of the plate, facing it, with feet a distance apart equal to shoulder width. Toes are now 12 inches from the plate, feet pointing straight ahead and parallel. Stance allows swing to cover entire plate. In "ready" position, bat is held diagonally upward back over right shoulder, not resting on it. Eyes sight over the left shoulder, which points at pitcher; batter tracks ball from movement of its leaving pitcher's fingers to its arrival at plate area. Right elbow is sharply bent and held away from body; left elbow is extended. Batter awaits pitch.

Grip

Bat is held at the knob end, trademark facing up, left hand at the bottom of handle, right hand above and close to it. If too heavy or too long, bat is "choked" up by moving both hands about four inches away from knob. Bat is gripped with left palm downward and right palm upward. Fingers are close together, the bat handle set in the heels of the hand.

Swing

In "ready" position, batter has weight on right foot, knees slightly bent. Swing starts with thrust of hips forward and twist of body to left as batter takes short step forward with left foot. Bat is swung parallel to the ground, making contact with the ball. Upon contact, wrists are snapped and rolled over, allowing smooth follow-through, during which body's weight is transferred from right foot to left. After second step toward first base, runner releases bat, dropping it effortlessly to the right, off the infield.

"Techniques" in contrast to "methods" reflect in detail the ultimate complexity of a skill, movement, or sport from which briefer, more general "methods" are derived. Teachers who are eager to get their handicapped pupils into the "mainstream" sometimes ask, "What difference does it make whether I'm teaching 'methods' or 'techniques' as long as everybody has fun?. Is there some practical advantage that one approach has over the other?" While it is true that the finer points of a skill or game may be lost to some youngsters, they should not be lost on

---

*Left-handed batter's technique is the same, but reversed. Specific dimensions may vary according to age and physical size of pupil.

the teacher. Mastery of a skill, game, or sport provides a range of teaching alternatives available to anyone with only a superficial grasp. Furthermore, underendowed children may benefit from seeing and hearing technical details about a movement or activity.

Stated another way, the relationship of technique to method is a part-to-whole "relationship;" once an impaired child has executed a part of a larger sequence, motivation improves. By acquiring a second skill and then a third, pupils may be motivated into an accumulation of interrelated movements that open up the possibility of team play. The rule of thumb dictates that students should be taught skill games and sports first by *methods,* then by *techniques.* To withhold techniques altogether would be to deny the handicapped child a right to know, to strive, and to succeed.

The question may be asked, "How many and what kinds of techniques should be offered in a physical activities program?" Every stage in an impaired youngster's development benefits from the appropriate activity, and most teachers believe in meeting student's needs "where they are." A different school of thought emphasizes fixed standards regardless of the constant change in performance levels; its proponents stress skill mastery through adherence to proper techniques. The conscientious instructor *balances* the appeal of "instant fun" with the deeper satisfactions that come with drills and practice.

Eager to move into techniques, some teachers ask:

- If I teach the techniques of a skill or game, how much time should I devote to each type?
- What degree of motor ability can I expect from each pupil?
- Is it better to teach techniques to a group or to individuals?

All three questions are premature unless the instructor has a clear educational philosophy and a firm knowledge of each pupil's handicap. These can only be acquired by working steadily and observing closely; the better approach is through methods, while techniques should wait until the groundwork is laid and interests are developed.

Breaking down any motor skill into its separate components and identifying each in relation to the total activity is known as *task analysis.* Such an analysis is the most effective way to determine whether or not a pupil has mastered the sequence thoroughly enough to go on to more complex activities. For a small child the mere act of sitting requires a control, usually taught, of hands and arms for balance. Similarly, some handicapped youngsters cannot stand or walk alone unless a teacher has guided them in body mechanics. In both instances the instructor analyzes and teaches such basic means as position, balance, and total body coordination.

In learning to sit or stand, an infant can receive various degrees of help by direct manual assistance or by the use of prosthetic appliances. The appropriateness of the individual techniques depends on an accurate task analysis.

If an impaired second-grader tries without success to kick a playground ball, she obviously needs someone who has analyzed this activity for what it is—a series of subtasks, or subresponses:

Keep your eyes on the ball.

Spread your feet comfortably.

Place the ball approximately one foot from your kicking foot.

Step forward one step on your nonkicking foot.

Swing your kicking foot, aiming at the center of the ball with your toe.

Follow through by extending your kicking leg in an upward arc.

Step forward on your kicking foot.

When the youngster has mastered the above components identified in the task analysis, her progress in kicking a playground ball will improve.

TEACHING SUGGESTIONS

Almost daily, teachers are confronted with problems that cannot be solved "by the book." However skilled in methods and techniques they may be, they soon learn that on-the-scene solutions call for inventiveness and imagination beyond neat and systematic theories. When instructors in physical education compare notes, they usually pool their experiences and come up with numerous practical suggestions and hints. The value of these suggestions and hints lies in their adaptability to specific handicapping conditions. Whenever teachers are unable to use methods and techniques effectively, a suggestion may be the solution. As the term implies, a suggestion proposes a way of teaching as desirable or fitting. A suggestion is offered for consideration as a possibility. It may serve as a fresh motivator for an instructor. The following suggestions—some of them simply "hints" or "tips for instruction"—are intended to present further ideas for the improvement of teaching.

General Suggestions Applicable to All Types of Impairments

Grouping. Should a class be grouped according to chronological age, mental age, kind of impairment, degree of impairment, physical size, or general motor competency? No formula exists that will provide an encompassing answer; random grouping is seldom effective. Much depends on the total number of pupils involved, which in turn depends on the school's pupil-teacher ratio. All of the factors listed above eventually enter the decision.

In a mainstreamed class, from one to three or four students with impairments may be successfully integrated with the nonhandicapped students. In the adapted physical education class, from 6 to 12 impaired students may be enrolled. Factors listed previously such as age, kind, and degree of impairment will enter into the success of the placements in the class. Careful planning of activities will help prevent mismatching, lopsided competition, and student resentment.

The number of groups should be dictated by the size of the class and the nature of the activities. A relay race, for example, would involve grouping a class of 12 into four teams of 3 pupils each, a division allowing for maximum individual action. In dodge ball, on the other hand, one would call for two teams of six each. The groupings should be changed for different activities to equate teams, develop leadership, and promote socialization.

Class Control. How can the teacher catch, and hold, each pupil's attention? Distractions may be everywhere. To contend with the noise of the gymnasium and playground, instructors must often train their voices for greater volume. The use of hand or arm signals may be helpful in gaining the attention of students. Whistles, if used at all, should be used sparingly and should preferably be replaced with clear instructions and challenging activities.

Giving Instructions. Verbal instructions should create a mental picture. The relative location of the speaker to the audience is important. Most activities can be taught to a class formed in a circle or semicircle, of which the teacher is an integral part. When demonstrating an activity, teachers often turn their backs on the class for the sake of realism; pupils do not have to transpose positions and movements from front to back or from left to right. Review and repetition are essential elements in the instructional process.

All children are imitators, and the impaired are no exception. Teachers should use this tendency to the fullest. New skills or activities should be introduced early in the instructional period. Handicapped pupils fatigue easily; once their learning curves have flattened, they lack stamina for novelty. The game approach may often be used to teach basic skills: rather than tedious drilling on how to kick a ball, the game of kickball may be used to teach the skills.

Leadership and Followership

Two concepts familiar to all physical education teachers are *leadership* and *followership*.

New ideas or movements require that either the teacher or the aide serve as leader, but they should recruit pupils as demonstrators and rotate leadership as much as possible.

Some children feel self-confident when they can initiate and create; others only when they can receive guidance support. Wise teachers put this basic difference in temperaments to good use; they do not force students to assume roles that lead to frustration, failure, or loss of self-respect.

A boy or girl may reject an invitation to lead a group at a given time. One technique is to have the shy or reluctant youngster join hands with the teacher or with the aide. While the activity proceeds, the teacher watches for the time the child's skill or interest matches the earlier suppressed impulse to lead; then the invitation can be extended to the student to lead the activity alone.

To the mentally retarded, as well as to many other impaired students, learning to follow is as important as learning to lead. This trait is probably more important than that of leadership.

Competition or Noncompetition

Which activities do teachers of the impaired prefer—competitive or noncompetitive? There are no easy answers. Some youngsters with impairments enjoy pitting their skills against others. For many, competition intensifies earlier anxieties and raises the spectre of failure. The soundest advice for teachers is initially to choose noncompetitive activities for students; stress those in which they may achieve success. Many pupils thrive on competitive activities. Self or individual competitive activities may appeal to one's sense of pride and one's idea of personal worth. Success in even the simplest activity can give both mentally retarded and physically disabled youngsters extreme satisfaction without a sense of "winner-loser" relationship, aggressiveness or fierce loyalty.

Discipline

Good leadership is the key to good discipline. If a youngster breaks off from a group or suddenly discontinues an activity out of impatience, boredom, or frustration, patience on the part of the teacher is needed. Knowledge of the characteristics of the child is important. When the teacher is occupied with the main activity, an aide may talk to or work with the boy or girl and attempt to have the child rejoin the group. In some cases a "cooling off" period is needed rather than a resumption of the activity. A different activity may be indicated.

Emotionally disturbed and mentally retarded pupils may disrupt the class because of communication failures. Resourceful teachers need to invent opportunities for such children to carry supplies or equipment, to perform simple manual tasks, or to assume leadership of a group. Rebellious or unstable children can thus reenter the scheme of things and at the same time restore their self-image. In many cases, trials and errors are the only solution to disciplinary problems.

Formations

The positioning of pupils in an activity area with reference to each other and to the teacher involves a number of formations. Those that are described include spread, circular, squad, semicircular, shuttle, modified shuttle, parallel lines, and couple formations.

   To assist student placements into the formations, the instructor may use masking tape, white shoe polish, beanbags, or cones. Beanbags, for example, may be thrown on the spots where the teacher wants pupils to sit or stand. Colored masking tape inscribed with pupils' names may be stuck to the floor at prearranged locations. In the following diagrams, the position of the teacher is indicated by a ''T'' and the position of the pupils by an ''X.''

   Spread Formation. Random dispersion of pupils located roughly equidistant from each other.

   Circle Formation. All children join hands. The teacher takes the hand of the first child and leads the group around in a circle. In this way, the teacher acts as an integral part of the circle rather than remaining inside it or outside it. The teacher can see and hear everyone and can be seen and heard by everyone.

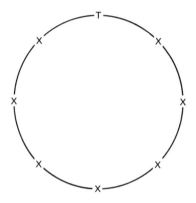

Squad, or Relay, Formation. For relays 3–6 in each group.

```
X   X   X
X   X   X
X   X   X
X   X   X
```

Semicircle Formation. For throwing, catching, or kicking. Wide application. Teacher observing.

Ball - - - -
Player_____

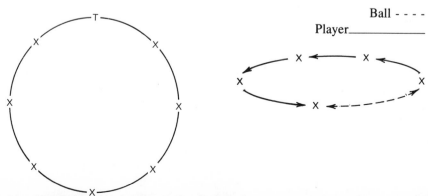

Shuttle Formation: After performing, each pupil moves across to the rear of the other line. (Used for passing, catching, and handing off.)

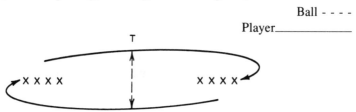

Modified Shuttle, or Relay Target. "Leader" faces the squad and throws an object to the first player in the line, who throws the object back, then goes to the rear of the line. After everyone has played, a new leader is designated, and leader goes to the end of line.

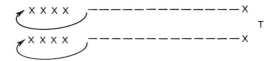

Parallel Lines. Two lines face each other at designated intervals. Many skills can be practiced from this formation.

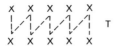

Couples, or Small Groups. Pupils establish groups of twos, threes, or fours. They may join hands. (Used for dance and couple activities.)

Colors

The use of colors in classrooms, gymnasiums, and playgrounds is remarkably effective in motivating physically and mentally impaired children and has met with the approval of physical educators. Brightly colored lines are painted or taped on floors to indicate lanes for relay and obstacle courses; colored starting lines, finish lines, and lanes may be used in running and jumping activities; clown-figures, cartoon characters, and multicolored targets, painted or taped on walls, serve as directional guides for throwing, volleying, or kicking targets.

Locker and Shower Room Supervision

In the absence of a physical education teacher, schools usually assign classroom or resource-room teachers the responsibility of conducting the instructional physical activity period. Male and female aides should be trained to supervise dressing, undressing, and showering, as well as to teach self-help skills to impaired students. Part of the instructor's responsibility includes encouraging personal habits of cleanliness. Are all impaired youngsters capable of taking showers? Is the shower room equipped to handle those confined to wheelchairs? Who is responsible for teaching children with bathing problems how to wash up after physical exertion? Proper locker room supervision results in improved personal habits, better grooming, greater self-sufficiency, and an enhanced self-image. If an impaired child wears a gym outfit, 10 to 15 minutes may be necessary to change from street clothes. Even more time—from 15 to 20 minutes—may need to be allowed after class for undressing, showering, and dressing again.

The question of gym uniforms for the impaired is bound to arise. Do most schools require or even recommend physical education regalia? Nationally, the situation is mixed, but the trend is toward a wider use of modified attire for all students participating in physical activities. Teachers feel that mentally retarded teenagers often respond positively to the wearing of T-shirts imprinted with the school name or insignia. From a safety point of view, sneakers or rubber soled shoes should be worn, except by those in wheelchairs, on the gymnasium floor.

Suggestions Applicable to Specific Impairments

Visual Impairments. In exploring an unfamiliar object, visually impaired pupils react in one of two ways. Either they associate the tactile sensation with a previous experience and promptly identify the object, or they go through a complex mental process not entirely understood by the psychologist. They may narrow down alternatives until identification is made. But if they do not, they may feel frustrated and defeated. Therefore, pieces of equipment or any item of supplies used by blind youngsters should be clearly described to them in terms of color, texture, size, and shape. At the same time students examine an object, the teacher should describe it.

The pupil should be helped to "feel" and follow the movements of a sighted classmate by placing one or both of the blind child's hands on the sighted child's arms, waists, legs, or feet.

Explanations should be given slowly so that students can comprehend the activity as well as memorize its location in the classroom, gymnasium, playground, or pool.

The prospects of the pupil joining sighted companions in an activity may be a good incentive to acquire skill and knowledge.

How one talks to a blind person—attitude, manner, and tone of voice—often communicates as much as, if not more than, *what* is said. A gentle reassuring tone can produce an intuitive response, whereas a flatly delivered set of instructions may be ignored.

Instructors should not feel uneasy about using the word "see" when communicating with these youngsters. They know it means "understand."

Keep students informed of the *location,* not only of their classmates, but also of the teacher.

Communication may be encouraged by helping pupils to identify themselves by name and to use the names of their classmates. If the sighted children talk, their blind classmates will soon recognize their voices.

Both verbal instructions and manual guidance should be used and closely coordinated.

Various sounds are useful as signals, especially those originating from target areas. In basketball, tapping on the rim of the basket or the ringing of a bell when the ball goes through are strategies to be used; in bowling, tapping on the floor near the pins is another. Metal keys or metal objects secured under the center section of the trampoline bed will help a pupil in bouncing near the center of the bed.

Audible balls with sound mechanisms are almost always helpful for soccer, softball, football, volleyball, and playground ball games. Balls with interior bells are now available and may be purchased from American Foundation for the Blind, 15 West 16th St., New York, N.Y. 10011 or from some sporting goods stores.

Music, as an accompaniment to various tempos and rhythms, should be used in teaching dance movements and patterns. Too much amplification, which interferes with instructions, should be avoided.

Blind students should not be left "stranded." If one or more of them are to be left alone even for a few minutes, tell them exactly where they are. It is a good idea to place them in actual contact with a wall, a bench, a chair, or some stable piece of equipment that will serve as an orientation point.

In a pool, ropes, floating corks on lines, and water lanes are essential for both the safety and instruction of visually impaired students.

Hearing Impairments. Prospective teachers of the deaf should be trained in sign language. Lip reading, interpreting facial expressions, eye and body movements are also skills to be learned. Courses in communication with the deaf and hard of hearing are offered in many colleges and community education centers throughout the country.

Instructors should enunciate clearly and speak slowly so that their lips may be read. They should remain at one location, preferably in front of the class. Distracting sounds should be avoided as much as possible.

Visual aids of all kinds should be used such as blackboards, diagrams, slides, films, loop films, and video tapes.

New activities should be visually presented, usually from start to finish, as the visual sense is heavily relied on by the deaf.

Deaf children usually respond best in *small* groups where social interaction is possible without the confusion caused by large numbers.

Balancing activities of all kinds will help to compensate for poor equilibrium. Activities that involve fast, sudden changes of direction are not recommended until they have been presented at a slower pace.

Neuromuscular and Orthopedic Impairments. Activities requiring time-limits that may discourage pupils should be avoided; nervousness and pressure often spoil concentration and lower performance; activities that demand excessive competition should be avoided—*participation,* rather than winning, should be emphasized.

In square dance classes, wheelchair collisions should be avoided; *arm* movements should be omitted and adequate space allocated for the various movements and turns; it is helpful to use hoedown (4/4 time) music so that the caller has time to tell the wheelchairs where to go.

Cardiovascular Impairments. The instructor must consider the type, duration, and frequency of each activity, and both its immediate and long-range effects when working with students who have cardiovascular impairments.

Static-held positions requiring little body movement such as standing while holding arms elevated, and rapid movements such as arm circles or jumping jacks, should be introduced with caution because they may induce stress and an overtaxed heartbeat.

High muscular resistance, requiring sudden outputs of strength, such as in lifting or throwing heavy objects, trying for speed or distance, or climbing under demanding conditions, should be closely supervised.

An emphasis on intense competition or participation in too vigorous an activity should be avoided; prolonged activity is inadvisable.

Respiratory Impairments. Fatigue and emotional stress resulting from overexertion or from overcompetitive activities should be avoided; pupils with severe asthma should not participate in strenuous body-contact activities.

Exercises with weights, when properly used, strengthen the respiratory muscles and diaphragm.

Because of dynamic shifts in positions, tumbling and trampoline activities are beneficial to asthmatic pupils.

Swimming should be encouraged as a means of utilizing all muscle groups and strengthening the entire respiratory system.

Mental Impairments. Teachers of the mentally retarded should observe the objectives of physical education, which are to develop motor skills, physical fitness, social adjustment, and emotional maturity; but they should keep these objectives in their proper perspective.

A structured warm-up consisting of exercises or jogging should be included in each activity class.

Less emphasis should be placed on perfection of skills and movements, and more emphasis on maximum participation and fun.

Formal or highly organized activities should be avoided.

Brightly-colored objects such as balls, targets or numbers on the floor seem to attract and hold the attention of students who have mental impairments.

Less emphasis should be placed on words than on actions; demonstrations are preferable to descriptions, especially when followed by practice by the students. If a teacher gives verbal instructions, they should be concrete, not abstract.

Since most mentally retarded students like to follow and to mimic, follow-the-leader games and mime activities should be used.

Praise generally produces a better reaction than a reprimand; the recognition and acknowledgement of a student's success in an activity is important.

Free play and creative movements that depend on the pupils' ability to recall the immediate past should be scheduled while the memories are fresh.

Some team sports are practical to be used with selected retarded students; experimentation may help in the selective process.

Obstacle courses are of interest and within the capability of retarded students if properly set up; they may include such items as mats, chairs, benches, ropes, and pieces of gymnastic apparatus.

Profoundly retarded pupils should be taught simple skills—crawling, creeping, rolling, walking, hopping, and ball rolling.

Emotional Impairments.   The behavior pattern of each emotionally impaired child should be recognized by the instructor.

Routines should be established early and maintained over a considerable period of time.

Gestures, facial expressions, body movements, and other student reactions should be learned and anticipated.

Short attention-spans are inevitable; when the doldrums set in, the instructor should be ready with alternatives; when children are withdrawn, shy, fearful, or hypersensitive, they should not be rushed; they should be allowed to watch their peers perform and, when possible, encouraged to imitate.

Younger autistic pupils need manual guidance in such basic skills as throwing, catching, batting, and kicking a ball.

Students should not be expected to stay in one position or be confined to a small area for any length of time.

A child who is quarrelsome or given to a temper tantrum will threaten the class order; make provisions through the use of a teacher's aide to separate this student from the rest of the class until the situation is calmed or resolved.

Too many strenuous activities in succession should be avoided.

Sudden noises may induce upsets or seizures; whistles, if used at all, should be used with restraint.

Activities should be selected that all class members can play or provisions should be made for alternatives for those who cannot participate.

Appendices

APPENDIX

SCHOOL HEALTH RECORD

HEALTH STATION: DATE:

Name of Child	Sex	Name of Mother	Year of Birth
Home Address		Occupation	Currently Employed ___ /Yes ___ /No
Telephone number		Name of Father	Year of Birth
Date of Birth Place of Birth (City, State)		Occupation	Currently Employed ___ /Yes ___ /No

During the day, this child is usually cared for by

___ Mother ___ Other (name) ___

RESPONSIBLE ADULT MAY BE
CONTACTED AT: ___ Home
Telephone No. ___

IF AN ILLNESS OR INJURY REQUIRES A DOCTOR'S ATTENTION, CALL

(name of doctor or clinic)

Telephone number

THIS CHILD IS ELIGIBLE FOR
MEDICAID   Yes ___ / No ___ /
IF YES, # ___

PERMISSION BY RESPONSIBLE ADULT

I give my permission for the above named child to receive a medical examination, immunization (see informed consent slips), laboratory specimen tests; and, referral to appropriate physician, dentist, occupational therapist, and others involved in Portland's preschool and school health activities.

Date ___   Signature ___

FAMILY HEALTH HISTORY (Record known, current and chronic health information)

Name of Family Member			Birthdate	Lives with child No	Yes	Health Status
Father						
Mother						
Siblings	M	F				
1.						
2.						
3.						
4.						
5.						
6.						

–1–

IMMUNIZATION HISTORY (enter immunization dates as given)

Antigen	Doses (put date)						Reactions
	#1	#2	#3	#4	#5	#6	
DPT							
DT							
Polio (oral)							
Rubeola (Measles)							
Rubella (German Measles)							
Mumps							

ILLNESS HISTORY (note any current illness, also)

Illness	Date illness present	Comments
Rubeola (Measles)		
Rubella (German Measles)		
Mumps		
Chickenpox		
Whooping Cough		
Impetigo		
Scabies (itch)		
Pediculosis (head lice)		
Thrush		
Bronchitis		
Rheumatism		
Pneumonia		
List Known Congenital Problem	Comment re treatment finished, treatment planned or no treatment given	

BIRTH HISTORY

Place of Delivery (Hospital, City, State) _____

Mother's health during pregnancy _____/excellent _____/Other (describe) _____

This child is mother's: gravida _____ para _____; Birthwt. _____

Delivery: _____/Normal _____/Breech _____/Caesarian

DEVELOPMENTAL HISTORY

Answer yes or no — Att'n Nurse:
(Attach current Denver Development if under 6 yr.)

Child able to sit _____ crawl _____ walk _____ talk _____ ‖ Toilet bladder _____

at approx. age _____   _____   _____   _____ ‖ trained: bowel _____

GENERAL HISTORY   Age:

Diet								
Iron								
Vitamins								
Fluoride (ask up to 10 yrs.)								
Allergies, Hives, Eczema								
Medications								
Hospitalization								
Operations								
Pica								
Fevers								

REVIEW OF SYSTEMS   Starred Items Appropriate for Infants—Detail Information After 3 Yrs.

HEENT—Headache								
Dizziness								
Eye Trouble								
*Ear Trouble								
Sore Throats								
Seizures								
Resp								
*Cough								
Asthma								
Wheezing								
CVS								
History of Murmur								
Difficulty Breathing								
GI								
*Appetite Loss								
Weight Loss								
*Vomiting								
*Diarrhea								
Abdominal Pain								
GU								
*History of Urine Infection								
Pain on Urination								
Frequent Urination								
Enuresis								
Discharge								
GYN								
Regular Periods								
Painful Periods								
Medications								
SKEL								
Deformity								
Joint Pain								
SKIN								
*Rash								
Acne								
Chronic Disease								

–3–

PHYSICAL EXAM   CODE * NOTE PHYSICAL FINDING

Date								
Age								
Height								
Weight								
Blood Pressure								
Nutrition								
Skin								
Lymphnodes								
Eyes L								
R								
Ears L								
R								
Nasopharynx								
Teeth & Mouth								
Heart								
Lungs L								
R								
Abdomen								
Genitalia								
Skeletal								
Extremities L								
R								
Femoral Pulse L								
R								

Examiner		Date	Test-Method	Results (Passed-Failed)

SCREENING TESTS

										Vision			
Hematocrit	Date									Vision			
	Result												
Urinalysis	Date												
	Result												
Blood Lead	Date												
	Result												
Tuberculin	Date												
(skin)	Result									Auditory			

–4–

APPENDIX B

Snellen Vision Test

Test procedures for the Snellen Vision Test* are as follows:

1. Pupil stands or sits at a distance of 20 feet from the chart; heels should touch a line on the floor for accuracy of distance.
2. Chart is placed so that the 20-foot line is approximately at the same level as the pupil's eyes.
3. Room should be quiet and free from visual distractions.
4. One pupil at a time is tested.
5. To discourage memorizing, pupils should be required to read the lines backwards.
6. Test each eye separately by using a covering card; the left eye is usually covered first to provide initial data for the dominant right eye.
7. Start with the 30-foot line on the chart; if satisfactorily read, proceed to the 20-foot line.
8. If the pupil fails the 30-foot line, move up to the 40-foot line and go progressively higher until a line is read with relative ease.
   Move pupils promptly from one line to the next above.
9. A line is considered read correctly when a minimum of three or four letters or symbols can be identified.
10. Scoring is recorded in fractions, the top number being "20" (the numerator represents the distance from the chart). The bottom number (denominator) represents the number of feet indicated on the line that is read successfully.

*Courtesy of the National Society to Prevent Blindness.

LETTER CHART FOR 20 FEET
Snellen Scale

E — 200 ft.

H N — 100 ft.

D F N — 70 ft.

P T X Z — 50 ft.

U Z D T F — 40 ft.

D F N P T H — 30 ft.

P H U N T D Z — 20 ft.

N P X T Z F H — 15 ft.

Developed and Produced by
National Society to Prevent Blindness
79 Madison Avenue, New York, N.Y. 10016

1/81

SYMBOL CHART FOR 20 FEET
Snellen Scale

M — 200 ft.

Ш E — 100 ft.

M Ш E — 70 ft.

Ǝ Ш M E — 50 ft.

Ш E Ǝ M — 40 ft.

Ǝ Ш M E Ш Ǝ — 30 ft.

M Ǝ E Ш Ǝ M — 20 ft.

Ш E M Ǝ E Ш — 15 ft.

Developed and Produced by
National Society to Prevent Blindness
79 Madison Avenue, New York, N.Y. 10016

1/81

Comments regarding Snellen Vision Test results:

The ratio 20/20 is considered *normal* vision: 20/200, 20/100, 20/70, 20/50, 20/40, and 20/30 are *less* than normal. Ratings of 20/15 or 20/10 are classed as *better* than normal.

Teachers should check each pupil for signs of eye strain, excessive blinking, tilting of the head, and uncommon facial gestures. Test results should be compared with the teacher's own personal observations of each pupil before referrals are made.

APPENDIX C

New York State Posture Rating Test*

NEW YORK STATE PHYSICAL FITNESS TEST · CUMULATIVE RECORD

pupil's name ___LAST___ ___FIRST___ ___INITIAL___

check one ___BOY___ ___GIRL___

GRADE							
DATE	Mo ___ 19___		Mo ___ 19___		Mo ___ 19___		Mo ___ 19___
AGE	Yrs___ Mos___		Yrs___ Mos___		Yrs___ Mos___		Yrs___ Mos___
HEIGHT	Ft ___ In___		Ft ___ In___		Ft ___ In___		Ft ___ In___
WEIGHT	lbs ___		lbs ___		lbs ___		lbs ___
COMPONENT	raw score	achievem't level	raw score	achievem't level	raw score	achievem't level	raw score	achievem't level
1. Posture		P		P		P		P
2. Accuracy		Ac		Ac		Ac		Ac
3. Strength		St		St		St		St
4. Agility		Ag		Ag		Ag		Ag
5. Speed		Sp		Sp		Sp		Sp
6. Balance		B		B		B		B
7. Endurance		E		E		E		E
Total Physical Fitness	SUM=		SUM=		SUM=		SUM=	

PROFILE

% ILES	P Ac St Ag Sp B E			
99 10				
98 9				
93 8				
84 7				
75 69 6				
50 5				
25 31 4				
16 3				
7 2				
2 1				
1 0				

PHYSICAL FITNESS

The physically fit person is the individual who is able to carry out his normal everyday tasks without undue fatigue and still have an ample reserve of energy to enjoy leisure and to meet emergencies.

*Courtesy of the New York State Education Dept.

Mo_____ 19____	Mo_____ 19____	Mo_____ 19____	Mo_____ 19____	Mo_____ 19____
Yrs_____ Mos__	Yrs_____ Mos__	Yrs_____ Mos__	Yrs_____ Mos__	Yrs_____ Mos__
Ft _____ In___	Ft _____ In___	Ft _____ In___	Ft _____ In___	Ft _____ In___
lbs _____	lbs _____	lbs _____	lbs _____	lbs _____

raw score	achievem't level	raw score	achievem't level	raw score	achievem't level	raw score	achievem't level	raw score	achievem't level
P		P		P		P		P	P
Ac		Ac		Ac		Ac		Ac	Ac
St		St		St		St		St	St
Ag		Ag		Ag		Ag		Ag	Ag
Sp		Sp		Sp		Sp		Sp	Sp
B		B		B		B		B	B
E		E		E		E		E	E
SUM=		SUM=		SUM=		SUM=		SUM=	

PROFILE PROFILE PROFILE PROFILE PROFILE

P Ac St Ag Sp B E

10 9 8 7 6 5 4 3 2 1 0

CUMULATIVE RECORD CHART
For Use with the New York State Physical Fitness Test (1958 Edition)
of the New York State Education Department

INSTRUCTIONS

The *Cumulative Record Chart* provides a convenient grade by grade record of pupil status and progress with respect to total physical fitness as measured by the New York State Physical Fitness Test.

The pupil's *total physical fitness level* in each grade is indicated by a solid horizontal line drawn across the profile at the appropriate place on the achievement level scale.

A pattern of the pupil's relative strengths and weaknesses is indicated by a solid heavy line connecting the series of points on the seven vertical lines, showing the achievement level for each of the seven components.

The shaded area on the profile chart represents the levels attained by the middle 50 percent or average group of New York State pupils. The white portion below and above the shaded area represents the physical fitness levels of pupils in the upper and lower quarters of the grade.

Form 1303 C. F. WILLIAMS & SON, ALBANY, N. Y.

POSTURE RATING CHART

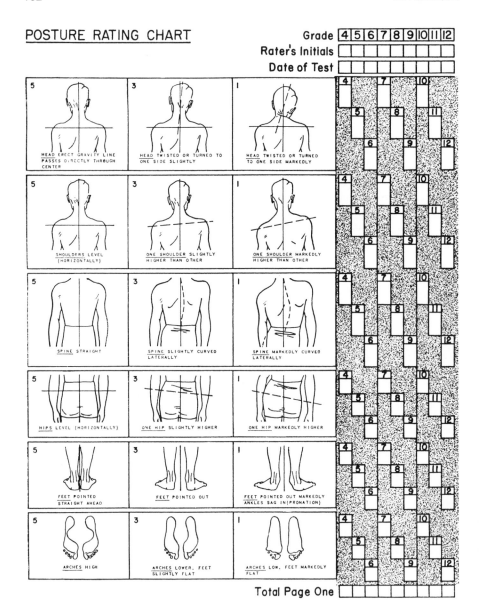

Grade	4 5 6 7 8 9 10 11 12
Rater's Initials	
Date of Test	

Total Page One

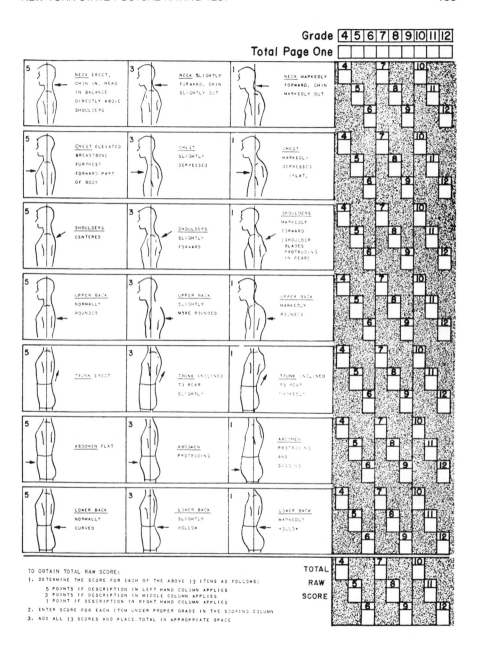

TO OBTAIN TOTAL RAW SCORE:

1. DETERMINE THE SCORE FOR EACH OF THE ABOVE 13 ITEMS AS FOLLOWS:

    5 POINTS IF DESCRIPTION IN LEFT HAND COLUMN APPLIES
    3 POINTS IF DESCRIPTION IN MIDDLE COLUMN APPLIES
    1 POINT IF DESCRIPTION IN RIGHT HAND COLUMN APPLIES

2. ENTER SCORE FOR EACH ITEM UNDER PROPER GRADE IN THE SCORING COLUMN

3. ADD ALL 13 SCORES AND PLACE TOTAL IN APPROPRIATE SPACE

APPENDIX D

Sixteen Developmental Steps in the Formation of the Body Image and the Body's Position in Space*

Following each step in this sequence are suggested testing activities purporting to evaluate the acquisition of the step involved. It is suggested that the teacher or parent should begin at step one and move down the check list attempting to determine when a child evidences the inability to accomplish the sub-tasks correctly. After this occurs for two to three steps, the check list should be temporarily abandoned and various tasks should be administered which are intended to improve the deficiencies identified. Many of these activities may be combined with various other motor training procedures suggested in the chapters which follow. For example, when attempting to heighten concepts of laterality the child may be encouraged to verbalize when he is rolling to the left or to the right on a mat. Thus, agility and laterality are being trained simultaneously. Similarly various tasks purporting to heighten balance can be combined with laterality training.

1. IDENTIFICATION OF BODY PLACES (FRONT, BACK, SIDES, TOP, BOTTOM).
   a. Touch the front of your body. ....
   b. Touch the top of your head. ....
   c. Touch your side. ....
2. BODY PLANES IN RELATION TO OBJECTS.
   a. Touch the wall with your back. ....
   b. Lie on the mat on your side. ....
   c. Place your front toward the chair. ....

*Selections from *Movement Activities for Neurologically Handicapped and Retarded Children and Youth,* by Bryant J. Cratty, reprinted with permission from Educational Activities, Inc., Freeport, New York.

184

3. OBJECTS IN RELATION TO BODY PLANES.
    a. Where is the ball—in front of you, behind you, or by your side? . . . .
    b. Is the ball by your feet or by your head? . . . .
    c. Is the chair to your side, to your back, or to your front? . . . .
4. BODY PART IDENTIFICATION (LIMBS, ETC.).
    a. Where are your feet? touch your feet. . . . .
    b. Where is your arm? . . . . touch your shoulder . . . .
    c. Where is your leg? . . . . touch your elbow . . . .
5. MOVEMENTS OF THE BODY.
    A. TRUNK MOVEMENT WHILE FIXED
        a. Bend forward toward the front . . . .
        b. Bend to the side; bend to the other side . . . .
        c. Bend slowly backwards . . . .
    B. GROSS MOVEMENTS IN RELATION TO BODY PLANES.
        a. Where is your side? . . . . Can you move sideways? . . . .
        b. Let's try forward . . . . . backward . . . . . and sideways movements. . . . .
        c. How can you jump up? . . . .
    C. LIMB MOVEMENTS.
        a. What can you do with your arms? Straighten arms . . . . bend
            arms . . . . . . lift arms at your shoulder . . . . . . turn your arms (rotate them
            both ways). . . . .
        b. What can you do with your legs? Straighten legs . . . . . . bend one leg at your
            knee. . . . .
        c. Lift one leg at your hip. . . . .
6. LATERALITY OF BODY.
    a. Touch your left leg. . . . .
    b. Touch your right arm. . . . .
    c. Climb this ladder using your left leg and left arm first. . . . .
    d. Touch your right ear. . . . .
7. LATERALITY IN RELATION TO OBJECTS.
    a. Place your left side nearest the chair. . . . .
    b. Put your left foot on the box. . . . .
    c. Go up to the wall and put your right side nearest the wall, now move and touch the
        wall with your left side. . . . .
8. STATIC OBJECTS RELATED TO LATERALITY.
    a. Is that box by your right side? . . . .
    b. Is that stick touching your right or left foot? . . . .
    c. Which arm is nearest the ball? . . . .
9. LATERALITY AND MOVING OBJECTS.
    a. You stand still and I'll move around you. You tell me where I am. When am I
        nearest your back, nearest your left, and nearest your right? . . . .
    b. Now I'll move a little faster. You tell me where I am now. . . . .
    c. Stand still and tell me where the rolling ball is. . . . .
        Is it to your left, your right, your back, or your front? . . . .
10. MOVING BODY'S LATERALITY IN RELATION TO OBJECTS.
    a. You walk around this chair and tell me where the chair is in relation to you. . . .

b. Using two chairs around which to walk a figure-eight, walk around the chairs and tell me where you are. When are your left and right sides of your body near the nearest chair? . . . .

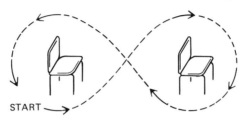

11. THE LEFT AND RIGHT OF OBJECTS (PERSONAL REFERENCE SYSTEM).
   a. Point to the left side of the table. . . . .
   b. Point to the right side of the chair. . . . .
   c. Show me the right and left sides of the paper. . . . .

In steps 12–16 the child is not moving, but is asked to make judgments of another's body parts or movements.

12. STATIC DIRECTIONALITY WITH OTHER PEOPLE (PROTECTION INTO ANOTHER'S REFERENCE SYSTEM).
   a. (Person opposite child) Show me my left arm . . . .

      b.   Touch my right elbow. . . . .

      c.   Touch my left ear with your left hand. . . . .

13.   LATERALITY OF OTHER PEOPLE IN RELATION TO STATIC OBJECTS.

      a.   Which side of my body is nearest the chair?. . . . .

      b.   As I walk around the figure eight (the two chairs) tell me which side of the object is nearest to me? . . . .

14.   RELATION OF STATIC OBJECTS TO LATERALITY OF OTHER PEOPLE.

      a.   (Teacher moves chair to a static position)

          Where is this chair in relation to me? . . . .

          Is it at my left or at my right? . . . .

      b.   Where is the ladder in relation to me?. . . . .

15.   MOVING OBJECTS IN RELATION TO OTHERS' LATERALITY.

      a.   Tell me where the ball is as it moves around my body.

          Is it to my right, my left, my front, or my back? . . . .

      b.   Where is the moving rope? Is it to my front, my back, my left, or my right? . . .

16.   LATERALITY OF OTHERS' MOVEMENTS.

      a.   Tell me, am I walking to my left or my right? . . . .

      b.   Which way am I moving?. . . . .

TRAINING PROCEDURES

Body image training *must* involve transfer (5) (23). The practice of a few favorite exercises to heighten laterality, for example, has been shown to train *only* those exercises and at times will fail to give the child a generalized concept that two sides of his body are independent of each other, that they can function independently or in unison, and that one is called "left," and the other is named "right." Thus a variety of tasks should be employed to aid the child to form the desirable perceptions. Some of these are obviously dictated by the level on the check list reached by the child. Others may be devised by the teacher. These activities fall into several categories.

    1. **Contact of body surfaces and body parts to various surfaces of the environment.** The child may be asked to roll to his back on the mat, later to his side, and last to his front. He may be asked to move against a wall and to place his back, side, or front toward the wall while maintaining contact. Limb movements may be made while contacting the vertical surfaces of walls, or the horizontal surfaces of matted floors. These movements may be paired with verbal cues from the teacher, or by verbalization on the part of the retarded. Several of the initial steps within the developmental sequence may be accomplished with this kind of approach, primarily numbers 1, 2, 3, 4, 5, and 6.

    2. **Pairing words with movements.** The extent to which the child can move or otherwise make correct judgments when asked to do so verbally has been assessed on the check list. This approach can be utilized in various training tasks after the child's perceptual limits have been ascertained. "Simon Says" games can be used here.

    3. **Drawing and Visual Inspection.** While lying or standing against a wall containing a writing surface the teacher or another child can outline the body, or some of its parts with a marking pen. The child can step away and study his body's conformations; perhaps color them, and in other ways discuss and think about what he has drawn and what it represents.

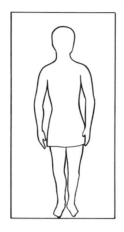

4. **Unilateral movements.** Movements to the left or right can be made in a variety of ways in response to word cues by the teacher, accompanied by word cues on the part of the child, or in response to word cues given by the child prior to his movements. An example of these activities include: rolling or tumbling movements to the left or right: jumping and turning to the left and right; crawling on the hands and knees; and calling out ''left and right'' as the hands touch the mat; jumping or moving laterally (sic) to the left or right: climbing and naming the hand used on each rung of a ladder; and kicking and/or throwing movements with accompanying verbalizations.

5. **Activities while one hand is occupied.** A ball may be held in one identified hand while walking the balance beam. Similarly a brightly colored cuff may be placed on one wrist. A variety of visual cues may be elicited to improve the child's awareness of his left-right dimensions.

SUMMARY

It is believed by many that the child's body forms the ''platform'' from which he makes perceptual judgments about space (49) (71). For example, it is easy to see that successful completion of step number 11 leads naturally to various left-right discriminations necessary to begin reading. Words must be read in correct order from left to right, letters must be placed in words in correct left-right order, and more basically many letters and numbers have individual left-right dimensions which must be perceived before the child can be expected to spell or to read.

It is believed that the perceptions which are covered in this chapter are basic to all kinds of learnings on the part of the retarded child. For if the child is unaware of where he is, what he is doing with himself, and where his body parts are, how can he be expected to engage in more exact judgments inherent in most classroom tasks?

APPENDIX E

Visual Tracking Rating Scale

Directions:

The student either sits or stands. No movement of the head is permitted. If, however, movement of the head is detected, it should be recorded. Eyes are fixed on the target, which is placed two feet away. The instructor watches the action of the student's eyes and makes assessment on each motor task. The scale can be used with youngsters between the ages of 4 to 18.

Ability to	Rating		
	Successful	Unsuccessful	Comments
Focus on a stationary ball with one eye covered			
Focus on a stationary ball with both eyes covered			
Focus both eyes simultaneously on a stationary ball for five seconds			
Identify letters and numbers attached to stationary ball or beanbag			
Identify size, color and shapes of objects			
Focus on a stationary ball while moving toward it			
Focus on a stationary ball while moving away from it			
Focus on a stationary ball placed to the right			
Focus on a stationary ball placed to the left			

Ability to

Ability to	Rating		
	Successful	Unsuccessful	Comments
Focus on a ball moving slowly from left to right			
Focus on a ball moving rapidly from left to right			
Focus on a ball moving slowly from right to left			
Focus on a ball moving rapidly from right to left			
Focus on a ball moving slowly in a vertical direction			
Focus on a ball moving rapidly in a vertical direction			
Focus on a ball moving slowly in a projectory			
Focus on a ball moving rapidly in a projectory			
Focus on a moving ball, losing it and retaining it			
Focus both eyes simultaneously on a fast moving ball			

APPENDIX

Activities of Daily Living

ACTIVITIES of DAILY LIVING

Name_____   Date_____

Type of Handicap_____

___I= Independent;   ___PI= Partial Independence without device___PW= Partial Independence with device;
___ID= Independent with device;_ _MW=Manual Wheelchair; -EW=Electric Wheelchair

I. Bed or Mat Activities

		YES	NO
1.	Move place to place..............		
2.	Turn, lie on abdomen.............		
3.	Sit erect from lying position and return.......................		
4.	Lift object from bedside table.....		

II. Personal Hygiene

		YES	NO
1.	Wash face, hands................		
2.	Brush teeth.....................		
3.	Comb, brush hair................		
4.	Makeup, shave...................		
5.	Clean, trim nails...............		
6.	On, off toilet..................		
7.	Adjust clothing for toilet needs....................		
8.	Ileal Conduit..................		

III. Eating Activities

		YES	NO
1.	Cut meat.........		
2.	Butter bread........		
3.	Eat with fork.......		
4.	Eat with spoon........		
5.	Drink from glass......		
6.	Drink from cup.......		
7.	Use straw............		

IV. Dressing & Undressing Activities

		YES	NO
1.	Pajamas. (Put on).....................		
2.	Shorts..(Put on)......................		
3.	Bra................................		
4.	Buttons - large size.................		
5.	Buttons - small size.................		
6.	Zipper.............................		
7.	Belt buckle........................		
8.	Hooks and Eyes.....................		
9.	Snaps.............................		
10.	Bows..............................		
11.	Lacing............................		
12.	Slip-over Garment.................		
13.	Slacks or Trousers................		
14.	Tie shoe laces....................		
15.	Braces............................		
16.	Prosthesis........................		
17.	Tie Necktie.......................		
18.	Night Casts.......................		

V. Hand Activities

		YES	NO
1.	Write Name only....................		
2.	Write full Name & Address..........		
3.	Turn page of book.................		
4.	Wind Wrist Watch..................		
5.	Open & Close Drawer...............		
6.	Open & Close Door Knobs...........		
7.	Open & Close Window...............		
8.	Pull Window Shade.................		

-2-

Name_____

V. (cont'd.) Hand Activities	YES	NO
9. Ring Door bell.........................		
10. Turn faucet............................		
11. Open & Close Safety pin..............		
12. Open & Close Bottle...................		
13. Strike Match..........................		
14. Open & Close Common Latches..........		
15. Safety Chain Door Fastener...........		
16. Sliding Bolt..........................		
18. Hinge Hasp w/Padlock & Key..........		
19. Cupboard Catch........................		

VI. Wheelchair Activities

	YES	NO
1. Mat to Wheelchair & Return.............		
2. Raising & Lowering Footrests...........		
3. Propelling wheelchair forward & stopping.................................		
4. Propelling wheelchair backward & stopping.................................		
5. Locking & unlocking brakes on wheel-chair....................................		
6. Pass through door with wheelchair......		
7. Wheelchair to chair & return..........		
8. Wheelchair to toilet & return..........		
9. Wheelchair to tub or shower.&.return...		
10. Wheelchair to car & return.............		

VII. Ambulation & Elevation

	YES	NO
1. Walk 30 ft. Forward....................		
2. Walk 30 ft. Backward....................		
3. Pass through Door.......................		
4. Up, Down, Ramp..........................		
5. Up stairs with Rail....................		
6. Down stairs with Rail..................		
7. Up stairs without Rail.................		
8. Down stairs without Rail...............		

VII. (cont'd.) Ambulation & Elevation

	YES	NO
9. Flights of Stairs.............		
10. Curb - Up & Down:		
a. 4" Curb..............		
b. 6" Curb..............		
c. 8" Curb..............		
11. Up Bus steps..................		
12. Down Bus steps................		

VIII. Travel Activities

	YES	NO
1. Cross Street on Green light...		
2. Get in Bus.....................		
3. From Bus to Street.............		
4. Walk to car, open door and enter car......................		
5. Walk with Package.............		
6. Carry Cafeteria Tray with Dishes.......................		

APPENDIX G

Physical Fitness Components Rating Scale

Physical Fitness Components	Rating		
	Fair	Good	Very Good
Agility			
Static balance			
Dynamic balance			
Coordination			
Muscular endurance			
Circulatory-respiratory endurance			
Flexibility			
Speed			
Strength			
Power			
Reaction time			

Fine Motor Skills Rating Scale

	Rating	
Ability to:	Successful	Unsuccessful
String ten small colored beads		
Print name		
Write name		
Cut a pattern from paper using scissors		
Pick up five toothpicks off the floor		
Color a simple pattern using crayons		
Paint a picture using water colors		
Group different colored beads together		
Place pegs in a pegboard		
Put together a simple puzzle		
Cut cloth using scissors		
Trace a picture by moving from dot to dot		
Copy a circle		
Copy a square		
Copy a rectangle		

Gross Motor Skills Rating Scale

	Rating	
Ability to:	Successful	Unsuccessful
Locomotor		
Crawl		
Creep		
Walk		
Run		
Jump		
Hop		
Slide		
Skip		
Gallop		
Nonlocomotor		
Bend and stretch		
Push and pull		
Swing and sway		
Twist and turn		
Fall and rise		

APPENDIX J

Ball Skills Rating Scale

Ability to:	Rating	
	Successful	Unsuccessful
Reach for a ball		
Grasp a ball		
Release a ball		
Roll a ball		
Bounce a ball		
Toss a ball with two hands		
Toss a ball with one hand		
Throw a ball underhand		
Throw a ball overhand		
Dribble a ball		
Catch a ball		
Kick a stationary soccer or playground ball		
Kick a soccer or playground ball in motion		
Punt a soccer or playground ball		
Bat a stationary ball on a tee		
Bat a thrown ball		

Movement Skills Rating Scale

Ability to:	Rating	
	Successful	Unsuccessful
Move around on a mat		
Balance on one leg (static)		
Balance on a balance beam (dynamic)		
Perform a forward roll		
Perform a vertical jump		
Perform a standing broad jump		
Move in, on, and around tires		
Use a hula hoop		
Toss a ring		
Toss a beanbag to hit various-sized targets		
Skip rope		
Climb a rope		

The Lincoln-Oseretsky Motor Development Scale

	Rating		
	Successful	Unsuccessful	Comments
1. Walking backwards.			
2. Crouching on tiptoe.			
3. Stork stand.			
4. Touching the nose.			
5. Touching fingertips.			
6. Tapping rhythmically with feet and index fingers.			
7. Jumping over a rope.			
8. Describing arcs.			
9. Standing heel to toe.			
10. Closing and opening hands.			
11. Making dots.			
12. Catching tennis ball.			
13. Making a ball.			
14. Winding thread.			
15. Balancing a rod crosswise.			
16. Tapping with each hand.			
17. Describing circles in the air.			
18. Placing coins and matchsticks in a box.			
19. Jumping and making one-half turn in the air.			

	Rating		
	Successful	Unsuccessful	Comments
20. Putting matchsticks in a box.			
21. Winding thread.			
22. Throwing a tennis ball.			
23. Sorting 40 matchsticks.			
24. Drawing horizontal lines.			
25. Cutting out circle with scissors.			
26. Putting coins in two boxes.			
27. Tracing maze with each hand.			
28. Balancing on tiptoes (eyes closed).			
29. Tapping with feet and fingers.			
30. Jumping, touching heels.			
31. Tapping feet and describing circles.			
32. Jumping and clapping.			
33. Standing on one foot.			
34. Balancing on tiptoe (eyes open).			
35. Opening and closing hands.			
36. Balancing a rod vertically.			

Source. William Sloan, "The Lincoln-Oseretsky Motor Development Scale," *Genet. Psych. Monogr.* 51:183–252, 1955.

The scale is published by: William Sloan. Chicago: C. H. Stoelting Co., 1955.

M

The Stott Moyes and Henderson Test of Motor Impairment

Areas of Function to be measured

1. Control and balance of the body while immobile.
2. Control and coordination of the upper limbs.
3. Control and coordination of the body while in motion.
4. Manual dexterity with emphasis on speed.
5. Tasks that emphasize simultaneous movement and precision.

Age Sub. 5	S	U
1. Standing heel-to-toe, eyes open.		
2. Building a bridge from three square rods.		
3. Jumping and clapping once before landing.		
4. Placing holed squares on a pin board one at a time.		
5. Placing match sticks simultaneously into a box.		

Age 5		
1. Balancing on tiptoes; feet together, eyes open.		
2. Bouncing a ball and catching it in two hands.		
3. Jumping over a cord at knee height.		
4. Posting coins into a bank box.		
5. Placing counters simultaneously into a box.		

Age 6

	S	U
1. Balancing on one leg; eyes open.		
2. Bouncing a ball and catching it in one hand.		
3. Hopping forward for 5 yards between two lines.		
4. Threading beads onto a lace.		
5. Tracing a circular track with a pencil.		

Age 7

1. Balancing on one foot with arms raised; eyes open.
2. Following a track of holes in a wooden board with a pencil.
3. Walking heel-to-toe along a line.
4. Placing pegs on a board, one by one.
5. Touching tips of the fingers in order.

Age 8

1. Balancing on one foot with other placed on the knee; eyes open.
2. Throwing a ball at a wall and catching the rebound.
3. Jumping sideways, three jumps with feet together.
4. Threading a lace through a series of holes in a wooden board.
5. Walking while balancing a bead on a board.

Age 9

1. Balancing on a wide board; eyes open.
2. Catching a ball in one hand.
3. Jumping and clapping twice before landing.
4. Placing a wooden pin through a series of holes.
5. Placing pegs simultaneously into a board.

Age 10

1. Balancing on a narrow board; eyes open.
2. Guiding a ball round an obstacle course on a table.
3. Jumping over a knee-height cord, taking off with two feet together and landing on one foot.
4. Placing match sticks in four small boxes.
5. Placing holed-squares simultaneously on two rods.

Ages 11–12

1. Balancing heel to toe on two narrow boards; eyes open.
2. Hitting a target with a ball.
3. Hopping sideways into two squares.

	S	U

4. Piercing holes in paper track.
5. Placing pegs on a board and squares on pins simultaneously.

Ages 13-14

1. Balancing on the toes of one foot.
2. Moving a ring along a rod.
3. Jumping backward and forward inside large circles.
4. Moving a pen round a track.
5. Piercing holes simultaneously with two styluses.

Source. S. E. Henderson and D. H. Stott, "Finding the Clumsy Child; Genesis of a Test of Motor Impairment," *Journal of Human Movement Studies,* Vol. 3, 1977, pp. 38–48.

Testing procedures are available from Brook Educational Publishing Ltd., P.O. Box 1171, Guelph, Ontario NIH6N3.

APPENDIX N

Dynamic Balance Skills Rating Scale

	Rating		
Ability to:	Poor	Fair	Good
Walk forward the length of the beam			
Walk backward the length of the beam			
Slide sideways to the left the length of the beam			
Slide sideways to the right the length of the beam			
Walk forward carrying a beanbag or eraser in each outstretched hand			
Walk forward carring an eraser on the head			
Walk backward carrying an eraser on the head			
Walk forward over obstacles on the beam			
Walk forward with eyes closed			
Hop the length of the beam on the right foot			
Hop the length of the beam on the left foot			

APPENDIX

Range-of-Motion
Rating Scale

Ability to:	Rating		
	Unable	Partial	Full
Rotate the head			
Rotate the arms			
Bend and extend the left arm			
Bend and extend the right arm			
Bend and extend the left hand			
Bend and extend the fingers on the left hand			
Bend and extend the right hand			
Bend and extend the fingers on the right hand			
Bend and extend the trunk (forward)			
Bend and extend the trunk (sideways)			
Bend and extend the trunk (backward)			
Rotate the trunk			
Bend and extend the hips			
Bend and extend the left leg			
Bend and extend the right leg			
Bend and extend the left foot			
Bend and extend the toes on the left foot			
Bend and extend the right foot			
Bend and extend the toes on the right foot			

APPENDIX P

The Purdue Perceptual-Motor Survey

	Rating	
	Successful	Unsuccessful
1. Balance and Postural Flexibility		
Walking Board		
Forward		
Backward		
Sideway		
Jumping		
Both feet		
One foot		
Skipping		
Hopping		
2. Body Image and Differentiation		
Identification of body parts		
Imitation of movement		
Obstacle course		
Going over		
Going under		
Going between		

Kraus-Weber test (evaluates physical strength and muscular fitness)
Angels-in-the-snow test (evaluates neuromuscular differentiation and sidedness)

	Rating	
	Successful	Unsuccessful
3. Perceptual-Motor Match		
Chalkboard		
Circle		
Double circles		
Lateral lines		
Vertical lines		
Rhythmic writing		
Rhythm		
Reproduction		
Orientation		
4. Ocular Control		
Ocular pursuits		
Both eyes		
Right eye		
Left eye		
Convergence		
5. Form Perception		
Visual achievement forms		
Form		
Organization		

Source. Eugene G. Roach and Newell C. Kephart, *The Purdue Perceptual-Motor Survey,* Columbus, Ohio, Charles E. Merrill Publishing Co. 1966.

APPENDIX Q

Southern California Perceptual-Motor Tests

1. *Imitation of Postures* (IP). The pupil is asked to imitate 12 postures demonstrated by the instructor.
2. *Crossing Mid-Line of Body* (CML). The pupil is asked to point at or touch the designated ear or eye using the left or right hand.
3. *Bilateral Motor Coordination* (BMC). The pupil is asked to use the palms of the hands to gently slap or touch the thighs with a rhythmical motion.
4. *Right-Left Discrimination* (RLD). The pupil is asked to identify his or her own left and right sides, those of another pupil, or of various objects.
5. *Standing Balance: Eyes Open* (SBO). The pupil is asked to balance himself or herself while standing on one foot, then change to the other foot. Each foot-balance is timed.
6. *Standing Balance: Eyes Closed* (SMC). This item is the same as number five except that eyes are kept closed throughout.

Source. Anna J. Ayres, Southern California Perceptual-Motor Tests, Los Angeles, California. Western Psychological Services, 1969. This test may be obtained from Western Psychological Services, 12031 Wilshire Boulevard, Los Angeles, California, 90025.

R

Aquatic Skills Rating Scale

NAME _____   DIAGNOSIS _____

MOVEMENTS CONTRAINDICATED _____

Skills	Successful	Unsuccessful	Comments
Entering pool			
Walking across pool			
Putting face in water			
Blowing bubbles			
Bobbing			
Face float, assisted			
Back float, assisted			
Kicking with board			
Beginner arm motion			

Skills	Successful	Unsuccessful	Comments
Face float alone			
Back float alone			
Use of lifejacket			
Beginner crawl			
Safety skills			

Source: Excerpt from *Adapted Aquatics,* Copyright © 1977 by the American National Red Cross, reprinted with permission.

S

Psychosocial and Emotional Behavior Traits

	Rating		
Psychosocial Behavior Traits	*Seldom*	*Frequently*	*Usually*
Has a positive self-image	1	2	3
Has a friendly personality	1	2	3
Makes friends with peers	1	2	3
Makes friends with adults	1	2	3
Liked by other pupils in the class	1	2	3
Exhibits leadership qualities	1	2	3
Exhibits followership qualities	1	2	3
Exhibits fairness	1	2	3
Is loyal to team and classmates	1	2	3
Cooperates with team and classmates	1	2	3
Volunteers to be on a team	1	2	3
Shows respect for school property	1	2	3
Likes to participate in individual activities	1	2	3
Likes to participate in group activities	1	2	3
Has communicative skill	1	2	3
Adjusts to new situations	1	2	3
Is talkative in group situations	1	2	3
Likes structured and organized play situations	1	2	3
Has self-confidence	1	2	3
Cooperates with the teacher	1	2	3

Emotional Behavior Traits	Rating		
	Seldom	Frequently	Usually
Exhibits pleasure	1	2	3
Exhibits excitement	1	2	3
Exhibits humor	1	2	3
Exhibits apathy or indifference	1	2	3
Exhibits anxiety	1	2	3
Exhibits fear	1	2	3
Exhibits anger	1	2	3
Exhibits depression	1	2	3
Reacts adversely to tense situations	1	2	3
Reacts adversely to criticism	1	2	3
Exhibits disappointment	1	2	3
Exhibits frustration	1	2	3

APPENDIX T

Student Social-Emotional Profile

Name: _____   Grade: _____

Student is:
   (sociable, quiet, passive, energetic, verbal, shy).
Learns best in an environment that is:
   (one to one, small group, large group).
In class, tends to be:
   (easily distracted, easily frustrated, conscientious, self-motivated).
Needs assignments that are:
   (creative, specific, concrete).
Needs:
   (successful learning experiences, constant support, encouragement).
Reacts under stress in a manner that is:
   (mature, defensive, frustrated, withdrawn).
Receives and processes information best:
   (visually, graphically, orally, mechanically).
Relationship to peers:
   (well-liked, fairly well-accepted, isolated, not well-accepted).
Self perception of relationship to peers:
   (well-liked, independent of, rejected).
Personal characteristics:
   _____kind and cooperative, friendly.
   _____attentive.

————enthusiastic.

————trustworthy.

————supportive with peers.

————sensitive and tactful.

————responsible.

————steadfast and forthright.

————insightful.

————well-organized and neat in his or her work.

————other _____

Social/emotional abilities:

———— verbally expresses his or her feelings rather than act them out.

———— trusts peers and staff.

———— accepts constructive criticism as valid feedback.

———— recognizes inappropriate and disruptive behavior.

———— recognizes and understands consequences of inappropriate behavior.

———— controls impulsive behavior.

———— generally judges sensibly and rationally.

———— improves upon his or her self-confidence and self-image.

———— initiates contact with others (to volunteer ideas and opinions in groups).

———— responds positively when confronted by staff on specific behavioral issues.

———— seeks staff assistance when upset, distressed, angry, losing control, or in agitated state.

Social/emotional difficulties:

———— verbally expressing feelings.

———— developing trust in staff and peers.

———— accepting constructive criticism as valid feedback.

———— recognizing inappropriate or disruptive behavior.

———— controlling impulsive behavior.

———— changing his or her negative attitude toward school.

———— developing a rational sense of judgment.

———— improving his or her self-image and confidence.

———— initiating contact with others (volunteering ideas and opinions in groups).

———— responding positively when confronted by staff on specific behavioral issues.

———— seeking staff assistance when upset, distressed, angry, losing control, or in agitated state.

APPENDIX U

Letter to Parents

Your School
Address
Your Town

_____   _____   _____
    (Student)   (Counselor)   (date)

Dear Parents:

We are attempting to modify the Health and Physical Education program at "Your School" so that every pupil who is able to be in attendance at school shall be able to participate in some part of the program.

The Physical Education Department is attempting to expand its adapted physical education program which is proving to be very successful.

The program is designed primarily to provide:

1. Corrective exercises, as recommended by physicians, for physically handicapped students, or for students who are exempt from a regular physical education class because of a temporary condition, including, but not limited to, injuries.

2. Exercises for body building of the students who, through testing or observation, are found to be in need of such a program.

3. Various types of activities for students who need corrective work to overcome obesity, abnormal posture, or who are limited in their ability to participate in regular programs.

214

At this time we feel that _____ will benefit by being assigned to
the adapted physical education program for the following reason:

    ___ Physical handicap   ___ Posture difficulty

    ___ Overweight   ___ Underweight

    ___ Insufficient strength and coordination. (When strength
        and coordination are improved, more personal satisfaction
        will be derived from participation in regular physical
        education classes and games.)

    ___ Other: _____

If you wish further information with regard to either the program or the reason
for your child being assigned to the program, please feel free to contact
J.J. Doe, Director of the Adapted Physical Education Program.

Your signature below will insure your child's participation in this program.

                            Sincerely yours,

                            Principal

Parent's Signature _____ Date _____

Parent's Remarks: _____

Source. Used with permission of the Illinois State Board of Education, all rights reserved. Subject
to the rights of the Department of Health, Education and Welfare under Public Law 94-142.

APPENDIX V

American Medical Association (AMA) Approved Prescription Form

ANY CITY PUBLIC SCHOOLS
SCHOOL HEALTH DEPARTMENT
PHYSICAL EDUCATION DIVISION

Dear Dr. _____

(This space can be used for information about state/local physical education requirements, rationale of adapted physical education, objectives and benefits of local programs, organization and administration of local classes, purposes, and uses of this form and related areas to improve understanding and communication among physicians, physical education teachers, parents, and others concerned with and involved in the education, health, and welfare of the student. Procedures for returning the form can be included in this section or at the end of the form.)

John J. Jones, M.D.   George T. Smith, Supervisor
Director, School Health Department   Division of Health, Physical
                                         Education, and Athletics

STUDENT INFORMATION

NAME _____
SCHOOL _____
HOME ADDRESS _____
City _____
State _____
Zip _____
HOME TELEPHONE ( ) _____
Grade and Section _____

CONDITION

Brief description of condition

Condition is   permanent   temporary

Comments _____

_____

_____

If Appropriate:
Comments about student's medication and its effects on participation in physical activities:

Student may return to unrestricted activity _____, 19__.
Student should return for reexamination _____, 19__.

FUNCTIONAL CAPACITY

Unrestricted - no restrictions relative to vigorousness of types of activities
Restricted - Condition is such that intensity and types of activities need to be
            limited (check one category below):
Mild - ordinary physical activities need not be restricted but unusally vigorous
       efforts need to be avoided
Moderate - ordinary physical activities need to be moderately restricted and
           sustained strenuous efforts avoided
Limited - ordinary physical activities need to be markedly restricted

ACTIVITY RECOMMENDATIONS

Indicated body areas in which physical activities should be minimized; eliminated,
or maximized.

	Maximized	Minimized	Eliminated	Both	Left	Right	Comments Including any Medical Contraindications to Physical Activities
Neck							
Shoulder Girdle							
Arms							
Elbows							
Hands & Wrists							
Abdomen							
Back							
Pelvic Girdle							
Legs							
Knees							
Feet & Ankles							
Toes							
Fingers							
Other (specify)							

REMEDIAL

Condition is such that defects or deviations can be improved or prevented from
becoming worse through use of carefully selected exercises and/or activities.
The following are remedial exercises and/or activities recommended for this
student. (Please be specific)

Signature of M.D. _____
Address _____
Telephone Number (   ) _____
Date _____

ANNOTATED LISTING OF FILMS WITH SOURCES

A CHILD IS A CHILD (16 mm, color, sound, 8 min.) Aims Instructional Media Services, P.O. Box 1010, Hollywood, California 90028.

This is a film that emphasizes that "a child is a child" and all children have similar needs. It shows that the trend toward special education for children with handicaps has gone so far that many educators tend to lose sight of the facts. The setting is a California State University preschool laboratory in which children with impairments—blind, mentally retarded, and emotionally disturbed—are integrated with nonhandicapped children.

AIDS FOR TEACHING THE MENTALLY RETARDED (16 mm, color, sound, 38½ min.) Thorne Films, Inc., 1229 University Avenue, Boulder, Colorado (available as one film or five separate films).

The films were taken at Laradon Hall School for Exceptional Children to show a functional approach to sequential instruction. The focus is on devices used to develop motor, sensory-perceptual, and integrated motor-perceptual skills and are unique in their application.

ALL THE SELF THERE IS (16 mm, color, sound, 13½ min.) American Alliance for Health, Physical Education, Recreation and Dance, 1900 Association Drive, Reston, Virginia 22091.

This film portrays physical education as individualized learning experiences designed to help pupils gain in various physical, social, psychological, and emotional ways. It presents movement education in the early years as a way for each child to feel successful and confident as individual movement patterns and coordinations are developed in stress-free environments. Individual and team activities add to the total development of children and offer them the means to explore and develop new interests.

AND A TIME TO DANCE (16 mm, black/white, sound, 10 min.) Commonwealth Mental Health Foundation, 4 Marlboro Road, Lexington, Massachusetts 02173.

This is a documentary film on Norma Canner, one of the earliest dancers to use creative movement with children. She is shown working with two classes of retarded children, one class in a community nursery and one in an institution.

AND SO THEY MOVE (16 mm, black/white, sound, 19 min.) Audio-Visual Center, Michigan State University, East Lansing, Michigan 48824.

This film shows the rationale, methods, procedures, and activities that are appropriate to movement for the mentally retarded and physically handicapped. Children are seen in purposeful and enjoyable movement experiences.

ANYONE CAN: LEARNING THROUGH MOTOR DEVELOPMENT (16 mm, color, sound, 27 min.) Bradley Wright Films, 309 North Duane Avenue, San Gabriel, California.

A film that provides teacher training through ideas for activities and methods of demonstration, and includes four areas: 1) rope handling skills, including activities designed to teach body image and spatial relationships, 2) ball handling techniques, 3) the stegel and its multiple uses, and 4) a few trampoline activities, mainly focusing on safety aspects. Problem solving approaches in which each child is encouraged to think and concentrate upon the tasks at hand are emphasized.

CAMP FRIENDSHIP (16 mm, color, sound, 13 min.) Minnesota Association for Retarded Children, 6315 Penn Avenue, South Minneapolis, Minnesota 55423.

This film presents activities and programs conducted at a residential camp for mentally retarded children and adults. The camp is owned and operated by the Minnesota Association for Retarded Children, Inc.

CAMP TOWHEE (16 mm, black/white, sound, 28 min.) Mrs. Doreen Kronick, 306 Warren Street, Toronto, Ontario, Canada.

Activities at a camp for children with learning disabilities are shown in this film. It illustrates a multisensory approach for language problems: gross motor, perceptual, and fine motor skills, as well as swimming and group recreation.

CAST NO SHADOW (16 mm., color, sound, 27 min.) Professional Arts, Inc., Box 8484, Universal City, California.

This is a unique film that vividly depicts a wide range of recreational activities for severely and profoundly mentally retarded, physically handicapped, multihandicapped, and emotionally disturbed children, teens and adults at the Recreation Center for the Handicapped in San Francisco, California.

CHALLENGE: A CAMP FOR ALL SEASONS (16 mm, color, sound, 12 min.) Easter Seal Society of Florida, 231 East Colonial Drive, Orlando, Florida 32801.

A story of Camp Challenge is presented. Children and adults, with a variety of impairing conditions, enjoy the summer camping sessions. They are seen participating in many recreational activities including arts and crafts, horseback riding, boating, fishing, bowling, dancing, and aquatics. A camp favorite is the Special Olympic Program. The facilities shown are both therapeutically functional and aesthetically attractive.

CHANGING EXPRESSIONS (16 mm, color, sound, 20 min.) Education Service Center, Region XIII, 816 East 53rd Street, Austin, Texas 78751.

This film presents the evaluation process and teaching methods used in a research project at Austin State School in Texas. It shows how instruction is specifically planned for the mentally retarded by dividing activities into small parts that can be learned by the participant. The focus is on conducting a functional and comprehensive physical education program for mentally retarded youth.

CHILDREN OF THE SILENT NIGHT (16 mm, color, sound, 27 min.) Film Library, Campbell Films, Academy Ave., Saxtons River, Vermont 05154.

This portrays the story of Perkins School, the largest and oldest school in the United States, where deaf-blind children are educated. It is a story of how deaf-blind children learn communication skills with the help of understanding and concerned instructors. The film points out the importance of physical education for the total development of the child, and these children are shown in their physical activity classes and during play. This film can help people understand the nature of the multiple impairment of deafness and blindness. It may also help people to better understand how the effects of the impairment can be lessened so these children can be mainstreamed into society.

CHILDREN'S PHYSICAL DEVELOPMENT CLINIC (16 mm, black/white, sound, 27 min.) Warren Johnson, College of Health, Physical Education and Recreation, Preinker Fieldhouse, University of Maryland, College Park, Maryland.

This film presents the Children's Physical Development Clinic at the University of Maryland: the clinicians, undergraduate and graduate students at the University, and the population the clinic serves. This clinic provides many physical/motor activities for youngsters who have a variety of physical, mental, emotional, and social deficiencies.

CIRCUIT TRAINING (16 mm, color, sound, 21 min.) United Association for Retarded Children, 225 East Milwaukee Ave., Milwaukee, Wisconsin 53202.

Practical and functional approaches for teachers and students to set up regular classrooms for circuit training are included in this film. Specific methods and techniques to meet special needs of mentally retarded youngsters are introduced. The film shows a class of moderately to severely retarded boys and girls participating in a circuit of activities such as bar press, box step, medicine ball exercise, half-squat, push-up, and bar curl.

COMMUNITY ADAPTIVE RECREATION PROGRAMS FOR THE HANDICAPPED (16 mm, color, sound, 7 min.) Recreational Adult Division, Milwaukee Public Schools, P.O. Drawer 10K, Milwaukee, Wisconsin.

The film shows a community adaptive recreation program designed to meet individual needs and satisfy personal interests. It demonstrates how fun activities become learning activities through adaptation, imagination, and creativity. Emphasized in the program philosophy is that these children are people first and impaired second.

CREATIVE KINDERGARTEN (16 mm, color, sound, 40 min.) Soundings, 2150 Concord Boulevard, Concord, California 94520.

An individualized program is shown based on diagnostic tests and prescriptive programs in which the objectives are to develop each youngster's creative potential and maximize the child's chances for educational success in later years. This individualized approach is more humane since it prevents failure. The focus is on developmental activities.

DEVELOPMENTAL PHYSICAL EDUCATION (16 mm, color, sound, 28 min.) Simenson and Johnson, Box 34, College Park, Maryland.

This film shows progressively arranged motor development activities in a school for moderately mentally retarded youngsters whose ages range from 6 to 15 years. The activities are demonstrated by students serving as instructors in a special clinic at the University of South Florida. The focus is on teacher-leader participation, creativity, and concern for the students. Many of the activities shown in this film do not require expensive equipment.

DISCOVERING RHYTHM (16 mm, color, sound, 11 min.) Universal Education and Visual Arts, 221 Park Ave. S., New York, New York, 10003.

In this film children are shown demonstrating that rhythm is an outgrowth of locomotor movements such as walking, running, jumping, hopping, skipping, and galloping. Basic concepts related to rhythm are taught.

EDUCATIONAL PRACTICES: ADAPTED PHYSICAL EDUCATION (¾ inch videocassette, color, sound, 28½ min.) Jo Anne Owens, State Consultant for Physical Education, Nebraska Department of Public Instruction, Lincoln, Nebraska.

An integrated class consisting of regular and special education students with various impairing conditions is shown participating in various physical and motor fitness activities and working on fundamental motor skills and patterns of a developmental nature. Different methods, approaches, and adaptations are shown.

EVERYBODY WINS (16 mm, color, sound, 22 min.) Bradley Wright Films, 309 North Duane Avenue, San Gabriel, California 91775.

Shown in this film are sequences for teaching skills of catching, throwing, kicking, and running to elementary school children. Logical progressions from the easiest level to the complex are presented.

FLOOR HOCKEY (16 mm, color, sound, 15 min.) Canadian Association for Mental Retardation, Kinsmen NIMR Building, York University, 4700 Keele Street, Downsview, Ontario, Canada.

This film on floor hockey is a very good team activity for both mildly and moderately mentally retarded youngsters. The film is directed at players and provides sequences and progressions. It introduces and expands floor hockey in physical education and recreation programs. The Special Olympic Floor Hockey championship between Philadelphia and Montreal in Maple Leaf Gardens, Toronto, is the climax of the film.

FOCUS ON ABILITY (16 mm, color, sound, 22 min.) American National Red Cross, Washington, D.C.

Designed to provide instructors with the basic techniques used in teaching swimming to children and adults with orthopedic, mental, emotional, and sensory impairments. This film clearly demonstrates that understanding between instructor and pupil should exist in order to make these techniques successful.

FUN WITH PARACHUTES (16 mm, color, sound, 12 min.) Documentary Films, 3217 Trout Gulch Road, Aptos, California 94003.

This film presents a visual presentation of selected parachute activities that add a new dimension to all levels of the physical education program. Because of its wide appeal and versatility, parachute play has been well received by all types, levels, and ages of impaired individuals.

HELLO EVERYBODY (six 10-minute-each color film strips with audiocassettes) James Stanfield Film Associates, P. O. Box 1983, Santa Monica, California 90406.

This series of film strips is designed to facilitate the mainstreaming process by acquainting teachers and students with the most common impairing conditions. Emphasis is on giving an understanding of each of the conditions presented and in looking at and accepting youngsters with these conditions on the same basis as other pupils and classmates.

JUST FOR THE FUN OF IT (16 mm, color, sound, 18½ min.) Orange County Department of Education, Educational Media Center), Civic Center Drive, Santa Anna, California.

This is a film that deals with ideas and activities for mentally retarded children. Activity areas include posture improvement, balance training, body and spatial awareness, strengthening muscle endurance, and increasing attention span.

LOOKING FOR ME (16 mm, black/white, sound, 29 min.) New York University Film Library, 26 Washington Place, New York, New York 10003.

A dance therapist reports on a research project in which she investigated the therapeutic benefits of patterned movement in her work with normal preschoolers, emotionally disturbed, autistic children, and adult teacher. Consideration is given to movement as an alternative to traditional approaches for reaching children with specific problems.

MAYBE TOMORROW (16 mm, color, sound, 28 min.) Adventures in Movement, 95 Danbury Road, Dayton, Ohio 45420.

The role and contributions of the Adventures in Movement program are vividly shown in this film. Blind, deaf, mentally retarded, cerebral palsied, and orthopedically impaired children are actively involved in movement activities. The use of basic movements, importance of success, achievement, and fun are stressed.

MOVEMENT EXPLORATION (16 mm. color, sound, 22 min.) Documentary Films, 3217 Trout Gulch Road, Aptos, California 94003.

Designed for kindergarten to sixth grade teachers, this film shows the concept of movement as it deals with various locomotor skills. In particular it shows children performing ball, hula hoop, jump rope, apparatus, and spatial awareness activities.

MOVEMENT TOWARD CONTROL (16 mm, color, sound, 27 min.) Andrea Boucher, Department of Physical Education, Towson State University, Towson, Maryland.

This film shows that movement is the basis of all learning—the first language of a child—children of different ages and abilities are served. Twelve handicapped and eight regular children are shown taking part in movement activities, educational gymnastics, creative dance, and sports.

OUT OF LEFT FIELD (16 mm, color, sound, 7 min.) American Foundation for the Blind, 15 West 16th Street, New York, New York 10011.

This film demonstrates how blind and visually impaired youths can be integrated with their sighted peers. A brief glance at these children swimming, playing basketball, using the trampoline, wrestling, singing, and dancing is shown in the film.

PARTNERS IN PLAY (16 mm, black/white, sound, 20 min.) United States Public Health Service, Audio-Visual Center, Chamblee, Georgia.

This film shows and discusses the experiences of personnel at Parsons State Hospital in Kansas. They successfully obtained a community recreation department's cooperation and support for integrating 65 mentally retarded and 80 nonretarded residents in a standard summer camping program. Included in this film are sequences showing methods, approaches, and procedures used in organizing and administering the camp, orienting the staff, and conducting activities.

PATTERNS (16 mm, color, sound, 17 min.) Education Service Center, Region XIII, 816 East 53rd Street, Austin, Texas 78751.

The need for physical education for trainable severely and profoundly mentally retarded persons is depicted in this film. Physical activities and equipment are demonstrated, showing how they promote motor development and improve physical fitness of retarded persons. Behavior changes are seen in severely and profoundly retarded persons through participation in a progressive physical education program.

PHYSICAL EDUCATION FOR BLIND CHILDREN (16 mm, color, sound, 20 min.) Dr. Charles E. Buell, 33905 Calle Acordarse, San Juan Capistrano, California 92675.

School children of a variety of ages who are visually handicapped are shown participating in a wide variety of physical education activities. Presented are the approaches to modify activities so these children can participate with their sighted classmates.

PHYSICAL EDUCATION: LEVER TO LEARNING (16 mm, color, sound, 20 min.) Stuart Finley, 3428 Mansfield Road, Lake Barcroft, Falls Church, Virginia 22041.

This film emphasizes the use of wholesome, vigorous physical activity as a means of motivating and challenging mentally retarded youngsters to improve performance and to stimulate total growth and development. A wide range of activities is shown so that all retarded children, regardless of age, background, experience, or functional level can discover activities to enable them to achieve and succeed.

RHYTHMIC BALL SKILLS (16 mm, color, sound, 11 min.) Martin Moyer Productions, 900 Federal Avenue East, Seattle, Washington, 98102.

Children in the first and third grades are shown participating in ball handling activities designed to teach them directions of up and down, right and left, and to learn concepts of clockwise and counterclockwise, around and between, and over and under, by manipulating a ball and directing their bodies through these movement patterns. A progressive sequence is also shown to help adapt these skills to games and sports.

ROPE SKIPPING (16 mm, color, sound, 16 min.) Martin Moyer Productions, 900 Federal Avenue East, Seattle, Washington, 98102.

Rope skipping is demonstrated in a physical education class. Contained in this film is a description of a variety of skipping steps and a short discussion of the values of rope skipping.

SAM (16 mm, color, sound, 20 min.) (also in videotape) OSPI Media Services, ETV/ITV, 325 South Fifth St., Springfield, Illinois 62706.

This is a film about an adapted physical education program in Centralia, Illinois, and Sam, an orphan, epileptic, and loner. He talks about his personal ambitions and problems as he runs; other students talk about their problems and aspirations as they watch others participate in a variety of physical activities.

SHOW ME (16 mm, black/white, sound, 30 min.) United World Films, Inc., 221 Park Avenue, South, New York, New York.

Some of the basic motor problems of severely mentally retarded children are depicted in this film. The major teaching method used and demonstrated is movement exploration. Many of the activities presented were new to these retarded boys and girls.

SPLASH (16 mm, color, sound, 21 min.) Documentary Films, 3217 Trout Gulch Road, Aptos, California 94003.

This film presents ways to use water environments—pans, sprinklers, wading pools, and swimming pools—along with aquatic activities to introduce and reinforce a variety of concepts. They are intended for the severely mentally retarded and multiply handicapped child, accenting self-help skills and readiness activities.

TESTING MULTIHANDICAPPED CHILDREN (16 mm, black/white, sound, 31 min.) United Cerebral Palsy Research and Education Foundation, 66 East 34th Street, New York, New York 10016.

This film discusses the assessment and diagnostic procedure of using three multihandicapped children. Ways and means of getting around sensory and motor problems and deficits that cover the actual potential of each child is shown. Emphasis is upon functional abilities, levels of understanding, and conceptual development of each child being tested.

P.L. 94-142—THE EDUCATION FOR ALL HANDICAPPED CHILDREN ACT (Film strips with audio cassettes) Council for Exceptional Children, The Bureau of Education for the Handicapped, 1920 Association Drive, Reston, Virginia 22091.

Three individual segments of this kit are entitled "Introducing P.L. 94-142," "Complying with P.L. 94-142," and "P.L. 94-142 Works for Children." These filmstrips are designed to meet the needs and answer questions of parents, administrators, and teachers about this law.

THE PACEMAKERS—LADY ALLEN OF HURTWOOD (16 mm, color, sound, 15 min.) The British Embassy, Washington, D.C.

This film shows and discusses a new playground designed especially for handicapped children. This playground is based on the idea of spaciousness and freedom of movement, and it offers play opportunities for children with a variety of handicapping conditions.

THE PROMISE OF PLAY (16 mm, color, sound, 22 min.) Bradley Wright Films, 309 North Duane Avenue, San Gabriel, California 91775.

This film portrays the successful integration of orthopedically handicapped children into the regular school programs through games and sports. Adapted equipment and activities to help each child succeed are shown, emphasizing the teaching of specific skills to enhance the pupil's physical health and self-concept. The adapted physical education instructor will find this film most interesting.

THERAPY THROUGH PLAY (16 mm, color, sound, 27 min.) Richard Switzer, Human Resources Center, Albertson, New York 11507.

This film shows physically handicapped children participating in a variety of activities including touch football, swimming, miniature golf, soccer, cage ball, relays, fencing, and bowling. Shown are several adaptations and modifications used in physical education in conjunction with approaches in other areas of the curriculum.

THINKING-MOVING-LEARNING (16 mm, color, sound, 20 min.) Bradley Wright Films, 309 North Duane Avenue, San Gabriel, California 91775.
    A wide range of perceptual motor activities used during a kindergarten class are skillfully taught by an experienced physical educator. Many of the activities demonstrated may be used with impaired children.

THOSE OTHER KIDS (16 mm, color, sound, 25 min.) Audiovisual Library Service, Continuing Education and Extension, University of Minnesota, 3300 University Avenue, S.E., Minneapolis, Minnesota, 55414.
    This film provides basic information about the development of special education. It presents legal developments that have guaranteed the right to education for every child regardless of the type or severity of his or her handicapping condition. The full continuum of special education services is discussed.

TOWARD MAINSTREAMING (color filmstrip with audiocassette, 13 min.) Recreation Center for the Handicapped, 207 Skyline Boulevard, San Francisco, California 94152.
    Mainstreaming is presented as both a goal and a process through activities, programs, and approaches carried out since 1952 at the San Francisco (California) Recreation Center for the Handicapped. Individuals of all ages and with all types and severities of impairments are shown participating in a variety of recreational activities.

UP AND OVER (16 mm, color, sound, 25 min.) Bradley Wright Films, 309 North Duane Avenue, San Gabriel, California 91775.
    This film thoroughly describes and illustrates the stegel, a versatile, rugged, and safe piece of physical education equipment. Activities are built around the movements of crawling, hanging, climbing, jumping, swinging, vaulting, and balancing. Clearly demonstrated is a teaching method that stresses individualization, repetition, and success.

WATER FREE (16 mm, color, sound, 35 min.) International Rehabilitation Films, Film Rental Department, 20 West 40th Street, New York, New York 10018.
    This film demonstrates the remarkable degree of mobility, independence, and enjoyment that individuals with all types of impairments can experience in a structured and progressive swimming program. The Halliwick method of teaching is stressed, which is based on the theory that once individuals experience the supportive nature of water in a variety of ways, they are well on their way to mastering a greater degree of freedom than they have ever known on land. Explanations and demonstrations of various techniques used in adapted aquatics are an integral part of this film.

WE CAN GROW (16 mm, color, sound, 13 min.) ACI Films Inc., Distribution Center, P. O. Box 1898, 12 Jules Lane, New Brunswick, New Jersey.
    This is a film that focuses upon children who are crippled, deaf, and blind, and how they get started in school. One sees them learning what regular children learn, and playing games children play, but in ways adapted to their impairing conditions.

WHO HANDICAPS THE HANDICAPPED (16 mm, black/white, sound, 14 min.) Frances Bush, Department of Physical Education, University of Portland, Portland, Oregon.

This film shows children with various impairing conditions, including cerebral palsy, muscular dystrophy, and hip disorders, discussing and performing basic movement activities.

WHY EXERCISE? (16 mm, color, sound, 12 min.) Associated Film Services, 3419 Magnolia Boulevard, Burbank, California.

This film presents the value of muscular activity as the human body makes adaptations to the exercise demands placed on it, in the form of increased strength, endurance, and improved flexibility. Included is a demonstration of the types of activities that develop each of these elements of fitness. Also shown is how good posture and proper body mechanics are maintained.

BIBLIOGRAPHY

Adams, Ronald C., Alfred H. Daniel, and Lee Rullman. *Games, Sports, and Exercises for the Physically Handicapped.* 2nd ed. Philadelphia: Lea and Febiger, 1975.

"Adapted Equipment for Physical Activities." *Practical Pointers.* **1** (5), (October, 1977).

American Alliance for Health, Physical Education and Recreation. *Special Fitness Test Manual for Mildly Mentally Retarded Persons.* Washington, D.C.: AAHPER, 1976.

_____. *Youth Fitness Test Manual.* Washington, D.C.: AAHPER, 1976.

_____. *Testing for Impaired, Disabled and Handicapped Individuals.* Washington, D.C.: AAHPER, 1976.

_____. Questions and Answers About P.L. 94-142 and Section 504. *Update.* Washington, D.C.: AAHPER, June, 1979, 12–13.

American Association for Health, Physical Education and Recreation. *Foundations and Practices in Perceptual-Motor Learning—A Quest for Understanding.* Washington, D.C.: AAHPER, 1971.

_____. *Special Fitness Manual for the Mentally Retarded.* Washington, D.C.: AAHPER, 1968.

American National Red Cross. *Adapted Aquatics.* Garden City, N.Y.: Doubleday, 1977.

Arnheim, Daniel D., David Auxter, and Walter C. Crowe. *Principles and Methods of Adapted Physical Education and Recreation.* 3rd ed. St. Louis: Mosby, 1977.

Auxter, David. "The Teacher of Individually Prescribed Instruction in Perceptual-Motor Development." *Journal of Health, Physical Education, and Recreation.* **42** (6), (June, 1971), 41–42.

Ayres, Anna Jean. *Southern California Perceptual-Motor Tests.* Los Angeles: Western Psychological Services, 1969.

Barrow, Harold M., and Rosemary McGee. *A Practical Approach to Measurement in Physical Education.* 3rd ed. Philadelphia: Lea and Febiger, 1979.

Bentley, William G. *Learning to Move and Moving to Learn.* New York: Citation Press, 1970.

Bird, Patrick J., and Bruce M. Gansneder. "Preparation of Physical Education Teachers as Required Under Public Law 94-142." *Exceptional Children.* **45** (6), (1979), 464–466.

Blackmarr, Syd, Martha Owens, and Susan Rockett. *Every Child a Winner: A Practical Approach to Movement Education.* Ocilla, Georgia: Irwin County Board of Education, 1974.

Boroch, Rose Marie. *Elements of Rehabilitation in Nursing.* St. Louis: Mosby, 1976.

Bradtke, Jane Silverman. "Adaptive Devices for Aquatic Activities." *Practical Pointers.* **3** (1), (September, 1979).

Brockport Invitational Task Force. "Implications of Section 504 of the Rehabilitation Act as Related to Physical Education Instructional, Personnel Preparation, Intramural, and Interscholastic/Intercollegiate Sport Programs." *Practical Pointers.* **3** (11), (February, 1980).

Broer, Marion R. *Efficiency of Human Movement.* 4th ed. Philadelphia: Saunders, 1979.

Buell, Charles E. *Physical Education for Blind Children.* Springfield, Ill.: Thomas, 1974

_____. *Physical Education and Recreation for the Visually Handicapped.* Washington, D.C.: AAHPER, 1973.

Burton, Elsie C. *The New Physical Education for Elementary School Children.* Boston: Houghton Mifflin, 1977.

Calhoun, James F. *Abnormal Psychology*. 2nd ed. Del Mar, Calif.: CRM, 1977.

Canadian Red Cross Society. *Manual for Teaching Swimming to the Disabled*. Toronto, Ontario: n.d.

Carron, Albert V. *Laboratory Experiments in Motor Learning*. Englewood Cliffs, N.J.: Prentice-Hall, 1971.

Christopherson, Victor A., Pearl Parvin Coulter, and Mary Opal Wolanin. *Rehabilitation Nursing*. New York: McGraw-Hill, 1974.

"Circuit and Station Activity Approaches." *Practical Pointers*. 1 (2), (August, 1977).

Clarke, Henry H. *Application of Measurement to Health and Physical Education*. 5th ed. Englewood Cliffs, N.J.: Prentice-Hall, 1976.

Close, John J., W. G. Allan Rudd, and Frank Plimmer. *Team Teaching Experiments*. New York: Humanities Press, Inc., 1975.

Corbin, Charles B. *Inexpensive Equipment for Games, Play and Physical Activity*. Dubuque, Iowa: Kendall/Hunt, 1976.

Council for National Cooperation in Aquatics. *A Practical Guide for Teaching the Mentally Retarded to Swim*. Washington, D.C.: Council for National Cooperation in Aquatics and AAHPER, 1969.

Cowart, Jim. "Teacher-Made Adapted Devices for Archery, Badminton, and Table Tennis." *Practical Pointers*. 1 (13), (May, 1978).

Cratty, Bryant J. *Adapted Physical Education for Handicapped Children and Youth*. Denver: Love Publishing Company, 1980.

_____. *Motor Activity and the Education of Retardates*. 2nd ed. Philadelphia: Lea and Febiger, 1974.

_____. *Movement Activities for Neurologically Handicapped and Retarded Children and Youth*. Freeport, N.Y.: Educational Activities, Inc., 1967.

_____. *Movement and Spatial Awareness in Blind Children and Youth*. Springfield, Ill.: Thomas, 1971.

_____. *Perceptual-Motor Behavior and Educational Processes*. Springfield, Ill.: Thomas, 1969.

_____. *Perceptual and Motor Development in Infants and Children*. 2nd ed. Englewood Cliffs, N.J.: Prentice-Hall, 1979.

Cruickshank, William M., and Orville G. Johnson., eds., *Education of Exceptional Children and Youth*. 3rd ed. Englewood Cliffs, N.J.: Prentice-Hall, 1975.

da Costa, Maria Irene Leita, trans., and Edgar A. Doll, ed. *Oseretsky Motor Proficiency Tests*. Circle Pines, Minn.: American Guidance Service, n.d.

Daniels, Arthur S., and Evelyn A. Davies. *Adapted Physical Education*. New York: Harper and Row, 1975.

Dauer, Victor P. *Essential Movement Experiences for Preschool and Primary Children*. Minneapolis: Burgess, 1972.

_____, and Robert P. Pangrazi. *Dynamic Physical Education for Elementary School Children*. 6th ed. Minneapolis: Burgess, 1979.

Davis, Patricia A. *Teaching Physical Education to Mentally Retarded Children*. Minneapolis, Minn.: Denison, 1968.

DeCecco, John P., and William R. Crawford. *The Psychology of Learning and Instruction*. 2nd ed. Englewood Cliffs, N.J.: Prentice-Hall, 1974.

DeHaven, G. E., and J. D. Bruce. *Individual Motor Achievement Guided Education*. Devon, Pa.: Devereux Industries, 1971.

Descoeudres, Alice. trans. Ernest F. Row. *The Education of Mentally Defective Children*. Boston: D. C. Heath, 1928.

DeWeese, David D., and William H. Saunders. *Textbook of Otolaryngology*. 2nd ed. St. Louis, Mo.: Mosby, 1973.

Donlon, Edward T., and Louise F. Burton. *The Severely and Profoundly Handicapped: A Practical Approach to Teaching*. New York: Grune and Stratton, 1976.

Daughtrey, Greyson. *Effective Teaching in Physical Education for Secondary Schools*. 2nd ed. Philadelphia: Saunders, 1973.

_____, and John B. Woods. *Physical Education Programs: Organization and Administration*. Philadelphia: Saunders, 1971.

Drowatzky, John N., *Motor Learning*. Minneapolis: Burgess, 1975.

_____. *Physical Education for the Mentally Retarded*. Philadelphia: Lea and Febiger, 1971.

Duane, James E. *Individualized Instruction, Programs and Materials*. Englewood Cliffs, N.J.: Educational Technology Publications, 1973.

Education for all Handicapped Children, Act of 1975. Public Law 94-142, 94th Congress, Washington, D.C., November 29, 1975.

Education of Handicapped Children: Implementation of Part B of the Education of the Handicapped Act. Federal Register **42** (163), Tuesday, August 23, 1977.

Ersing, Walter F., and Ruth Wheeler. "The Status of Professional Preparation in Adapted Physical Education." *American Corrective Therapy Journal*. **25** (4), (July/August, 1971), 111–118.

Fait, Hollis F. *Experiences in Movement: Physical Education for the Elementary School Child*. 3rd ed. Philadelphia: Saunders, 1976.

_____. *Special Physical Education: Adapted, Corrective, Developmental*. 4th ed. Philadelphia: Saunders, 1978.

Ferster, C. P., Stuart Culbertson, and Mary C. P. Boren. *Behavior Principles*. 2nd ed. Englewood Cliffs, N.J.: Prentice-Hall, 1975.

Fisher, Seymour. *Body Consciousness: You Are What You Feel*. Englewood Cliffs, N.J.: Prentice-Hall, 1973.

Fitts, William Howard. *The Self-Concept and Performance*. Nashville: Dede Wallace Center, 1972.

_____. *The Self-Concept and Self-Actualization*. Monograph (3). Nashville: Dede Wallace Center, 1971.

_____. *Tennessee Self-Concept Scale Manual*. Nashville: Counselor Recordings and Tests, 1965.

_____. *The Self-Concept and Behavior*. Nashville: Dede Wallace Center, 1972.

Frederick, Bruce A. *202 Ideas for Making Low-Cost Physical Education Equipment*. Danville, Ill.: School Aid Co., 1971.

French, Ronald W., Paul Jansma, and Joseph P. Winnick. "Preparing Undergraduate Regular Physical Educators for Mainstreaming." *Amer. Corr. Ther. J.* **32** (2), (March-April, 1978), 43–48.

Frostig, Marianne, *Movement Education: Theory and Practice*. Chicago: Follett, 1970.

Gagne, Robert M. *The Conditions of Learning*. 3rd ed. New York: Holt, Rhinehart and Winston, Inc., 1977.

Gallahue, David L. *Developmental Play Equipment for Home and School.* New York: Wiley, 1975.

Galloway, Charles M. "Teaching is More Than Words." *Quest.* Monograph XV. (January, 1971), 67–71.

Gecas, Victor, James M. Calonico, and Darwin L. Thomas. "The Development of Self-Concept in the Child: Mirror Theory Versus Model Theory." *Journal of Social Psychology.* **92** (1), (February, 1974), 67–76.

Geddes, Dolores. *Physical Activities for Individuals with Handicapping Conditions.* 2nd ed. St. Louis, Mo.: Mosby, 1978.

Gellert, Elizabeth. "Children's Constructions of Their Self-Images." *Perceptual and Motor Skills.* **40** (1), (February, 1975), 307–324.

Gesell, Arnold Lucius. *Infant and Child in the Culture of Today: The Guidance of Development in Home and Nursery School.* rev. ed. New York: Harper and Row, 1974.

Gilliam, Bonnie C. *Basic Movement Education for Children.* Reading, Mass.: Addison-Wesley, 1970.

Goodenough, Florence L., and Dale B. Harris. *Goodenough-Harris Drawing Test.* New York: Harcourt, 1963.

Gordon, Ira J. *How I See Myself Manual and Test.* Gainesville, Fla.: Florida Educational Research and Development Council, n.d.

Grossman, Herbert J., ed. *Manual on Terminology and Classification in Mental Retardation.* American Association on Mental Deficiency. Special Publication No. 2. Baltimore: Garamond/Pridemark Press, 1973.

Groves, Lilian, ed. *Physical Education for Special Needs.* London: Cambridge University Press, 1979.

Hackett, Layne C. *Movement Exploration and Games for the Mentally Retarded.* Palo Alto, Calif.: Peek Publications, 1970.

Harris, Dale B. *Children's Drawings as Measures of Intellectual Maturity.* New York: Harcourt, 1963.

Harrison, Tinsley Randolph, editor-in-chief. *Principles of Internal Medicine.* 9th ed. New York: McGraw-Hill, 1980.

Hedbring, Charles, and Carole Holmes. "Getting It Together With P.L. 94-142: The IEP in the Classroom." *Education and Training of the Mentally Retarded.* October, 1977.

Henderson, S. E., and D. H. Stott. Finding the Clumsy Child: Genesis of a Test of Motor Impairment." *Journal of Human Movement Studies.* **3**, (1977), 38–48.

Hilgard, Ernest R., and Gordon H. Bower. *Theories of Learning.* 5th ed. Englewood Cliffs, N.J.: Prentice-Hall, 1981.

Hilsendager, D. A. *Basic Motor Fitness Test.* Philadelphia: Department of Physical Education, Temple University, n.d.

Hobbs, Nicholas, gen. ed. *Issues in the Classification of Children.* San Francisco: Jossey-Bass Publishers, Vol. I and II, 1975.

Humphrey, James H. *Child Learning Through Elementary School Physical Education.* 2nd ed. Dubuque, Iowa: Brown, 1974.

Hurt, H. Thomas, Michael D. Scott and James C. McCroskey. *Communication in the Classroom.* Reading, Mass.: Addison-Wesley, 1978.

Illinois Office of Education. *Adapted Physical Education: Related Legislation, IEP Development and Programmatic Considerations for Illinois.* Springfield, Ill.: IOE, 1978.

"Individualized Education Programs." *Practical Pointers*. 1 (6), (October, 1977).

"Individual Education Programs: Assessment and Evaluation in Physical Education." *Practical Pointers*. 1 (9), (February, 1978).

"Individualized Education Programs: Methods for Individualizing Physical Education." *Practical Pointers*. 1 (7), (December, 1977).

Information and Research Utilization Center in Physical Education and Recreation for the Handicapped. *Adapted Physical Education Guidelines: Theory and Practice for the Seventies and Eighties: a project of Bureau of Education for the Handicapped*. U.S. Office of Education, Department of Health, Education, and Welfare, prepared and distributed by Physical Education and Recreation for the Handicapped: Information and Research Utilization Center (IRUC), Washington, D.C.: American Alliance for Health, Physical Education and Recreation, 1976.

Information and Research Utilization Center in Physical Education and Recreation for the Handicapped. *Early Intervention for Handicapped Children Through Programs of Physical Education and Recreation*, (developed by Liane Summerfield). Washington, D.C.: American Alliance for Health, Physical Education and Recreation, 1976.

Information and Research Utilization Center in Physical Education and Recreation for the Handicapped. *Integrating Persons With Handicapping Conditions Into Regular Physical Education and Recreation Programs: A Bibliography and Literature Analysis*. Revised ed. Washington, D.C.: American Alliance for Health, Physical Education and Recreation, 1977.

Information and Research Utilization Center in Physical Education and Recreation for the Handicapped. *Physical Activities for Impaired, Disabled and Handicapped Participants*, (prepared by Linda Tibaudo). Washington, D.C.: American Alliance for Health, Physical Education and Recreation, 1976.

Information and Research Utilization Center in Physical Education and Recreation for the Handicapped. *Physical Education and Recreation for Cerebral Palsied Individuals*, (assembled by Nancy Graue). Washington, D.C.: American Alliance for Health, Physical Education and Recreation, 1976.

Information and Research Utilization Center in Physical Education and Recreation for the Handicapped. *Physical Education, Recreation, and Related Programs for Autistic and Emotionally Disturbed Children*, (prepared by Liane Summerfield). Washington, D.C.: American Alliance for Health, Physical Education and Recreation, 1976.

Information and Research Utilization Center in Physical Education and Recreation for the Handicapped. *Physical Education, Recreation, and Sports for Individuals With Hearing Impairments*, (prepared by Kristina Gilbertson). Washington, D.C.: American Alliance for Health, Physical Education and Recreation, 1976.

Information and Research Utilization Center in Physical Education and Recreation for the Handicapped. *Professional Preparation In Adapted Physical Education, Therapeutic Recreation, and Corrective Therapy*, a project of U.S. Department of Health, Education, and Welfare, Office of Education, Bureau of Education for the Handicapped. Sponsored by American Alliance for Health, Physical Education and Recreation, Unit on Programs for the Handicapped. Washington, D.C.: The Center, 1976.

Institute for Physical Education. *Handbook of Physical Education and Activities for Exceptional Children*. Old Saybrook, Conn.: IPE, 1975.

Itard, Jean-Marc. *The Wild Boy of Averyon*. New York: Appleton-Century-Crofts, 1962.

Johnson, Barry L., and Jack K. Nelson. *Practical Measurements for Evaluation in Physical Education.* 3rd ed. Minneapolis: Burgess, 1979.

Johnson, Leon, and Ben Londeree. *Motor Fitness Testing Manual for the Moderately Mentally Retarded.* Washington, D.C.: American Alliance for Health, Physical Education and Recreation, 1976.

Joint Committee of the Lifetime Sports Education Project and the Project on Recreation and Fitness for the Mentally Retarded. *Physical Activities for the Mentally Retarded: Ideas for Instruction.* Washington, D.C.: Project on Recreation and Fitness for the Mentally Retarded, 1968.

Kanner, Leo. "Childhood Psychosis: A Historical Overview." *Journal of Autism and Childhood Schizophrenia,* (1971).

"Austistic Disturbances of Affective Contact." *Nervous Child.* **2,** (1943), 217–250.

Kephart, Newell C. *The Slow Learner in the Classroom.* 2nd ed. Columbus, Ohio: Merrill, 1971.

Kirchner, Glenn. *Physical Education for Elementary School Children.* 4th ed. Dubuque, Iowa: Brown, 1978.

————, Jean Cunningham and Eileen Warrell. *Introduction to Movement Education.* 2nd ed. Dubuque, Iowa: Brown, 1978.

Kirk, Samuel A., James J. Gallagher. *Educating Exceptional Children.* 3rd ed. Boston: Houghton-Mifflin, 1979.

Knapczyk, D. R., and W. P. Liemohn. *Theme Instruction: An Inter-Disciplinary Model for Service and Training in Special Education.* Bloomington: Indiana University Developmental Training Center, 1973.

Krusen, Frank H., ed. *Handbook of Physical Medicine and Rehabilitation.* 2nd ed. Phildelphia: Saunders, 1971.

Lawrence, Elizabeth A., and James F. Winschel. "Self-Concept and the Retarded: Research and Issues." *Exceptional Children,* **3** (1973), 310–319.

Lawther, John D. "Directing Motor Skill Learning." *Quest.* Monograph VI, (1966), 68–76.

————. *The Learning and Performance of Physical Skills* 2nd ed. Englewood Cliffs, N.J.: Prentice-Hall, 1977.

Lerch, Harold A., et al. *Perceptual-Motor Learning: Theory and Practice.* Palo Alto, Calif.: Peek Publications, 1974.

Levy, Ronald B. *Self Revelation Through Relationships.* Englewood Cliffs, N.J.: Prentice-Hall, 1972.

Mahler, Margaret S. "On Child Psychosis and Schizophrenia: Autistic and Symbiotic Infantile Psychosis." *Psychoanalytic Study of the Child.* New York: International Universities Press, 1952, 7.

Marlow, Dorothy R. *Textbook of Pediatric Nursing.* 5th ed. Philadelphia: Saunders, 1977.

Marsallo, Michael. "Innovative Developmental Physical Activities for Early Childhood and Special Education Students." *Practical Pointers.* **3** (8), (January, 1980).

Massachusetts Acts of 1972, Chapter 766, Boston, Mass.

Mathews, Donald. *Measurement in Physical Education.* 5th ed. Philadelphia, Pa.: Saunders, 1978.

Matthews, Lillian B. "Improving the Self-Image of the Socially Disabled." *Journal of Home Economics.* 67 (May, 1975), 9–12.

May, Elizabeth Eckhardt, Neva R. Waggoner, and Ebaner Boettke Hotte. *Independent Living for the Handicapped and the Elderly.* Boston: Houghton-Mifflin, 1974.

Means, Louis E., and Harry A. Applequist. *Dynamic Movement Experiences for Elementary School Children.* Springfield, Ill.: Thomas, 1974.

Mercer, Jane R. *Labeling the Mentally Retarded.* Berkeley, Calif.: University of California Press, 1973.

Miller, Arthur G., John F. Cheffers and Virginia Whitcomb. *Physical Education: Teaching Human Movement in the Elementary Schools.* Englewood Cliffs, N.J.: Prentice-Hall, 1974.

Montessori, Maria. *The Montessori Method.* 5th ed. New York: Frederick A. Stokes Co, 1912.

Moran, Joan May, and Leonard Harris Kalakin. *Movement Experiences for the Mentally Retarded and Emotionally Disturbed Child.* 2nd ed. Minneapolis: Burgess, 1977.

Morris, Peter, H. T. A. Whiting. *Motor Impairment and Compensatory Education.* Philadelphia: Lea and Febiger, 1971.

National Society to Prevent Blindness. *Snellen Eye Charts.* New York: NSPB, n.d.

Neilson, Neils P., and Clayne R. Jensen. *Measurement and Statistics in Physical Education.* Belmont, Calif.: Wadsworth, 1972.

Nelson, Waldo E., Victor C. Vaughan, and James R. McKay. *Textbook of Pediatrics.* 11th ed. Philadelphia: Saunders, 1979.

Nomenclature and Criteria for Diagnosis of Diseases of the Heart and Great Vessels. 8th ed. Boston: Little, Brown and Co., 1979.

O'Donnell, Patrick H. *Motor and Haptic Learning.* San Rafael, Calif.: Dimensions Publishing Co., 1969.

Orpet, R. E. *Frostig Movement Skills Test Battery.* Los Angeles: Marianne Frostig Center of Educational Therapy, 1972.

_____, and T. L. Heustis. *Move-Grow-Learn: Movement Skills Survey.* Chicago, Ill.: Follett, 1971.

Oxendine, Joseph B. *Psychology of Motor Learning.* New York: Appleton-Century-Crofts, 1968.

Pennsylvania Association for Retarded Children, Nancy Beth Bowman, et al. *Plaintiffs versus Commonwealth of Pennsylvania.* David H. Kurtzman, et al., Civ. A, No. 71-42, United States District Court, E. D. Pennsylvania, October 8, 1971, 334 Federal Supplement 1257 (1971).

Peter, Laurence J. *Individual Instruction.* Hightstown, N.J.: McGraw-Hill, 1972.

Piers, Ellen V., and Dale B. Harris. *Piers-Harris Self-Concept Scale.* Nashville: Counselor Recordings and Tests, 1969.

Price, Robert J. *Physical Education and the Physically Handicapped Child.* London: Lepus Books, 1980.

Priest, L. "Integrating the Disabled in Aquatics Programs." *Journal of Physical Education and Recreation.* **50** (2), (February, 1979), 57–59.

"Principles and Practices for Championship Performances in Wheelchair Field Events." *Practical Pointers.* **3** (7), (January, 1980).

Quay, Herbert C. "Patterns of Aggression, Withdrawal, and Immaturity." In *Psychopathology Disorders of Childhood.* ed. Herbert C. Quay and John S. Werry. New York: Wiley, 1972, 1–29.

Raimy, Victor. *The Self-Concept as a Factor in Counseling and Personality Organization.* Columbus, Ohio: State University Libraries, 1971.

Rarick, G. Lawrence, D. Alan Dobbins, and Geoffrey D. Broadhead. *The Motor Domain and Its Correlates in Educationally Handicapped Children.* Englewood Cliffs, N.J.: Prentice-Hall, 1976.

Rathbone, Josephine L., and Carol Lucas. *Recreation in Total Rehabilitation.* Springfield, Ill: Thomas, 1970.

Reid, G. "Mainstreaming in Physical Education: The Concept and Its Implications." *McGill Journal of Education.* **14**, (Fall, 1979), 367-77.

Roach, Eugene, and Newell C. Kephart. *The Purdue Perceptual-Motor Survey.* Columbus, Ohio: Merrill, 1966.

Roos, P. "Current Issues in the Education of Mentally Retarded Persons." In *Conference on the Education of Mentally Retarded Persons.* ed. W. J. Cegelka. Arlington, Texas: National Association for Retarded Citizens, 1971.

Salkin, Jeri. *Body Ego Technique: An Educational and Therapeutic Approach to Body Image and Self-Identity.* Springfield, Ill.: Thomas, 1973.

Saronson, Irwin G. *Abnormal Psychology.* 2nd ed. Englewood Cliffs, N.J.: Prentice-Hall, 1976.

Schurr, Evelyn L. *Movement Experience for Children: A Humanistic Approach to Elementary School Physical Education.* 2nd ed. Englewood Cliffs, N.J.: Prentice-Hall, 1975.

Seguin, Edward. *Idiocy: Its Treatment by the Physiological Method.* New York: Teachers College, Columbia University, 1907.

Seymour, Mary, and Don Megale. *Guide for Planning the Program in Physical Education in the Elementary Schools.* Corvallis, Ore.: O.S.V. Book Stores, 1977.

Sherrill, Claudine. *Adapted Physical Education and Recreation: A Multidisciplinary Approach.* Dubuque, Iowa: Brown, 1976.

Shivers, Jay A., and Hollis Fait. *Therapeutic and Adapted Recreational Services.* Philadelphia: Lea and Febiger, 1975.

Shontz, Franklin C. *Perceptual and Cognitive Aspects of Body Experience.* New York: Academic Press, 1969.

Short, Francis X. "Team Teaching for Developmentally Disabled Children." *Journal of Health, Physical Education and Recreation.* **46** (8), (October, 1975), 45-46.

Simon, Jerald, Jr. "Emotional Aspects of Physical Disability." *The American Journal of Occupational Therapy.* **25** (1971), 408-410.

Singer, Robert N. *Motor Learning and Human Performance: An Application to Physical Education Skills.* New York: The Macmillan Co., 1975.

————, and Walter Dick. *Study Guide Teaching Physical Education: A Systems Approach.* Boston: Houghton-Mifflin, 1974.

Sloan, William. *The Lincoln-Osertsky Motor Development Scale.* Chicago: C. H. Stoelting Co., 1955.

Snodgrass, Jeanne. "Self-Concept: A Look at Its Development and Some Implications for Physical Education Teaching." *Journal of Physical Education and Recreation.* **48** (9), (November/December, 1977), 22-23.

Sorrell, Howard M. "Innovative Perceptual-Motor Activities: Programming Techniques That Work—Part II." *Practical Pointers.* **3** (3), (November, 1979).

Sosne, Michael. *Handbook of Adapted Physical Education Equipment and Its Use.* Springfield, Ill.: Thomas, 1973.

Special Olympics, Inc. *P.L. 94-142: It's the Law: Physical Education and Recreation for the Handicapped*, Washington, D.C.: The Joseph P. Kennedy, Jr. Foundation, n.d.

State Department of Education (Division of Special Education) *Individualized Educational Plans*. Baltimore, n.d.

Stein, Joe. *Developing Ball Skills Through Movement Exploration*. Campbell, Calif.: Enrichment Materials Co., 1969.

Stein, Julian U., and Lowell A. Klappholz. *Special Olympics Instructional Manual. . . From Beginners to Champions*. Washington, D.C.: American Association for Health, Physical Education and Recreation, 1972.

Stein, Thomas A., and Douglas H. Sessoms. *Recreation and Special Populations*. 2nd ed. Boston: Holbrook Press, Inc., 1977.

Steindler, Arthur. *Kinesiology of the Human Body*. Springfield, Ill.: Thomas, 1973.

Stenner, A. Jackson, and William G. Katzenmeyer. "Self-Concept Development in Young Children." *Phi Delta Kappan*. **58** (1976), 356–357.

Telford, Charles W., and James M. Sawrey. *The Exceptional Individual*. 4th ed. Englewood Cliffs, N.J.: Prentice-Hall, 1981.

Thomas, John Bernard. *Self-Concept in Psychology and Education: A Review of Research*. Windsor: NFER, 1973.

Thorpe, Lewis P., Willis W. Clark, and Ernest W. Tiegs. *California Test of Personality*. New York: McGraw-Hill, 1939, 53.

"Tips on Mainstreaming: Do's and Don'ts in Activity Programs." *Practical Pointers*. **1** (10), (March, 1978).

Torres, Scottie. *A Primer on Individualized Education Programs for Handicapped Children*. Reston, Va.: Foundation for Exceptional Children, 1977.

University of Minnesota. *Mainstreaming*. **2** (2), Minneapolis, (Spring, 1976).

Vannier, Maryhelen. *Physical Activities for the Handicapped*. Englewood Cliffs, N.J.: Prentice-Hall, 1977.

_____, M. Foster, and D. L. Gallahue. *Teaching Physical Education in Elementary Schools*. 6th ed. Philadelphia: Saunders, 1978.

_____, and Hollis F. Fait. *Teaching Physical Education in Secondary Schools*. 4th ed. Philadelphia: Saunders, 1975.

Vodola, Thomas M. *Individualized Physical Education Program for the Handicapped*. Englewood Cliffs, N.J.: Prentice-Hall, 1973.

Walker, Jeanette, editor and arranger, in cooperation with the National Association of State Directors of Special Education and the Kentucky Department of Education Bureau of Education for Exceptional Children. *Functions of the Placement Committee in Special Education: A Resource Manual*. Washington, D.C.: NASDSE, 1976.

Walters, Etta. "Prediction of Postnatal Development from Fetal Activity." *Child Development*. **36** (1965), 801–808.

Warwick, David. *Team Teaching*. New York: Crane Russak Co., 1971.

Webster, Murray, Jr., And Barbara Sobieszek. *Sources of Self-Evaluation; A Formal Theory of Significant Others and Social Influence*. New York: Wiley, 1974.

Weiss, Raymond, and William B. Karper. "Teaching the Handicapped Child in the Regular Physical Education Class." *Journal of Physical Education and Recreation*. **51** (2), (February, 1980), 32 ff.

Wessel, Janet A., ed. *Planning Individualized Education Programs in Special Education: With Examples from I CAN Physical Education*. Northbrook, Ill.: Hubbard, 1977.

Wheeler, Ruth Hook, and Agnes M. Hooley. *Physical Education for The Handicapped.* 2nd ed. Philadelphia: Lea and Febiger, 1976.

Willgoose, Carl E. *The Curriculum in Physical Education.* 3rd ed. Englewood Cliffs, N.J.: Prentice-Hall, 1979.

————. *Health Education in the Elementary School.* 5th ed. Philadelphia: Saunders, 1979.

Winnick, Joseph P. *Early Movement Experiences and Development Habilitation and Remediation.* Philadelphia: Saunders, 1979.

————. "Issues and Trends in Training Adapted Physical Education Personnel." *Journal of Health, Physical Education and Recreation.* **43** (8), (October, 1972), 75–78.

Wylie, Ruth C. *The Self-Concept: A Review of Methodological Considerations and Measuring of Instruments.* Rev. ed. Lincoln: University of Nebraska Press, 1974.

York, Lilla Jean. *The Background, Philosophy and Purposes of Team Teaching.* Dallas: The Leslie Press, 1971.

Photo Credits:

pp. 110, 111; Courtesy of *Agassiz Village,* W. Poland, Me.

pp. 114, 118, 121, 127, 128, 131; Courtesy of *Cotting School for Handicapped Children,* Boston, Ma.

pp. 136; Courtesy of *Camp Waban,* Sanford, Me.

pp. 124, 129, 130; Courtesy of *Pine Tree Camp for Crippled Children and Adults,* Rome, Me.

pp. 123; Courtesy of *University of Southern Maine,* Portland, Me.

pp. 46, 115, 116, 119, 122, 125, 127, 132, 134, 135; Courtesy of *Woodfords-West Educational Center,* Portland, Me.

Index